Noah Knowles Davis

Juda's Jewels

A Study in the Hebrew Lyrics

Noah Knowles Davis

Juda's Jewels
A Study in the Hebrew Lyrics

ISBN/EAN: 9783743393677

Manufactured in Europe, USA, Canada, Australia, Japa

Cover: Foto ©Thomas Meinert / pixelio.de

Manufactured and distributed by brebook publishing software (www.brebook.com)

Noah Knowles Davis

Juda's Jewels

JUDA'S JEWELS

A STUDY IN

THE HEBREW LYRICS

BY

NOAH K. DAVIS, Ph.D., LL.D.
Professor in the University of Virginia

NASHVILLE, TENN.
PUBLISHING HOUSE OF THE METHODIST EPISCOPAL CHURCH, SOUTH
BARBEE & SMITH, AGENTS
1895

Entered, according to Act of Congress, in the year 1895,
BY NOAH K. DAVIS,
In the Office of the Librarian of Congress, at Washington.

PREFACE

The chief aim of this work is to indicate some of the rhetorical graces of the Hebrew lyrics. A large number are quoted in full, carefully annotated, and followed by a general exposition. Besides this endeavor to make clear the true meaning and force of the text, I have thought it needful, in order to its higher appreciation, to give the probable historical setting of each lyric, to depict vividly the scene, and thus to bring into relief the significance of many figurative expressions and their underlying sentiment.

In the translation as well as in the interpretation I have had numerous helps, too many to be named, in standard commentaries and special treatises, English and foreign, the early and the later, even the latest. Ever ready to modify my views, I have neglected no available source of information; yet the candid reader who is acquainted with the voluminous literature of the subject will, nevertheless, accord to me a fair measure of independence. The renderings have been compared word by word with those of the Canterbury Revision. Being in hearty sympathy with its reverence for the classic diction of the Authorized Version, I have not deviated from one or the other except where it was impossible for me to adopt the phraseology of either. In appropriating the views or renderings of others I have not always been careful to give credit, hoping that the frequent credit given and this general acknowledgment will be deemed sufficient.

Much pains has been taken to present to the eye not only the parallelism of the verses, but also the strophic structure of each lyric. Upon the strophic forms there is as yet no general consensus, and I have been obliged, with little or no help, to venture on those presented, hoping that a bold essay in this direction may lead to approved and permanent results. The principles guiding me in the formal distribution are discussed in the seventh chapter.

The work was begun and well-nigh completed with no thought of publication, but it is now issued in the hope of arousing more general attention to the unmatched excellence of this marvelous literature, and inducing a reverential study of its many graces. The subject is familiar to biblical scholars and ministers of religion, so that I hardly expect to interest them; but I am sure they will unite with me in the wish that laymen who love the Scriptures may find the little book, written by one of themselves, both interesting and useful.

To Professor Collins Denny, of Vanderbilt University, I am gratefully indebted for kindly approval, for helpful criticism, and for the several valuable notes to which I have appended his name. NOAH K. DAVIS.

University of Virginia.

CONTENTS

		PAGE
I.	The Plain	9
II.	The Cavern	38
III.	The Desert	76
IV.	The Mountain	119
V.	The Valley	159
VI.	Verses	212
VII.	Stanzas	255
VIII.	Lyrics	300

(5)

David the son of Jesse
>   The man who was raised on high
>   > The anointed of the God of Jacob
>   > > The sweet psalmist of Israel

ANNOTATED CITATIONS

PSALMS.

	PAGE
II. Why do the nations rage?	295
VII. O Lord, my God, in thee do I put my trust...	56
VIII. O Lord, our Lord, how excellent is thy name.	22
XV. Lord, who shall abide in thy tabernacle?.....	154
XIX. The heavens declare the glory of God	26
XXIII. The Lord is my shepherd; I shall not want...	18
XXIV. The earth is the Lord's, and the fullness thereof.	148
XXVII. The Lord is my light and my salvation.......	97
XXIX. Give unto the Lord, O ye mighty............	35
XXXI. In thee, O Lord, do I put my trust..........	83
XXXIV. I will bless the Lord at all times............	70
XXXIX. I said, I will take heed to my ways..........	182
XLII. As the hart panteth after the water brooks...	191
XLIII. Judge me, O God, and plead my cause.......	194
XLV. My heart overflows with a goodly theme.....	324
LI. Have mercy upon me, O God	165
LVII. Be merciful unto me, O God	93
LXVIII. Let God arise, let his enemies be scattered...	136
XC. Lord, thou hast been our dwelling place......	308
XCI. He that dwelleth in the covert of the Most High.	345
XCV. O come, let us sing unto the Lord	285
CI. I will sing of mercy and judgment..........	125

		PAGE
CIV.	Bless the Lord, O my soul....................	337
CXXX.	Out of the depths have I cried unto thee.....	253
CXXXVII.	By the rivers of Babylon..................	332
CXXXIX.	O Lord, thou hast searched me............	203
CXLII.	I cried unto the Lord with my voice.........	66
CXLIII.	Hear my prayer, O Lord....................	63

2 SAMUEL.

I.	Gazelle of Israel, slain on thine own mountains.	114
XXIII.	The last words of David, the son of Jesse.....	208

(*Other citations are not annotated.*)

JUDA'S JEWELS

I.—THE PLAIN

THE most ancient of all songs are sweetest and noblest of all. The first in time are the first in worth. Poetry is an art which accumulates, but does not progress; or rather it is not an art, since its early, untutored, spontaneous efforts are its best. Centuries before Pindar, before Homer, there was a bard in Judah whose songs have ever since been singing by millions more and more, and will still be singing when all others are forgotten. He, the Adam of song, typical of mankind, touched the utmost verge of every possible human experience; step by step he trod all paths of joy and sorrow; one by one he traversed all avenues to honor and dishonor; and he wandered from boyhood to old age, harp in hand, singing all the changeful way in tones that echoing hearts will never allow to die. That the ear may catch the divine perfection of this melody, the eye must see the songster where he stands. Let us then go along his way, and when he stops to sing we too will pause with listening eyes and ears.

§1. David, the son of Jesse, appears first as a shepherd boy on the plains east of Bethlehem. He is the youngest of eight brothers. Two elder sisters are also named, but his mother's name is nowhere given. The great prophet and judge, Samuel, comes to their home at Bethlehem to select and anoint a new king over Israel.[1] The eldest of the sons, the tall, handsome, and haughty Eliab, is rejected; and so successively the others. And Samuel said unto Jesse: "The Lord hath not chosen these. Are here all thy children?" David is sent for. He comes; a handsome lad, of rather short stature, in contrast with Eliab, Saul, and Goliath; but his frame is compacted for both agility and strength. Thus he says of himself:

> It is God that girdeth me with strength.
> He maketh my feet like hinds' feet;
> He teacheth my hands to war,
> And mine arms to bend the brazen bow.[2]

His dress is probably a simple frock, leaving his neck and arms bare, girdled about the waist, and reaching his knees. His hair is auburn, his eyes

---

[1] 1 Samuel xvi.
[2] Psalm xviii. 32-34. Achilles is called πόδας ὠκύς.—*Il.*, i. 58. We are also reminded of the bow that Ulysses left at Utica.

beautiful and bright, his complexion ruddy with the flush of youth and health.[1] "And the Lord said: Arise, anoint him, for this is he." So the symbolic oil is poured upon his head, and the Spirit of the Lord came upon David from that day forward.

We will presume that David returned for a time to the care of his sheep. His anointing, viewed merely as an objective fact, must have had a powerful effect in developing his character. We may doubt if he fully understood its import until long afterwards,[2] but not that the mystery was food for his wondering thought. His peaceful and solitary pursuit promoted reflection, and as he pondered his destiny the currents of his thought deepened their channels.

> Muse amid thy flocks awhile,
> At thy doom of greatness smile,
> Bold to bear God's heaviest load,
> Dimly guessing at the road.[3]

When, moreover, we remember that the Spirit of the Lord was now upon him, it is evident that this was a great epoch in his mental history, and the true beginning of his wonderful career.

Another fact must have made a deep mark on

---

[1] See Stanley, *Lectures on the Jewish Church*, Lecture xxii.
[2] Josephus says that Samuel whispered it in his ear.—*Ant.*, vi. 8, § 1.
[3] *Lyra Apostolica*, lvii.

his character. By his father and brothers he was disdainfully consigned to a menial occupation, and it became the subject of taunt.[1] Endowed with a highly sensitive nature, he felt this keenly. But the exclusion from the family circle, the humiliation, the mortification, however bitter to the lonely lad, became in his healthful mental organization, and doubtless under the influence of the Spirit, a means of discipline and strength, of self-mastery. The sculptor has blunt chisels, which, under heavy blows, break off rude masses of marble, but he also has sharp chisels, with which he perfects his work.

David's mother no doubt was in sympathy with him. That there were strong points in her character may be surmised from Jesse's apparent weakness and the unquestionable powers of her children. Her youngest was naturally her darling, and so she called him, for the name "David" means "beloved." As a faithful mother she had in early years taught him many lessons of love and duty. Kneeling at her knees, with his palms together and upraised, he had learned from her the name "Jehovah;" and when he was driven out to hard service and solitude, her tears softened him, her love went with him and animated him, and he

---
[1] 1 Samuel xvii. 28.

remembered and practiced the lessons of her piety. What matters it that we know not her name? She, type of the virgin mother, is immortal in her son.[1] It seems to me we may often note in David's conduct, even in late periods of his life, the unmistakable marks of his mother's hand, especially in his generous, gentle, and kindly impulses; yet never does he name her, and only once refers to her. In an agony of prayer he cries, "Save the son of thine handmaid;" thus resting his plea on her desert.[2] But why this reticence? In every true man's heart there are some things too sacred for utterance; there is an inviolable inner shrine. A mother's name is never a light thing. A man of deep and fine feeling, as was this man, does not at any time talk much about his mother, and when death adds its sanctity, how the heart shuts up on her name!

Another fact is worthy of note as making an impress on David's character in his early youth. He was thrown into constant communion with nature. Her sweet and healthful influences, her gentle and stern aspects developed his strength, deepened his emotions, and peopled his fancy. The plains of Bethlehem, which for three thousand years have

---

[1] The earlier rabbis attempt to establish the immaculate conception of David.

[2] Psalm lxxxvi. 16. *Cf.* verse 16 of Psalm cxvi., a post-exilic imitative composition.

been sheep pastures, are remarkable for landscape beauty, a beauty that must have been far greater in David's day, when foliage was more abundant there than now. There he learned to love the sky, the mountain, the distant sea, the brawling brook, the green field, the perfumed flower. There he took his first lessons in that various language of nature with which his poetry abounds; for

> To him who, in the love of nature, holds
> Communion with her visible forms, she speaks
> A various language; for his gayer hours
> She has a voice of gladness, and a smile
> And eloquence of beauty, and she glides
> Into his darker musings with a mild
> And healing sympathy that steals away
> Their sharpness ere he is aware.[1]

But there were frowns in the landscape whose features were symbolic of his life. Before him, in the dim eastern distance where earth met sky, there lay in a deep valley of gloom the sea that was for all time the emblem of death and God's hate of sin. Nearer, stretching north and south, lay the haunted wilderness, which afterwards overheard the great temptation, already occupied by ferocious beasts that came thence like emissaries of Satan to ravage the flocks. In the lower

[1] Bryant, *Thanatopsis*.

grounds were horrible pits of slime and springs of bitter, poisoned waters. Still nearer were abrupt precipices pierced with gloomy unknown caves, the refuge of crime. The edge of the cliffs was broken here and there by ravines leading from the plains above, deepening dangerously and filled with the shadow of death. But as yet his feet trod the green and sunny slope, and flowers bloomed on the pathway leading from the home of his birth.

Let us remember that David was a poet and a musician born. Probably untaught, he cultivated for himself the native impulse to pour forth in song the overflow of his heart, beguiling his lonely and quiet hours with a harp which he invented, and, after a rude fashion, had made.[1] Thus he attuned both melody and harmony with verse.

The fame of his harp went beyond Bethlehem, and reached the court at Gibeah.[2] He is sent for to play before the king. He goes afoot, like the mediæval minstrel, his harp, muffled with lilies, hanging from his shoulders. Its sweet tones, drawn out by the native skill of a loving hand, soothe the dark hours of the fierce and gloomy king, and quiet the evil spirit that troubled him,

---

[1] Amos vi. 5, They "that chant to the sound of the viol, and invent to themselves instruments of music, like David."

[2] 1 Samuel xvi. 18.

thus "lifting Saul's name out of sorrow, and weaving a spell to sustain him where song had restored him."[1] When David returned to his home we do not see that he was at all elated by this brilliant episode in his boy life. Still we must believe that it quickened his thoughts like wine. He was not yet a man, but his manhood was rapidly developing.[2]

§ 2. Let us think of David now as returned from court to the plains, resuming his peaceful pursuits, tending the sheep, musing on nature, playing the harp, and singing his own songs out of a fresh, innocent, impulsive, boyish heart. Let us try to picture the scene: The sun is near meridian. Sunken in the deep blue of the oriental sky, he sheds from the center of the dome his golden glories down to the far horizon. The gay green fields respond. They sparkle and almost glow with brilliance. These sunlit pastures lie eastward from Bethlehem on the table-land which just beyond breaks precipitously down to the

---

[1] From Browning's *Saul*, the gem of his *Dramatic Lyrics*, and inferior to nothing he has written.

[2] There is an old and curious tradition that David was very small, but that after Samuel anointed him he grew rapidly, and soon reached the stature of Saul. Hence Saul's armor fitted him when he was making ready to fight the giant. (See Baring-Gould's *O. T. Legends*, p. 319.)

valley of the Jordan and the sea. The watered meadows of this lower level are reached by deep ravines breaking through the cliff that overhangs the valley. David leads his sheep from the pastures above into one of these to seek the meadows. The ravine is a narrow, dark, and gloomy valley. There are dangerous precipices to skirt, and steep descents to make. But he leads in the right paths, and guides with his shepherd's crook the silly sheep, watchful to catch and save the one whose feet may slide. They follow trustfully, and by the good shepherd's care reach and traverse the depths in safety, and very soon emerge from the dark shadow into the sunny meadows. Here he makes them lie down to rest in the cool grass, beneath the tamarisk shade, nigh to the quiet stream hindered by rushes. He is seated on a rock, watchfully near, for the great wilderness is hard by, and once there came a lion out of the wood and seized a lamb of the flock. But David smote him, and slew him, and delivered the lamb.[1] Now he watches, that his sheep may feast and rest securely in the very presence of their enemies.

David's mother, as I think, had taught him to offer habitually at set times praise and prayer to Jehovah. He made a rule.[2] It is this:

---

[1] Samuel xvii. 34, 35.   [2] Psalm lv. 17.

Evening, morning, and at noon will I pray and cry aloud;
And he shall hear my voice.

The midday season has now come. He thinks of the anointing, and of the generous king at whose court he was recently a guest, with perhaps a presage of danger; then of God's love, and bounty, and protecting care. He takes his harp in his hand to sing. Music and poetry are the wings of his devotion. Hear his noonday song:

The LORD is my shepherd; I shall not want.

I

He maketh me to lie down in green pastures;
He leadeth me beside the still waters.
He restoreth my soul; [name's sake.
He guideth me in the paths of righteousness for his

II

Yea, though I walk through the valley of the shadow
I will fear no evil; [of death,
For thou art with me;
Thy rod and thy staff they comfort me.

NOTES.—The first line announces the general subject. Shepherd applies more particularly to strophes 1 and 2; and I shall not want, to strophe 3. The psalm begins and ends with Jehovah (LORD), not elsewhere named.

Strophe 1.—Jehovah refreshes and guides.—leadeth; in the East flocks are not driven, but led.—the paths are straight, right, direct.—for his name's sake, not for any desert of mine.

Strophe 2.—Jehovah protects and comforts.—the valley; re-

III

Thou preparest a table before me in the presence of [mine enemies;
Thou hast anointed my head with oil;
My cup runneth over. [of my life;
Surely goodness and mercy shall follow me all the days
And I will dwell in the house of the LORD forever.

A few general remarks upon this delicious little pastoral lyric before passing. It is the familiar Psalm xxiii., which we all got by heart when we were children, but I doubt if any of us have yet exhausted it.

Observe the arrangement in parallel lines, and the distribution into three strophes or stanzas, each

---

member Bunyan's allegorical expansion of this figure. The brevity of the second and third lines renders them emphatic. Omit art. The rod to defend; the staff to support. We have here the first direct expression of the religious idea of a shepherd, which has taken so deep root in the heart of Christendom. For *rod* DeWitt puts *scepter;* Cheyne, *club.*

Strophe 3.—The guest of Jehovah. A change of figure; the transition is in the first line, which may be referred to the shepherd protecting his sheep at pasture, or to what follows, the royal host making a feast.—oil, the symbol of grace.—cup, the symbol of joy.—goodness and mercy are personified; the twin guardian angels, who will never forsake him during all this present life. But his aspirations rise higher;—forever is a flash of light from the eternal world, a glimpse of immortality. Thus the song begins on earth, and ends in heaven. Faith awakens Hope, who, with the golden key of promise, unlocks and throws open the gates of everlasting bliss, and as the eye of Love gazes into its limitless expanse, her lips cry out *forever.*

containing a complete thought, the whole being preceded by an independent line giving the subject. This highly artistic form is almost wholly obscured in our common version, as usually printed, and in no arrangement that I have seen is it properly exhibited.

The title is: A Psalm of David.[1] Its historical place has been disputed. Biblical critics very generally allow its Davidic authorship, but refer it in turn to almost every period of David's life. As these authorities differ so widely, we may think for ourselves. Its freshness and simplicity, the vivid figures from nature, its childlike faith, the absence of the warrior, the outlaw, and the king, and more, the entire absence of any consciousness of sinfulness—all are good grounds for referring it to David's youth. The chief reasons for assigning it to a later period are founded on the mention of his enemies and of the house of Jehovah. Let us observe that, *beth* [house] in early Semitic usage is any lodging place; *e. g. Beth-el*, Genesis xxviii. 19. Moreover, may not both be anticipations? The latter one is expressly future. We may add that the figure of the guest of a king (strophe 3) would readily suggest itself to one who had recently been actually entertained at court. But our historical view is not essential to its highest beauties. It is a gem not needing a setting, or rather, a fixed star shining by its own light.

---

[1]The titles prefixed to a majority, nearly three-fourths, of the psalms are very ancient; being found in the Septuagint Version, which dates from the third century, B.C. They are not, however, considered of equal authority with the text. The critics pronounce some of them incorrect. About this one, however, there should be no doubt—the psalm is David's.

§3. Let us now pursue our fancies. The noonday devotions are over. The afternoon is passing. David leads his flock up again to the higher ground, to a more secure place nearer Bethlehem. The sun sets, night is coming on, and the voiceless stars are looking down from heaven. David has gathered his sheep together on the spot where a thousand years afterwards shepherds were watching their flocks by night and the starry angels came singing down from heaven, announcing the advent of the Good Shepherd, of whom David was the unconscious type.[1]

The hour for his evening devotions is at hand. The calm but brilliant glories of an oriental night fill his soul with sweet solemnity. He has not yet lost the instinct of childish innocence that finds God in everything. "Blessed are the pure in heart; for they shall see God." So his heart bows before the manifest Presence, and his eyes drink the luster of his jewels; for night is God's crown. And when the full-orbed moon rises over the heights of Abarim and mounts the sky, he adores the Creator who has set his glory upon the heavens. He feels that it is given to him, though a mere babe in knowledge, to lift up a voice of per-

---

[1] Luke ii. 8 ff.; John x.

fected praise which shall confound those that deny the excellent name of the Lord of the heavens and the earth. Yet, he reflects, how insignificant am I! But no; for God made man in celestial mold, and appointed him to rule the world. Aroused by this inspiring thought, he touches his lyre, and night and the silent stars listen to his evening hymn:

O LORD, our Lord, how excellent thy name in all the
Who hast set thy glory upon the heavens. [earth!

I

Out of the mouth of babes and sucklings
Hast thou established strength,
Because of thine adversaries,
That thou mightest still the enemy and the avenger.

NOTES.—The first distich is a proem, an overture involving the theme, and expressing the occasion of devotion. We omit *is* of the A. V. and R. V., as needless and a blemish.

Strophe 1. The first and fourth lines are antithetically parallel. There is a depreciating allusion of the singer to himself. Perhaps his exorcism of the evil spirit from Saul suggested the thought. But the best possible comment is found in the following words: "And when the chief priests and scribes saw the wonderful things that he did, and the children crying in the temple, and saying, Hosanna to the Son of David! they were sore displeased, and said unto him, Hearest thou what these say? And Jesus saith unto them, Yea; have ye never read, Out of the mouth of babes and sucklings thou hast perfected

II

When I consider thy heavens, the work of thy fingers,
The moon and the stars which thou hast ordained;
What is man that thou art mindful of him?
And the son of man, that thou visitest him?

III

For thou hast made him but little lower than the angels,
And crownest him with glory and honor;
Thou madest him to have dominion over the works of
[thy hands.

IV

Thou hast put all under his feet;
All sheep and oxen, yea and the beasts of the field;
The fowl of the air, and the fish of the sea,
Whatsoever passeth through the paths of the seas.

O LORD, our Lord, how excellent thy name in all the
[earth!

---

praise?" (Matthew xxi. 15, 16.) The quotation of our Lord is made from the Septuagint.—avenger, rather *revenger*, one who avenges himself; one violent and arrogant.

Strophe 2. Note the marvelous beauty of the English diction here. *Cf.* Psalm cxliv. 3.

Strophe 3. Than the angels, rather, *than deity*. The whole strophe is an echo of Genesis i. 26, 28. Man is God's vicegerent. See also Hebrews ii. 6, and 1 Corinthians xv. 27.

Strophe 4 is an expansion of the last line of strophe 3. We omit *things* of the A. V. and R. V.—**sheep and oxen**, the domestic animals, small and great.—**beasts of the field**, wild ani-

This is the beautiful and profound Psalm viii. We should read it by moonlight. Spurgeon calls it "the song of the astronomer." Its subject is, Man's superior dignity as conferred by Jehovah. The title attributes it to David, and is indisputable. The historical occasion here indicated is, in general, that assigned to it by Nachtigal, Tholuck, Perowne, and other good critics; the reasons are similar to those given for the place of Psalm xxiii. The thought descends from the heavens to the earth, Christlike; and in the Epistle to the Hebrews ii. 5–8, the psalm is applied to Christ's humiliation. Most interpreters regard it as Messianic; if so, its depths are immeasurable.

If we study closely the parallel phrases, and the succession and relation of thoughts, the Psalm, after we have set apart the proem and epode, seems to fall naturally and clearly into four strophes of four lines each, excepting strophe 3, which has but three lines. Is there not a poetic reason for this exception? The first and last lines of this strophe are pretty closely parallel. The intermediate one does not seem clearly synonymous. If there were a line parallel to this beginning the strophe, then it also would be a quatrain, having the alternate lines parallel. Now look at the sense: In strophe 2 the poet sinks into despondency at the humiliating thought of man's comparative insignificance. May we not suppose a pause, a mo-

---

mals; always the meaning in Scripture of this phrase.—whatsoever, all unknown sea monsters. The leviathan? Job xli.

The last line is an epode, and a repetition of the first. Thus the picture is set in a frame of praise. "The ends are wound together as a wreath." (*Delitzsch*.) Jehovah occurs only at the beginning and at the close, as in Psalm xxiii.

ment's silent meditation in the very middle of the song, poetically expressed by the elision of a line? Then comes a sudden rebound of feeling, arousing the singer to highest exultation. Observe further that the illative *for* ('כ) can make no proper connection in sense with what precedes. If we disregard the illation and force a connection, as is done in the versions of Conant, Cheyne, and De Witt, then the tone of depression continues, and sinks, in strophe 3, lower still; thus destroying one chief poetic beauty of the lyric, the sudden revulsion, besides leaving strophe 4 standing alone, almost meaningless. Let us rather conceive that *for* connects with the elided thought, which the mind of the reader easily and naturally supplies, something like this: Yet is there not essential and even higher dignity in man? Surely there is, "for thou hast made him," etc.

When the sculptors of Italy were called upon to restore the lost arm of the Apollo Belvidere they declined; but at last Montorsoli was persuaded, after long study, to undertake the task. It was the audacity of genius. But not even Milton would dare to write a line to take this vacant place. And indeed there is no mutilation here, but a poetical enthymeme, more effective and beautiful than any expression.

§ 4. Our shepherd boy, we will now imagine, having finished his evening devotions, prepares for rest, saying:

I will both lay me down in peace, and sleep;
For thou, Lord, only makest me dwell in safety.[1]

---
[1] Psalm iv. 8.

His young blood, his vigorous health, his duties arouse him in the early morning from his balmy, refreshing sleep in the pure air of the open plain, and his first thought is:

> I laid me down and slept;
> I awaked; for the Lord sustained me.[1]

The moon and the stars are still shining, and remind him by their silent eloquence of the glory of the Creator, and by their westward movement that they thus speak to all who dwell under the canopy of the sky. But the glowing flush, rapidly spreading upward from the eastern hills, hastens him to his morning devotions. He tunes afresh his humble lyre, saying:

> My voice shalt thou hear in the morning, O Lord;
> In the morning will I direct my prayer unto thee,
> And will look up.[2]

He kneels on one knee, his face eastward, his eyes on the waning stars. He sweeps the sounding strings, and his morning song awakens the sleeping echoes and bids farewell to night.

I

> The heavens declare the glory of God;
> And the firmament sheweth his handiwork.
> Day unto day uttereth speech,
> And night unto night sheweth knowledge.

---
[1] Psalm iii. 5. [2] Psalm v. 3.

II

There is no speech nor language,
Where their voice cannot be heard.
Their line is gone out through all the earth,
And their words to the end of the world.

NOTES.—*Strophe 1.* Celestial objects are personified, and utter voices.—firmament, expanse.—Day unto day; a chain of tradition.

Strophe 2. Theirs is not a language that cannot be heard—*i. e.*, understood (*Moll, et al.*). Hence it would be better to read *Whereby* instead of *Where*. Translated literally, the first distich gives: "No speech and no words without their voice heard." The passage has been very variously interpreted. Many, influenced perhaps by *Where* (supplied by the translators), interpret *speech* and *language* to be that of the various nations in different parts of the earth. So Conant: "Whatever may be the speech or language of the people." This is too prosaic for its highly figurative surroundings, the bold personifications. Moreover, it passes awkwardly from the utterances of the heavens to the literal speech of men, and then back again to the voices and words of nature. How much better that the language throughout be that of the subject, of nature. Others omit *Where*, as the Revised Version, which reads: "Their voice cannot be heard." Likewise we have what is equivalent in "There is neither speech nor language; but their voices are heard among them." (*Prayer Book version.*) So, also, Ewald. This cuts off all direct connection with what precedes, and with what follows, and the passage becomes a parenthetical explanation, very prosaic, trite, and superfluous, that the preceding statement is not literal but figurative. This view is intolerable. Cheyne accepts the latter interpretation, but rejects the distich as a gloss.—line, primarily a measuring line;

. Night is turning into day. The curtains of the eastern heavens unfold, and joyously the greater light begins his appointed course:

III

In them hath he set a tabernacle for the sun,
Which is as a bridegroom coming out of his chamber,
And rejoiceth as a strong man to run his course.
His going forth is from the end of the heaven,
And his circuit unto the ends of it;
And there is nothing hid from the heat thereof.

He is reminded of something not unlike the sun, but higher and holier than he; something more animating and enlightening, more delightful and pure, more stable and true. And he sings:

IV

The law of the LORD is perfect, restoring the soul;
The testimony of the LORD is sure, making wise the
[simple.
The precepts of the LORD are right, rejoicing the heart;
The commandment of the LORD is pure, enlightening
[the eyes.

---

hence, rule of conduct, precept, decree. (See Romans x. 18.)

Strophe 3. Sunrise.—tabernacle, tent.—bridegroom, reminds us of Christ.—strong man, hero (*Delitzsch*).—his circuit, is from one horizon over to the other.

Pagans worshiped the sun, but here he disappears in the greater light of God's law.

The fear of the LORD is clean, enduring forever;
The judgments of the LORD are true, and righteous
[altogether.

V

More to be desired are they than gold, yea, than much
[fine gold;
Sweeter also than honey and the drip of the honeycomb.
Moreover by them is thy servant warned;
And in keeping of them there is great reward.

But oh, who can keep them? David is not conscious of overt sin, but the light of God's holy law shining down into his heart reveals—for by

---

Strophe 4. A eulogy of the law. The writer of Psalm cxix. has expanded it into one hundred and seventy-six verses.—**restoring, refreshing.**—**simple,** uneducated and docile.—Bishop Patrick says: **The law** is the whole as given by Moses; **testimony,** the law relating to commemorative observances—*e. g.* the passover; **precepts,** the statutes of the ceremonial law and positive ordinances; **commandments,** the moral law, the Decalogue; **judgments,** the civil law. (See 1 Kings ii. 1–3.)—**fear,** is probably put by metonymy for such precepts as regulate private conduct. There are twelve eulogiums, related as sumption and conclusion, inspiration and aspiration, which Martin Luther compares to the twelve fruits of the tree of life. (Revelation xxii. 2.)

Strophe 5. The last line of strophe 4 contains only a sumption, whose conclusion is expanded into strophe 5. The judgments of the Lord are most precious and most sweet.—**thy servant,** personal application to self.

the law is knowledge of sin—such a bewildering maze of desires and motives, such strong impulses to evil, that in dismay he can sing no more. A sigh breaks from him:

VI
Who can understand his errors?

With this sigh, the hushed harp is laid aside on the soft grass, both knees are bent, the palmed hands upraised, and with the light of God's sun shining down into his eyes, and with the brighter light of God's love shining forth from his eyes, the dear boy prays—a prayer which saints have been ever since repeating:

VII
Clear thou me from hidden faults.
Keep back thy servant also from presumptuous sins;
    Let them not have dominion over me;
Then shall I be perfect,
And I shall be clear from great transgression.

VIII
Let the words of my mouth,
And the meditation of my heart,
Be acceptable in thy sight,
O LORD, my rock, and my redeemer.

Strophe 7. **Hidden**, secret sins of ignorance, in contrast with —**presumptuous**, purposed, deliberate, boastful sins.—**keep**

THE PLAIN   31

This Psalm xix. is David's according to its title, and beyond question.[1] Its historic place is generally admitted to be in his early life. It is plainly a sunrise hymn. The subject is, The glory of God as manifest in his works, and in his revealed will. Says Bacon: "The heavens declare the glory, but not the will of God; this is known only by his law." We might perhaps say that the harmony of natural and revealed religion is the theme.[2]

There are clearly three parts. The first is rich

---

[1] The well-known paraphrase, "The spacious firmament on high," is commonly attributed to Addison, but has been claimed also for one Andrew Marvel (died 1678). Let him have it. I am glad to believe that the author of *Cato* was not guilty of the travesty. See, however, Macaulay in the *Edinburgh Review*, No. lxxviii., pp. 203, 211, 259.

The Prayer Book version of the Psalter is taken from *The Great Bible*, published in 1539, which was a revision of Mathew's by Coverdale. See Westcott, *History of the English Bible*, p. 185 margin, and pp. 74, 206.

[2] Kant concludes his great work on the *Metaphysic of Ethics* (*Kritik der praktischen Vernunft*—Beschluss) with a famous peroration, beginning: "Two things there are, which, the oftener and the more steadfastly we consider them, fill the mind with an ever new, an ever rising admiration and reverence—*the* STARRY HEAVEN *above, the* MORAL LAW *within.*" This is the double theme, and what follows is an unconscious expansion of David's psalm. Hamilton, without recognizing its progenitor, quotes the passage at length in three several places (*Metaphysics*, pp. 28, 630, and *Discussions*, p. 310), saying: "I do not know a better example of the sublime, in all its three forms." The two productions strikingly contrast the poet and the philosopher, the boy and the man, the heart and the head, the ancient and the modern.

---

back, a very suitable prayer with which to begin a day, not knowing what it may bring forth. Lead us not into temptation.

Strophe 8. **Lord,** Jehovah, seventh time.—**rock,** in whose strength only can I keep the law.—**redeemer,** deliverer from the guilt and consequence of breaking the law.

in natural imagery; the second, in profound doctrine; the last, in holy emotion. In the first is God the creator; in the second, Jehovah the lawgiver; in the third, Jehovah the redeemer. The difference of tone and rhythm between the first and second parts (strophes 1, 2, 3, and 4, 5) has induced some critics (Ewald, Köster, DeWette, Cheyne, and the higher critics generally) to pronounce them independent compositions, most probably by different authors. But the change of style corresponds finely with the change of subject, and is a poetic merit. DeWitt's view accords with ours. We find a similar change, quite as marked, when we enter upon the third part (strophes 7, 8), the prayer. The line—for it can hardly be called a strophe—marked VI, stands by itself, and expresses the transition of thought and feeling from the hymn to the prayer. Strophes 3 and 4 are each double tristichs, containing the chief matter, what precedes and follows being merely accessory.

§ 5. Besides his appointed hours, we may well believe that other occasions moved David to worship. The phenomena of the firmament seemed especially to fire his imagination; the peculiar bent of his genius was upward. Nature in her extraordinary aspects always seems to us a near manifestation of the Deity. In storms, above all, does he seem immediately present; we tremble at his wrath, we hear his voice, we almost see his awful form. Storms of most fearful character often break over the region of Palestine. Wilson at Baalbec, quoted by Tholuck, says: "I was here overtaken by a storm; it came down in a moment, and raged with fearful fury. A horrible darkness covered the whole land, all the floodgates of heaven seemed at once opened, the rain poured down in rivers and, dashing along the sides of the mountains, enveloped everything in impenetrable mist and horror." Dr. Stewart, in a similar scene at Sinai, says: "Every thunderbolt as it burst with the roar of a cannon seemed to awake a series of distant echoes on every side. They swept like a whirlwind among the higher mountains, becoming faint as some mighty peak intervened, and bursting with undiminished volume through some yawning cleft, till the very ground trembled with the concussion."

Such scenes could not fail to be celebrated by David. Let us conceive his attention caught by the signs of a coming tempest. Having hastily sheltered his flock, he climbs a rocky eminence, and taking his stand aloft, harp in hand, appears against the blue sky like a statue erected to poesy. Looking far northward he sees the dim outline of Lebanon covered with forests of cedar,[1] and the

---

[1] These mountains, Stanley and Thomson tell us, can be seen from various points through the whole extent of Palestine.

snowy peak of Hermon. Above them, in midheaven, there is an ominous gathering of dark clouds. A storm is about to sweep from the north in the usual course through the Ghor, the valley of Jordan, and through the wilderness, even to Kadesh in the far south. But the poet's eye, glancing from earth to heaven, sees in the clear cerulean above these lowering clouds the throne of Jehovah, and a host of mighty angels, clothed in priestly vestments, preparing for a special service of praise. Roused by the vision, David sounds his lyre, and with exalted song leads the celestial choir in the hallelujah. The tempest spreads its black wings, shuts out the cerulean, and swoops down. Peal after peal of thunder, first from the distant mountains, afterwards along the valley, reverberates with a thousand shouting echoes among the hills. Amid the roar of the tempest, David's voice of praise is heard mingling with "the voice of Jehovah" (ever the childish name for thunder), and his song does not cease until the storm has swept far southward, and the rainbow of peace—God's smile—beams from the retiring cloud.

Here is his storm song, beginning in heaven—*gloria in excelsis*—ending on earth—*pax in terris:*

THE PLAIN

I

Give unto Jehovah, O ye sons of God,
Give unto Jehovah glory and strength.
Give unto Jehovah the glory of his name;
Worship Jehovah in the beauty of holiness.

II

The voice of Jehovah is upon the waters;
The God of glory thundereth,
Even Jehovah upon the great waters.
The voice of Jehovah is powerful;
The voice of Jehovah is full of majesty.

III

The voice of Jehovah breaketh the cedars;
Yea, Jehovah breaketh in pieces the cedars of Lebanon.
He maketh them also to skip like a calf;
Lebanon and Sirion like a young buffalo.
The voice of Jehovah cleaveth out flames of fire.

NOTES.—*Strophe 1.* The proem, an overture. It sounds the keynote of preparation in heaven, and reminds us of the prologue to Job.—**sons of God,** see Job i. 6.—**beauty of holiness,** holy vestments.

Strophe 2. In the upper sky.—**waters,** the lowering clouds.

Strophe 3. In the far north.—**breaketh,** with lightnings.—**skip,** see Psalm cxiv. 4.—**Sirion,** Hermon; the Sidonians called it Sirion, meaning "breastplate," suggested by its rounded, snowy summit reflecting the sunlight.—**buffalo,** wild bull of Bashan. The Scripture *unicorn* (A. V.) is the rhinoceros.—**cleaveth fire,** forked lightning; the only time mentioned. The construction of this line in the Hebrew might be called zigzag.

IV

The voice of Jehovah shaketh the wilderness;
Jehovah shaketh the wilderness of Kadesh.
The voice of Jehovah maketh the hinds bring forth,
And strippeth the forests bare;
And in his temple everyone shouts, Glory!

V

Jehovah sat enthroned above the flood;
Yea, Jehovah sitteth King forever.
Jehovah will give strength unto his people;
Jehovah will bless his people with peace.

This Psalm xxix. is ascribed to David by its title, which is unquestionable. There is nothing to indicate its historic place except its style of youthful freshness and vigor. Of the five strophes, the proem and epode have four lines each; the others, especially descriptive of the storm, have five each. The variations in the parallelism admitted by the pentastich avoid monotony in construction, and thus leave the fine poetic monotony in the repeti-

---

Strophe 4. The storm is moving south.—Kadesh, Numbers xiii. 26.—bring forth, prematurely because of terror.—bare, of foliage and branches, by wind or lightning.—his temple, or palace, the universe.—Glory, the reply to the call in strophe 1. The mountains, by their echoes, join in the choral anthem.

Strophe 5. The epode restores calm (no more thunder) and ends with the sweet assurance of blessing and peace.—flood, a reminiscence of that great judgment (*Ewald*), suggested by the deluge of rain and the swelling torrents.—forever, the God of the flood is still King, now and forever, and will fulfill his ancient covenant.—peace, the bow of promise.

tion of "the voice of Jehovah" to its full unmingled effect. The whole arrangement is symmetrical and artistic in the highest degree. Our deviations from the text of the Authorized Version are considerable, mostly in accordance with Conant, or Moll, or the Revised Version. Jehovah is named eighteen times; in the body of the psalm, ten times. "The voice of Jehovah" occurs seven times, reminding us of the seven thunders of the Apocalypse. (Revelation x. 4.)

The psalm is only secondarily a description of a storm. The storm is merely an occasion for a call to worship and trust in Jehovah. Spurgeon says: "Rehearse it under the black wing of the tempest, by the gleam of the lightning. The call to worship chimes in with the loud-pealing thunder, which is the church bell of the universe, ringing kings and angels, all the sons of earth and of heaven, to their devotions." Among all the hymns to Thor, or to thundering Zeus, where is its equal? Pindar, sublime as he is, has no ode comparable to this.

II.—THE CAVERN

§ 1. It has been well said that throughout the Psalter runs a threefold cord of personal experience, of sympathetic utterances on behalf of humanity, and of Messianic prophecy. The Psalter has its roots in the events of David's life. In the providence of God his life was varied wonderfully, so that his songs and prayers might express every phase of religious feeling which can move within the human heart. The prophecy, being unconscious, was more exclusively the work of the Spirit.

David possessed extraordinary intellectual gifts. Added to these were delicate feelings, as sensitive to passing influences as the bosom of the sea to a zephyr's breath, but readily deepening into stormy impulses so profound and powerful that they would have overmastered any other than an equally great will. His career was so ordered that all these powers were brought to their fullest development, and tested to their utmost strength. He was destined to rise in early life to the height of youthful ambition, and thence to be degraded to the lowest depths of humiliation and disgrace that a clear conscience can know. He was destined to rise thereafter to a throne, and then again to be minished and brought low through affliction, oppression, and sorrow, to know the anguish of bereavement, the pangs of violated trust, and the sharper serpent's tooth of filial ingratitude. Moreover, he was destined to holy and heavenly communion with God, and to descend from this loftiest height into base crime, and to know the hell of a guilty conscience; thence to rise by grace at last to perfect peace in the sweet sense of a forgiveness of sins. These extreme alternations, presenting a range of experiences unparalleled in recorded history, discovered all the secret depths of his nature. His changing moods and passions, even his sin and crime, which with their swift and fearful punishment form a domestic tragedy of rare terror and pathos, opened fountains of humility, of comfort, of gratitude. The hand of God was upon him, and he was kneaded like dough preparing for the oven. The providence is clear. He was to learn in suffering what he taught in song. Every refreshing stream has its source in a smitten rock. It pleased the Lord to bruise him for our sake.

The words of David while he was being made perfect through sufferings, the gold and silver refined by fire, are treasured in the Psalter. So it is that every man, under any pressure of prosperity or adversity, in any phase of feeling, may here find sympathy, consolation, instruction, and strength for every Godward struggle. The excellence of the Psalter is its universality. It is, says Luther, "the manual of all the saints." Here is prayer, or praise, or penitence, or faith, or adoration, according to our need. Let our state be what it may, we are here taught, as nowhere else, how we may approach God acceptably. All other books of the Bible are the words of God addressed to man, in law, in history, in prophecy, in exhortation, and in doctrine. In this we have the words of man addressed to God—of man in his griefs and fears, doubts and hopes, his joys, cares, and anxieties—words, too, inspired, so that we know they are right words, moving words, acceptable words. They are not suited to one age, but to all; not to one country, but to all. Every new emergency in human affairs has discovered new mines of wealth in the Psalter. It has retained its hold on the veneration and affections of Jews and Christians alike. However devious the doctrines of the Church, its songs are one. All warring sects unite in harmonious devotion. How many millions of all peoples are to-day singing these songs and offering these prayers, and how is their influence deepening and widening as the ages roll on!

David's psalms record his subjective experiences. For the very reason of this entire subjectivity do they need to be illustrated by the circumstances that gave them birth, by his objective experiences. Thus only can we have sure ground for explicating the subtile thoughts and occult allusions to facts, and to account for and interpret the mass of feeling. In part to this end it may be that his is the longest and most minute biography in the Old Testament. Indeed, it may properly be said we have two histories of David, one of his outward life as recorded in the books of Samuel, the other of his inward life as recorded in the Psalter. In the latter his heart is laid bare as no other heart has ever been, so that we of to-day may know him more intimately, more thoroughly than we know anyone that lives or has lived, aye, more than we know ourselves. But to attain this we need the light of objective facts, hence the special value of the detailed story of his outer life. Like as a simple, colorless engraving in mere outline is used as a key to an elaborate painting, so the sharp-cut lines of the prose narrative reveal to us the chiefest glories and depths of the Psalter. Let us, then, follow David in his first rise and fall, that we may better understand the words of his mouth, and the meditation of his heart, and see how tribulation worketh patience, and patience experience, and experience hope, and hope maketh not ashamed because the love of God is shed abroad in his heart.

§ 2. The hour has come when David can no longer be a shepherd lad on the plains. He is drawn into public life.[1] The Philistines are renewing their efforts to subjugate Israel. The armies encamp against each other about fourteen miles west of Bethlehem.[2] Jesse's elder sons are there, and the old man, wishing to hear the news, sends David on an errand to them. What follows is well known to every child: David's spirited indignation at the defiance of the gigantic champion; the quite elder-brotherly way in which Eliab snubs him; the calm, gentle reply, showing, perhaps, the mother's training, but showing certainly his great superiority to Eliab, and that he had already conquered and kept in bonds a stronger than Goliath—his own spirit. Then

---

[1] 1 Samuel xvii. [2] At Ephes-dammin—The Bound of Blood—*i. e.*, the contested frontier.

comes the famous duel, the overthrow of the giant,[1] the rout of the enemy, the royal audience, the triumphant march to the capital, the songs of the women who came out to meet them with timbrels and dances. Josephus says that when the matrons sang, "Saul has slain his thousands," the maidens responded, "But David his ten thousands." This is quite a brilliant bit of fancy for the dusty old Flavius. However, it may be true; for David, when the giant fell, ceased to be a boy, entered upon his manhood, and was from that day and forever the hero of Israel; and maidens on

---

[1] *Cf.* the victory of Odysseus over Polyphemus. We cannot forbear to note here a curiosity in Hebrew literature. The number of the canonical psalms is one hundred and fifty; but in the Septuagint version, and hence in the Syriac, Arabic, and Ethiopic, there is extant another, Psalm cli. Adam Clarke's translation of it is as follows:

"A psalm in the handwriting of David, beyond the number of the psalms, composed by David when he fought in single combat with Goliath.

I

I was the least among my brethren;
And the youngest in my father's house;
And I kept also my father's sheep.

II

My hands made the organ;
And my fingers jointed the psaltery.
And who is he who taught me?
The Lord himself, he is my master,
And the hearer of all that call upon him.

such occasions are prone to be more enthusiastic and less conservative than matrons.

Soon David is an established leader in Israel. He is placed in command of a considerable military force. By a display of valor, and by uniform success in numerous expeditions, he confirms his national reputation, and becomes the popular idol. He is, too, a recognized member of the court of Saul. Apparently he enjoys the highest favor of

III

He sent his angel, and took me away from my father's sheep;
And anointed me with the oil of his anointing.
My brethren were taller and more beautiful than I;
Nevertheless the Lord delighted not in them.

IV

I went out to meet the Philistine,
   And he cursed me by his idols.
I cast three stones at him,
   In the strength of the Lord.
I smote him in the forehead,
   And felled him to the earth.
I drew out his own sword from its sheath,
   And cut off his head,
And took away the reproach from the children of Israel."

This morceau is very ancient, and is found in the Codex Alexandrinus; but it is not found in any Hebrew text. It is undoubtedly spurious, and was uniformly rejected by the fathers, and by the councils of the Christian Church. It has not a particle of David's genius, is thoroughly vapid and flat, but will answer a good purpose here in showing by contrast the excellence of his genuine productions.

the king, and Jonathan, the heir apparent, bestows on him the confidence of most ardent friendship. With all this he seems not elated, but acts and speaks with great modesty and discretion. Thus he grows in wisdom, and in favor with God and man.

Moreover, there was a beautiful princess at court, the younger sister of Jonathan. The consequence is obvious. Here was a handsome young hero, admired by everybody, who, in addition to his other knightly accomplishments, played the harp and sang delightfully. Of course, love and courtship, and the princess becomes his bride. Putting all together, what more could a young man's heart desire? It seems like one of our fairy tales, where everything is perfect—an unknown, handsome young knight kills the giant that no one dared to fight, delivers the kingdom, takes command of its army, and marries the king's daughter. Imagination can invent nothing more fascinating to youth, and hence this history is the common stock of romances. At the happy culmination, however, our story books stop; but this narrative runs on, deepens into tragedy, and rides the billows of an eventful life.

From such a giddy height every path must lead downward. "They that stand high have many blasts to shake them, and if they fall, they dash themselves to pieces." The king's favor was only apparent. Saul had formerly been afflicted by an evil spirit which the magic of David's lyre had power to exorcise—a service it has ever since been doing for kings and for beggars as well. Affliction has become familiar with the charm, and calls for its music in every hour of distress and pain. But a demon of greater power had now entered the king's soul, one that will not down at the bidding of holy song—jealousy. The story is too familiar to be repeated.[1] But I fancy when the maddened king "eyed" the harper, poised his ponderous javelin, and hurled it at his life, that, missing its deadly aim, it crashed through the upraised lyre, an ineffectual shield, tearing out its delicate strings, and then sank quivering into the wall beyond. No more songs for thee, O king! The sweet songster has fled; his lyre is in ruins before thee. A deadly, sure blow at thine own peace. Whenever I hear man or woman cast a sneer at the songs of Israel's bard, I think of Saul's spear.

The lyre of David's boyhood, the joyful harp of innocence and peace, is destroyed. He must now attune another, and learn the notes of sorrow.

---
[1] 1 Samuel xix. 9, ff.

§ 3. *The descent begins.* The first humiliation is that this intrepid young warrior must flee to his wife for protection, into the women's apartments, which, by oriental custom, were safe from other intrusion.[1] After some days she lets him down outside the city wall through a window,[2] and he steals away alone under the cover of night, like a base and guilty thing.

Jonathan intercedes, and narrowly escapes murder at his father's hand.[3] David and his friend meet stealthily and part with bitter tears. No wonder "David's grief exceeded" when he felt this new humiliation—that he had alienated father and son, and been the occasion of the father's attempted murder of his brother and only friend. We say only friend, for the friendships of the sycophants who throng a court move with the humor of the king.

It seems, however, that some two or three young comrades in arms joined him and followed him to Nob, where the tabernacle at that time stood.[4]

---

[1] Psalm lix., see title.

[2] We are reminded of a similar escape from Jericho, and of one from Damascus.

[3] 1 Samuel xx. 27, ff.

[4] 1 Samuel xxi.; *cf.* Mark ii. 25. Nob was close to Jebus, the future Jerusalem.

David's faith in God is evidently failing, for here he descends to a mean deception of the simpleminded priests, if not to a barefaced lie, which afterwards brings them to bloody death, like cattle in a slaughter pen.[1] The fallen prince begs for bread. Then the stripped warrior asks for arms. Girded anew with the sword of Goliath, which had been laid up as a trophy in the tabernacle, his martial pride returns. That trust by which he had won it is now reposed in the trophy itself, which soon betrays him to a further fall.

Down, down, how rapidly he sinks! Whither now shall he go? He resolves to seek refuge in the fortress of his enemies, the enemies of his country, and of his God. Many centuries afterwards, Themistocles and Coriolanus each found, by a similar step, safety and protection. How was it with this falling hero? His few companions refuse to follow him, and he goes entirely alone to the court of King Achish of Gath.[2] This Philis-

---

[1] 1 Samuel xxii. 18, 19.

[2] It ought to be observed that, contrary to a very common notion, the Philistines were at this time far superior to the Israelites in the arts of peace and of war, and in all the attainments of a civilized state. The court of Saul was a barbarous affair compared with that of Achish; and Achish himself, though a heathen, seems to have been a right royal and refined gentleman. See his conduct here, and in 1 Samuel xxvii. and xxix.

tine capital was a short day's journey southwest from Nob. We suppose David reached Gath in the afternoon. He seems to have been blind in his audacity; for here, in the very home of the slain giant, he was soon recognized, probably by means of the well-known sword in which he was trusting. The mob, infuriated by the sight of this trophy, seize and bring him to the king. David's quick wit saves him, but how basely! He feigns madness.[1] His being at Gath and alone might have been proof enough, but he adds lunatic behavior, and scrabbles on the doors of the gates, and lets his spittle drip down upon his beard. What a fall is here! King Achish, disgusted, sharply reproves his courtiers for admitting such a fellow into the royal presence. They have him away. They wrest the sword of Goliath from him. Though they know that this is David, the hero warrior of Israel, who had slain his thousands, yet they disdain to pollute their knightly swords with his debased blood. The rabble hoot him through the streets. He is kicked out of the gate, and chased with stones.[2]

---

[1] So did Ulysses in similar circumstances.

[2] Psalms xxxiv. and lvi. are referred by their titles to this event, but cannot be so interpreted. For a different view respecting the first, see §7.

He escapes eastward toward the hills, and night, the friend of the fugitive, coming on, he is safe again. But how forlorn! Without arms, without companions, without friends, without food or shelter; degraded, ashamed, insulted, scorned by the heathen; beaten off from their habitations, a thing too mean to kill—what a pitiable state! He sits beside the highway in the moonless night, despised and rejected of men, it may be thinking that the foxes have holes, and the birds of the air have nests, but he not where to lay his head.

And now in such condition would not man's heart, guiltless of crime, turn yearningly back to the scenes of his youth, to his father's house, to his mother's side? There at least he is sure of love. So we will think of David as rising with a sigh, and setting his face eastward. He climbs the hills toward Bethlehem, some fifteen miles distant, and labors through the night along the old battlefield, where his public career began, the sunrise of his little day of glory, which had so quickly passed, so darkly closed. He retraces the path he so blithely trod to bring his father's message to his brothers. The waning moon has risen. By its little but welcome light, from the heights which on the west and south overlook the town, he gazes wistfully on the home of his childhood sleeping peacefully before him. His aged father is there, his true and valiant brothers, his gentle mother, unconscious of the fierce and rapid disasters that have befallen her darling. May he enter and rest and be soothed by the kindly sympathies of home? No, he dares not enter, lest he should bring on his home the vengeance of the tyrant who seeks his life, and the slaughter of the innocents be anticipated by a thousand years. Heartsick, he turns away. He remembers the green pastures and the still waters. He wanders down into the valley where his truly happiest days were spent. But even here he dares not linger, for the dawn approaches, and the fugitive from man's eye must burrow in the jackal's home, and hide by day in the darkness of a den.

§4. Not far from the sheep pastures east of Bethlehem is the traditional cave of Adullam.[1]

---

[1] The correct location of this cave is a matter of dispute among the best informed writers. Only two places can thus far fairly claim any right to consideration: the cave in the Wady Kureitun, and that on the hill of Aid el Ma. The Bible mentions two places named Adullam, if they be two: one a city in the lowland (Joshua xv. 33, 35), probably the one mentioned in Genesis xxxviii. 1, 12, 20; the other a cave (1 Samuel xxii. 1; 2 Samuel xxiii. 13; 1 Chronicles xi. 15).

The cave in the Wady Kureitun is about four and a half miles southeast of Bethlehem, in lat. 31° 39′, long. 35° 14′. A

With Dr. Thomson and other good authorities, we hold the tradition to be correct. The site is five miles southeast of the village, approached by a path which descends rapidly the entire distance. "From the low ground of the neighborhood," says Mr. Bonar, "the cave is reached by climbing a precipitous ascent, the full height of which is a thousand feet. Half-way up you find a

---

tradition "that cannot be traced behind the Crusaders" favors this site. The suitability of this place for David's purposes is shown in the following: "It is one of the most remarkably situated caves in the side of one of the grandest and wildest gorges in Palestine, the narrow path to it blocked by a fallen rock, so that a few resolute men could defend it against a host. . . . . There are three caves, opening one into the other, of which the first is lofty and of considerable size, and could easily accommodate four hundred men. We found the floor dry and dusty even toward the end of the rainy season. It was in David's own country, 'the wilderness of Judea,' where he was accustomed to feed his sheep—1 Samuel xvii. 28." (*Brass.*) This site agrees with the indications in the Bible better than the other (2 Samuel xxiii. 13; 1 Chronicles xi. 15; 1 Samuel xxii. 1, 3, 4).

The hill Aid el Ma is about twelve miles west-southwest of Bethlehem, in lat 31° 39' 20", long. 34° 59' 50". In the name "it is possible to hear Adullam." This is the most suitable site yet discovered for the city of Adullam, for a number of places named in connection with this city lie close by (Joshua xv. 35; Nehemiah xi. 30; Micah i. 15; 2 Chronicles xi. 7). From Bethlehem one goes *down* more to Aid el Ma than to Wady Kureitun (1 Samuel xxii. 1; 2 Samuel xxiii. 13). Jose-

slope that leads off to a ledge of rocks. Along this ledge, overhanging a precipice of five hundred feet, you walk for half a mile, the path presenting many difficulties. When you reach the entrance of the cave, you find it guarded by masses of rock, over which you make your way into the cavern, and are soon lost in a succession of many chambers. Each of these is a sort of hall in which you might imagine the rocks to be Gothic pillars. Some of the chambers are only a few feet high, others are like the inside of a church. The whole mountain of rock seems to be honeycombed; it is all natural excavation. No one has explored more than a few hundred yards of it; though the natives believe that it reaches as far south as Hebron, about sixteen miles." From this and other accounts, it is evident that the cave is hollowed in that vast table of limestone rock which

---

phus says the cave was "by the city of Adullam." (*Ant.*, vi. 12, 3.) This makes a strong case for Aid el Ma. But "the site is" *not* "entirely suitable," and "it cannot be said that there is enough resemblance in the modern name to place it beyond doubt as Adullam." If all of David's four hundred men hid in the cave of Adullam at one time, Aid el Ma could not have been the place, for this "low, smoke-blackened burrow" is too small. The row of small caves at Adullam is "separated from" the city "by a narrow valley."

The following authorities favor Wady Kureitun: W. M.

constitutes the "hill country" of southern Palestine, and that its entrance is in the steep escarpment of this rock looking toward the Dead Sea, the ledges being the outcropping of its nearly horizontal strata. David, from his early years, must have known this cave as a place of resort. He and his youthful companions had often scrambled up to its entrance and explored its recesses, little thinking of its predestined history.

In the morning twilight, after his nocturnal journey from Gath, we find David standing near the mouth of the cavern, solitary and sad. The situ-

---

Thomson, *The Land and the Book*, "Southern Palestine and Jerusalem," pages 330-335; Rev. W. F. Birch, in *Palestine Exploration Fund Quarterly*, 1884, page 61; 1886, page 31; Rev. Henry Brass, in *Palestine Exploration Fund Quarterly*, 1890, page 180; Henry A. Harper, *The Bible and Modern Discoveries*, pages 223, 224; Horatius Bonar, *Land of Promise*, pages 244-247.

The following authorities favor Aid el Ma: Major C. R. Conder, *Tent Work in Palestine*, pages 153, 276, *sq.*; Major Conder, in *Palestine Exploration Fund Quarterly*, January, 1876, page 41; George Armstrong, *Names and Places in the Old and New Testament and Apocrypha, with Their Modern Identifications* (revised by Colonel Sir Charles W. Wilson and Major Conder), page 6; Canon Tristram, in *Picturesque Palestine, Sinai, and Egypt*, Vol. I., page 142; A. F. Kirkpatrick, in *Cambridge Bible for Schools*, on 1 Samuel xxii. 1; George Adam Smith, *The Historical Geography of the Holy Land*, pages 229, 230.—*Denny*.

ation is symbolic. Though his foot is firm on the solid rock, there is a mountain behind him, there is a dizzy precipice at his feet. Far below and away eastward stretches the fearful wilderness toward the sea, which now begins to glimmer in the light dawning over the heights of Abarim.[1] So the dawn in his soul betokens returning day, a return of that faith in his God which, in the gloom of his troubles, seems almost to have forsaken him. He has reached the lowest depth, and with renewing trust, the ascent begins. He feels that in God, and in him only, are help and deliverance. Yet there is a burning sense of injustice at the hands of Saul and his minions, made hotter by consciousness of innocence. God shall be his judge. His heart impels him to the divine tribunal. Shall not the Judge of all the earth do right? Relying on God's righteousness, he will appeal to him to overthrow the wicked and establish the just. Let us think of him as kneeling on the dizzy ledge of rock, once again toward the rising sun, and, with his hands outstretched, uttering this fervid prayer:

---

[1] The range of Nebo, the mountains beyond Jordan and the Dead Sea, the northern end of the Moab mountain-wall as seen from the west. See Numbers xxvii. 12.

O Lord my God, in thee do I put my trust.

I

Save me from all them that pursue me,
And deliver me, lest he tear my soul,
Like a lion rending it in pieces,
While there is none to deliver.

II

O Lord my God,
If I have done this,
If there be iniquity in my hands,
If I have rewarded evil unto him that was at peace
                        [with me,
(Yea, I delivered him that without cause is mine
                      .   [adversary,)
Let the enemy pursue my soul and overtake it,
Yea, let him tread down my life to the earth,
And lay mine honor in the dust.

NOTES.—The first line Delitzsch calls the *Capitatio Benevolentia;* with which cry of faith, hope, and love David begins a number of his psalms.

Strophe 1. **Them—he:** this abrupt change of number is frequent with David. Here it may indicate, first the minions of Saul, and then the king himself.—**soul,** life.—**lion,** we have supposed David's eyes were overlooking the wilderness where the lion lurked from which he had delivered the lamb.

Strophe 2. An indirect but strong asseveration of innocence. Compare Paul's appeal: "I stand at Cæsar's judgment seat, where I ought to be adjudged: to the Jews have I done no wrong, as thou very well knowest. For if I be an offender, or

III

Arise, O LORD, in thine anger,
Lift up thyself against the rage of mine adversaries,
Awake for me; judgment hast thou ordained.
Let the congregation of the peoples surround thee;
And over them return thou on high.
The LORD ministereth judgment to the peoples.

IV

Judge me, O LORD,
According to my righteousness,
And according to mine integrity that is upon me.
Oh let the wickedness of the wicked come to an end,
But establish thou the righteous,
Trying the hearts and reins,
Righteous God.

---

have committed anything worthy of death, I refuse not to die; but if there be none of these things whereof these accuse me, no man may deliver 'me unto them. I appeal unto Cæsar." (Acts xxv. 10, 11.) The parenthesis may allude to the deliverance of Saul from Goliath and the Philistines.

Strophe 3. The poet arranges a judgment scene. He calls upon God to arise, to awake, to prepare for judgment. Let him assemble the peoples to witness the vindication of justice. Let them encircle the tribunal; to which high seat, the assembly being convened, the Judge then returns, and sits to hear the causes of the peoples. (A different view of *return thou on high* is taken by many commentators; but this seems best, and is supported by Perowne, Hupfield, Calvin, Kimchi, *et al.*)

Strophe 4. Now into the presence of the Judge rushes the

The prayer is ended. Meditation follows:

V

My shield is with God,
Who saveth the upright in heart.
God is a righteous Judge,
Yea, a God that is angry every day.
If a man turn not, he will whet his sword;
He hath bent his bow, and made it ready,
He hath aimed at him weapons of death,
He maketh his arrows fiery shafts.

---

oppressed one, crying for justice, pressing his suit, asserting his innocence, demanding retribution. If this be not poetry, where shall we look for it? (*Cf.* Corneille's *Le Cid*, Act 2, sc. 8.) —mine integrity upon me, as a robe.

 I put on righteousness, and it clothed me,
 My judgment was as a robe and a diadem. (Job xxix. 14.)

—hearts and reins: with the Hebrews "the heart was the seat of the understanding and will; the reins, of natural impulses and affections; both in contrast to mere outward appearances." (*Canon Cook.*) The rhythm of this fourth strophe is panting with breathless haste and earnestness.

 Strophe 5. With God: more accurately, *upon God.*—my shield: having claimed the protection of God, he looks to him for defense, and will no longer attempt it for himself. Thus he has placed his shield upon God's arm, and trusts him to interpose it.—angry, with the wicked.—bent: literally, *trodden his bow*, which is poetically more vivid and forcible; a large, strong bow, requiring the aid of the feet to bend it.—fiery shafts, tipped with fire, as in ancient sieges.

VI

Behold, he travaileth with iniquity,
He hath conceived mischief,
And brought forth falsehood.
He hath digged a pit,
And hollowed it out,
And is fallen into the ditch he made.
His mischief shall return upon his own head,
And his violence shall descend upon his own crown.

I will praise the LORD according to his righteousness,
And will sing praise to the name of the LORD most
[high.

This Psalm vii. is generally admitted on internal evidence to belong to David's early life. "It is remarkable for vivacity, rapid and vigorous transitions, and vivid imagery—points recognized by Ewald and other critics as marking a genuine production of David's youth." (*Cook.*) But there is nothing to mark its place more definitely. As it seems to express admirably David's feelings at

---

Strophe 6. **He, his enemy.**—shall return, the sides of the pit cave in upon him. The figures are homely, but very strong.

The close. The LORD—*i. e.*, Jehovah—occurs seven times. "Sœpe oratio, quem pene desperantem recipit, exultantem relinquit." (*Bernard.*) The final words of this psalm are like a flower opening its petals to the morning sun. The night had made the flower bend its head, dripping with dew, but now, as it lifts itself to greet the dawn, the tears of darkness have become diamonds around its coronet.

this epoch of his life, we have so used it without other warrant.[1]

Its structure is unsettled, Ewald, Köster, Moll, Cheyne, De Witt, and Maclaren each dividing it differently. The divisions here indicated are grounded primarily on the sense, and are submitted without discussion to the judgment of the reader. The term *Shiggaion*, occurring in the title, means an excited, irregular dithyrambic ode, and accordingly we find it unsymmetrical, yet not so much so as to hide its artistic features.

In the present rendering there are deviations from the defective translation of the Authorized Version and also from the Revised Version. No change, however, has been made but what seems requisite to a correct expression of the original sense, and each is supported by excellent authority. By these changes several obscurities, both of sense and structure, are cleared.

§5. The prayer and meditation are ended. The sun has risen. David has retired into the cave, and is lost to sight in the gloom of its recesses.

---

[1] The title runs thus: "Shiggaion of David, which he sang unto the Lord, concerning the words [or business] of Cush the Benjamite." That is, A dithyrambic ode of David concerning the words or conduct of Cush. Some interpreters consider Cush to be Saul himself. Many other guesses have been made. We may adopt the conjecture that Cush (meaning *Ethiopian*) was one of Saul's confidential adherents, who, himself jealous, had set himself malignantly to poison his master's mind against David by lying slanders while David was yet at court, and that he continued his false and inflammatory accusations during David's sojourn in the wilderness. The supposition will explain a number of indignant expressions in the psalms of this period. (See strophe 2.)

When one reads the Cave Psalms of David, one who has never himself been minished and brought low through oppression, affliction, and sorrow, it is for him well-nigh impossible to catch more than a glimpse of their celestial beauty, or to apprehend aught of their divine power. He may ponder their contents, and then perhaps will only wonder why they have been cherished and extolled through so many ages as the most precious heritage of early antiquity. He is standing as it were in the sunshine, outside the cave, peering into its gloom, and seeing nothing there. But of such as sit in darkness, and in the shadow of death, bound in affliction and iron, of the soul that is melted because of trouble, these saintly words glide like seraphic music into the darker musings, with a mild and healing sympathy. Paul and Silas in the prison at Philippi, the early Christians in the Roman catacombs, the Scottish Covenanters in the caves of the Highlands, Bunyan in Bedford jail, Judson in the Burmese dungeon—these are but few of thousands—all Christian martyrs, all Christian sufferers in mind, body, or estate, thousands of thousands in all ages have been soothed and comforted in their hours of darkness, have been fortified and inspired to saintly heroism by the heavenly spirit breathing in these psalms.

Their beauty to such as these is clear as the beauty of the skies; their power, divine.

If we stand outside the cave of Adullam, in the clear sunshine, gazing into the unfathomable darkness of its unknown recesses, we see nothing. But if we enter, and now immersed far within its deepening gloom, turn and look upward and outward, what a brilliant and glorious view of the illumined landscape and the blue sky, made tenfold brighter by contrast with the dark sides and roof of the cavern, the cold, rough rocks that frame the glowing picture. One who has never been within a cave, and thus looked out on the sunlit world, can scarcely imagine this vision of beauty, so like a vision of paradise, like looking into heaven.

And now, while gazing with dilated eyes on the revelation, we may hear from the far deeper recesses the voice of a suppliant. An interval of reflection has brought David to feel that in the sight of the Judge he is not so entirely guiltless as to be clearly justified. But he relies on God's righteousness rather than on his own, and as his servant, humbly prays for acquittal. He renews his complaint, remembers the days of old, avows his trust, and asks to be delivered from the realm of darkness into the land of uprightness:

THE CAVERN

I

Hear my prayer, O LORD,
Give ear to my supplications;
In thy faithfulness answer me,
And in thy righteousness,
And enter not into judgment with thy servant;
For in thy sight no man living is righteous.

II

For the enemy hath persecuted my soul,
He hath smitten my life down to the ground,
He hath made me to dwell in darkness,
As those that have been long dead.
Therefore is my spirit overwhelmed within me;
My heart within me is desolate.

III

    I remember the days of old,
    I meditate on all thy works,
    I muse on the work of thy hands.
    I stretch forth my hands unto thee,
    My soul thirsteth after thee,
    As a thirsty land.

IV

Hear me speedily, O LORD,
My spirit faileth;
Hide not thy face from me,
Lest I become like them that go down into the pit.

Cause me to hear thy loving-kindness in the morning,
For in thee do I trust;
Cause me to know the way wherein I should walk,
For I lift up my soul unto thee.

V

Deliver me, O LORD, from mine enemies,
I flee unto thee to hide me.
Teach me to do thy will;
For thou art my God,
Thy spirit is good;
Lead me into the land of uprightness.

VI

Quicken me, O LORD,
For thy name's sake;
For thy righteousness' sake,
Bring my soul out of trouble.
And of thy mercy cut off mine enemies,
And destroy all them that afflict my soul;
For I am thy servant.

There are no means of determining with certainty the historic place of this Psalm cxliii., since it contains no distinct historic allusions, but is simply a mournful wail *de profundis*. It is David's by its title, and in its style, and is referable to his early days, since it is without those marks that commonly characterize his later compositions, particularly a deep consciousness of personal sinfulness. In some copies of the Septuagint and in other versions there is added to the title, "When Absalom his son pursued him." This is irreconcilable with the closing sentiment of the psalm, and is considered of no authority.¹

The language here adopted is, with slight exceptions, that of the Authorized Version and Revised Version, which pretty closely correspond. The formal structure is very simple, but is, however, quite artistic, and without calling for remark, merits attention. The sentiment also is so simply and directly expressed, that a thoughtful reader needs no aid of comment. It may be observed, however, that in the last line of strophe 5 "land of uprightness" is more literally *land of a level region or plain*. We call attention to the distribution of the vocative "O LORD," which occurs four times. The general feeling is that of humble trust. An alternate rise and fall is beautifully marked in each strophe, particularly in strophe 4, forming almost regular undulations. Toward the close the feeling becomes more earnest, marked by the shortened phrases, making us think of the quicker panting of a thirsty soul.

§ 6. In after days David remembered his deep humiliation at this time, he remembered the striving of his soul, and he remembered with gratitude the prompt deliverance which was granted in answer to his prayer. Psalm cxlii. is entitled, "A prayer when he was in the cave," being a subsequent account of his forlorn condition, and of his prayer, in the following words:

---
¹ It is the last of the seven Penitential Psalms, so called by the Jews; but I cannot see why this one should be included under that title. The seven are: Psalms vi., xxxii., xxxviii., li., cii., cxxx., cxliii. All are entitled David's except cii. and cxxx.

I

I cried unto the LORD with my voice,
With my voice unto the LORD did I make my suppli-
I poured out my complaint before him,   [cation.
I shewed before him my trouble.
When my spirit was overwhelmed within me,
Then thou knewest my path.

II

In the way wherein I walked
They had privily laid a snare for me.
I looked on my right hand, and beheld,
But there was no man that would know me;
Refuge had failed me;
No man cared for my soul.

III

I cried unto thee, O LORD;
I said: "Thou art my refuge,
And my portion in the land of the living.
Attend unto my cry,
For I am brought very low.
Deliver me from my persecutors,
For they are stronger than I.
Bring my soul out of prison,
That I may praise thy name."

IV

The righteous shall compass me about;
For thou shalt deal bountifully with me.

The general interpretation of this psalm as indicated above is in accord with the rendering of the Authorized Version, here adopted. But the revisers and other good Hebraists prefer to translate the verbs of strophes 1 and 2 in the present tense. If we read it so, we cannot consider the psalm a subsequent description. With this view, however, the unquestionable preterits in the first and second lines of strophe 3, *I cried*, *I said*, seem inconsistent. We therefore prefer the Authorized Version, which on linguistic grounds also is defensible.

§7. The presence of David in the cave of Adullam soon became known at Bethlehem. It was now harvest time, and the Philistines, as was their custom at this season, made a predatory raid on the fields of Judah, and took and for some time

---

NOTES.—Strophe 2 is suggested by the last line of strophe 1. It may be understood to refer to the machinations of his enemies while at court, those who shared and fostered the jealousy of Saul. In the fourth and last lines he for a moment forgets Jonathan, and below declares that God is his only portion in the land of the living.

Strophe 3. This prayer consists of a claim, followed by three distinct yet parallel petitions. They look not so much like the prayer itself as like an enumeration of the points for which he had prayed.

Strophe 4. The description being finished, this closing distich seems to express independently and generally a present grateful confidence in the continuance of God's goodness to him. It is a manner of closing quite characteristic of the Davidic psalms, especially those referring to persecution—*e. g.* Psalm xiii. 5, 6.

held possession of Bethlehem. In consequence, David's brethren and all his father's house went down to Adullam unto him. Besides these, everyone that was in distress, and everyone that was in debt, and everyone that was discontented gathered themselves unto him, and he became a captain over them; and there were with him about four hundred men.[1]

David's aged father and mother had fled to him. His first care was to provide for their safety and comfort. So he took them, guarded by his band, around to the east of the Dead Sea, and secured for them a home and protection in the land of Moab, the native land of his great-grandmother Ruth. He honored his father and mother, and so inherited the promise. While tarrying in Moab, the prophet Gad, probably sent by Samuel, appears and commands his return. Then David departed, and came into the forest of Hareth, which

---

[1] 1 Samuel xxii. 1, 2. These included David's nephews, Joab, Abishai, and Ashael. His followers became passionately attached to him; for he possessed largely that personal magnetism which has always characterized great leaders. See the romantic incident, occurring at this time, but recorded in 2 Samuel xxiii. 13-17, in which his conduct recalls Alexander's in the deserts of Gedrosia, and Sir Phillip Sydney's last hours. (*Cf.* 4 Maccabees iii. 6-16.)

was most probably in the western portion of the district of Judah.¹

As we picture him and his band loitering in the pleasant groves of Hareth, we cannot help thinking of the romantic Robin Hood, and of the exiled duke and his gentle followers in the forest of Arden. We will imagine David employing these sunny hours by inditing a delightful ode in grateful acknowledgment of God's mercies to him, and, wishing to encourage and benefit the devoted followers who share his outlawed condition, addressing it to them. No doubt many of them were godly men ("saints," strophe 3). Others, perhaps the younger men, he exhorts to piety, assum-

---

¹ 1 Samuel xxii. 3-5. There has been some difficulty about Hareth. The LXX. reads "city" for "wood." "Very probably the name is preserved in that of Kharas, a village in the Hebron mountains between Hulhul and Adullam [Aid el Ma], where dense patches of scrub abound." (*Names and Places*, page 80.) "No woods now exist, but it would be too much to say they did not, for pine woods existed in this very district and around Hebron as late as the times of the crusades, though not a single tree can now be found. The site of David's hiding place at Hareth we have, I think, been the first to discover in the strong ruined site of Kharas, which lies in the higher hills above Keilah, scarcely more than a mile [fully two miles] from it, among inaccessible ravines, but easily reached from the valley of Elah." (Major Conder in *Palestine Exploration Fund Quarterly*, January, 1876, page 42.)—*Denny.*

ing a parental tone (strophe 4), and encourages in them a reliance on God by reference to his own experience, and its happy results:

I

I will bless the LORD at all times;
    his praise shall continually be in my mouth.
My soul shall make her boast in the LORD;
    the humble shall hear thereof and be glad.
Oh magnify the LORD with me,
and let us exalt his name together.

II

I sought the LORD and he answered me,
and delivered me from all my fears.
    They looked unto him, and were lightened;
    and their faces were not ashamed.
This poor man cried, and the LORD heard him,
and saved him out of all his troubles.
    The angel of the LORD encampeth round about
    and delivereth them.   [them that fear him,

NOTES.—*Strophe 1.* His resolution, and an invitation to his companions to praise.—the humble, meek sufferers, or distressed ones in general.

Strophe 2. The reason, furnished by his own and their experience.—were lightened, became bright. All who steadfastly look on the Lord reflect the light of his countenance. The contrast is the face dark with shame.—poor man, distressed one.—the angel of the Lord, the captain of the Lord's host. (Joshua v. 14.) Very appropriate to the supposed military situation of David and his band. (See also Genesis xxxii. 1, 2.)

III

Oh taste and see that the LORD is good;
    blessed is the man that trusteth in him.
Oh fear the LORD, ye his saints;
    for there is no want to them that fear him.
The young lions do lack, and suffer hunger;   [thing.
but they that seek the LORD shall not want any good

IV

Come, ye children, hearken unto me,
and I will teach you the fear of the LORD.
    What man is he that desireth life,
    and loveth many days, that he may see good?
Keep thy tongue from evil,
and thy lips from speaking guile.
    Depart from evil, and do good,
    seek peace and pursue it

Strophe 3. Exhorting the saints, his godly companions, to trust and fear.—**taste and see**, "*nisi gustaveris, non videbis.*" (*Bernard.*) On account of this expression, the psalm was used at communion by the early Christian Church.—**young lions**, even the young ones, who are so strong, active, and fierce, do lack. An allusion also very appropriate to the supposed situation in the forest of Hareth, which was probably a wild region in western Judah.

Strophe 4. Instructing the children, *juvenes*, his young followers, how to attain good. (See 1 John ii. 1, *et al.*).—**tongue** (*cf.* James iii. 2, 10).—**pursue**, aspire after; young warriors long for battle.

V

The eyes of the LORD are toward the righteous,
and his ears are open unto their cry.
 The face of the LORD is against them that do evil,
 to cut off the remembrance of them from the earth.
The righteous cry, and the LORD heareth,
 and delivereth them out of all their troubles.
The LORD is nigh unto them that are of a broken heart,
 and saveth such as be of a contrite spirit.

VI

Many are the afflictions of the righteous;
but the LORD delivereth him out of them all.
 He keepeth all his bones;
 not one of them is broken.
Evil shall slay the wicked;
 and they that hate the righteous shall be condemned.
The LORD redeemeth the soul of his servants,
 and none of them that trust in him shall be con-
 [demned.

Strophe 5. The Lord's attitude toward the righteous, the wicked, and the contrite; the poet's experience and observation. (See 1 Peter iii. 12.)—**the remembrance**, the dread lest it should be cut off is characteristically Semitic. (*Cf.* Job xviii. 17.)

Strophe 6. The Lord's dealing with the righteous and the wicked; the poet's experience and observation.—**he keepeth**, etc.: probably not prophetic, but applicable to our Lord. (John xix. 36. See also Exodus xii. 46.)—**evil**, is personified. The evil of the evil-doer slays him. A poetical expression for moral suicide.—**condemned**, held guilty.

Here David has given us another most precious psalm, written in remembrance of his dark hours, but overflowing with gratitude and praise for the redemption which God wrought for him. It is Psalm xxxiv. Commentators generally agree that it is an early psalm, because of its entire freedom from that consciousness of deep guilt which is discoverable in nearly all his late psalms. The tone is didactic and reflective, but warmly grateful. It is obviously designed to give instruction to those about him. The distichs have rather a parabolic or gnomic character. This style is inconsistent with a lyrical effusion occurring at the time of the event it celebrates, as in case of psalms already quoted, but it entirely accords with circumstances such as those under which we have supposed it was written.

The title says that it was his psalm "when he changed his behavior before Abimelech; who drove him away, and he departed." Abimelech was probably the dynastic name of the kings of Gath, and Achish the personal name of the one then reigning. We cannot interpret the psalm in accordance with this title, unless we suppose that the incidents at Gath are taken as representative of this whole period of humiliation in which they were so prominent.

The structure merits special attention. It is alphabetic, a species of acrostic. In this case, the initial letters of the distichs taken in succession are the letters of the Hebrew alphabet in their order, twenty-two in all. In the rendering here this feature is marked by giving a capital initial only to the alphabetic lines. There are one or two irregularities which we need not now pause to note. The object of the artifice was probably to assist memory. It is therefore not a poetic or rhetorical, but a mnemonic feature, yet entirely in accord with the didactic character of the psalm, showing that David intended that his followers should memorize it.

The first four strophes alternate—*i. e.*, the first is similar in construction to the third, and the second to the fourth. The first and third consist each of a quatrain and an added distich; the second and fourth, of four distichs each, which in the second strophe clearly alternate both in form and sense. The last two strophes are similar to each other, consisting each of two distichs and a quatrain. This construction is a compound of the preceding, increasing the variety, while holding to the fundamental plan and symmetrical arrangement.

It has commonly been thought that the Alphabetic Psalms have no strophe structure beyond what the alphabetic arrangement indicates. Hence Moll and Cheyne, for example, mark each distich here as a distinct strophe, influenced, perhaps, also by the gnomic style; others, as De Witt and the Revised Version, mass the whole without any division. Alexander, in speaking of Psalm cxlv., very strangely says: " In form it is an Alphabetic Psalm, and, like others of its class, admits of no analysis." This cannot be allowed. Surely no one can read Psalm xxv., which in alphabetic arrangement is exactly similar to this, and fail to observe its sharply distinct and nearly equal divisions into prayer and meditation, and then meditation and prayer; the two meditations being separated by a cry occurring right in the middle of the psalm (verse 11). If in the one before us the divisions are not so obvious, yet they appear sufficiently clear when we attend to the succession of thought. In the notes an attempt is made to unfold this logical order.

The structure exhibited here may be deemed too elaborate, and be rejected either as not really existing, or as not intended by the poet. Whether it exist or not, I must leave to the judgment of the candid and critical reader. If he contemplate it until its marvelous and symmetrical beauty takes hold on him, he will not readily dismiss it as a fancy wholly baseless. If admitted to exist, then it may be asked, Is it the unconscious result of poetic fervor, the natural rhythmical movement of thought when impelled by waves of feeling, yet undiscerned by the thinker, and hence not a premeditated design; or did the poet become conscious of these complex subjective undulations, and bring them under control, and give them expression in the outline of his design? Let it be remembered that this is not a lyrical effusion of the moment, the offspring of passion, like the more simply constructed psalms previously quoted; but a work done in calm retirement, deliberately perfected at leisure, and having a conscious ulterior purpose—all which is attested by the didactic tone, by the forms of address, and by the alphabetic arrangement. May we not believe that the artist expended pains on the form of his poem, and deliberately elaborated it, wishing to make it more acceptable to those whom he proposed to instruct, and more adherent to their memories?

III.—THE DESERT

§1. THE ascent of David from the humble station of a shepherd boy to the giddy height of the favorite of the court and nation was rapid, smooth, and joyous as a lark mounting with song into sunshine. His descent was abrupt as a bird with broken wing. The humiliation was bitter and deep, but it was short. Already has he begun to rise again. Now the way upward is long, toilsome, dangerous, demanding hard struggles, and full of snares. It is marked by peculiar experiences, developing new phases in his character, and before it terminates at the throne, he has become a man of mature years. The songs of this perplexed period were dear to Wallace, and especially dear to Alfred, himself a harper, a songster, and a fugitive king. Not only to the fugitive, but to all who suffer contumely and persecution, are they replete with celestial power. We must sketch the reascent, that we may better understand the poet's feeling, and more justly prize the gems he scattered on his way.

We left David and his armed band of four hundred men lingering in the solitudes of Hareth, in a desert region. He and his followers are often spoken of as outlaws. This is hardly just. True, he was condemned to death, and hunted by the king; but such was the misrule and disorder of the time, that he, now becoming recognized as heir to the throne, was the best, and perhaps the only, representative of law in all that section. As the irresponsible chieftain of an armed force, he might be expected to become a disorganizer of society; but, so far as we can learn, his influence was conservative, and his course calculated to maintain justice. Hence, during the weak and failing administration of Saul, the independent position of this second Jephthah was a boon of Providence to all southern Judah. The term "outlaw" is also apt to be accompanied by the notion that he lived by exaction, if not by robbery; but, on the contrary, he was the protector of his people from oppression and robbery, and lived by their voluntary and grateful offerings.

We have an immediate illustration of these relations. While in Hareth, word came to David that the Philistines had made a descent on the threshing floors of Keilah, a fortified town, situated in western Judah.[1] He promptly, under divine direction, marched to its relief, drove off the enemy, and remained a welcome guest of the citizens. Probably he tarried here some months, and meantime his band increased to six hundred men.

While enjoying the hospitalities of the grateful city, he heard of one of those terrible tragedies that cast their shadows all along his life.[2] Saul had been enraged and alarmed at his escape. Doeg, an Edomite, the king's equerry, who happened to witness David's interview at Nob with Ahimelech the high priest, told Saul of it, adding

---
[1] Keilah: Now the village Kila, in the Hebron mountains eight miles northwest of Hebron. See *Names and Places*, p. 109. "A fortified city (1 Samuel xxiii. 7), named in Joshua xv. 44 as one of a group of cities in the *Shephelah* or 'Lowland,' which included the low limestone hills bordering on the Philistine plain. It was perched on a steep hill above the valley of Elah, about three miles south of Adullam [Aid el Ma], where the name, Kila, still survives to mark the site." (Kirkpatrick on 1 Samuel xxiii. 1 in *Cambridge Bible for Schools*.) "Keilah is probably the present Kela, a hill covered with ruins on the Judean side of the valley." (Smith's *Historical Geography*, p. 230.) "The valley of Elah has its head near Hebron, and runs northward and westward past Keilah, Hareth, Adullam [Aid el Ma], and Socoh, debouching into the Philistine plains at Tell es Safy, the probable site of Gath." (Conder in *Picturesque Palestine*, Vol. I., p. 204.)—*Denny*.

[2] 1 Samuel xxii. 6, ff.

the lie that Ahimelech had consulted the ephod for David.¹ To have done so would have been owning allegiance to David as chief ruler; for this oracle was only for the vicegerent of Jehovah. Saul probably inferred from this statement that Ahimelech was fully aware of David's altered relations to him. The king sent for all the priests. They were eighty-five in number, and we see them now standing in order before his throne, clothed in their holy vestments. The king charges them with treason. Ahimelech, as chief priest and spokesman, not aware of the deceit that David had practiced upon him, makes a calm and truthful but vain defense. Saul commands his bodyguard to fall on the priests and slay them; but they would not, dared not. He then gives the bloody order to Doeg, who, being a foreigner, obeys. The scene becomes sublime. These holy men fear neither Saul nor the sword of Doeg, but calmly standing, silent and unmoved, they await the death stroke that hews them down one after another, until high priest and all lie mangled and bloody at the king's footstool. It must have been so, else how could one swordsman, all others having refused, accomplish this complete slaughter? Some, at least,

---

¹For a different view, see Lange's *Commentary* on the defense of Ahimelech, and remarks of Dr. Toy.

might have escaped. There is no parallel in history, unless it be the slaughter of the Roman senate in the forum by the Gauls. Josephus well pronounces it the culminating crime of Saul's career.[1] Abiathar, the son and successor of the high priest, had probably been left in charge at Nob, and thus escaped. With the ephod in his hand, he fled to David at Keilah.[2] Thus the oracle of the vicegerent is transferred to David. When

---

[1] In order to understand Saul's conduct in his attempts on the life of David, in the slaughter of the priests, and in his subsequent hot pursuit of David, we should consider that the "jealousy," to which it is briefly attributed, was not merely because of David's prowess and the praises of the people, nor was it the mere whim of a madman; but that it probably arose when he became aware of David's anointing, and the consequent claim upon the throne. That he himself was rejected, and Jonathan set aside from the succession, was sufficient, as things go in history, to excite the attempt on David's life; though in this case its criminality was vastly intensified in that it was an attempt to thwart by violence a known divine decree. But when David escaped, Saul had reason to fear that he would organize and lead a rebellion against his throne. Hence the charge of treason on the priests. And when David had collected a force, and was enlisting the sympathies of southern Judah, Saul, to all outward appearance, had good cause for alarm, and, but for the divine element, we would say he was justified in taking the most active measures to crush what was evidently to him incipient rebellion.

[2] 1 Samuel xxii. 19, 20; and xxiii. 6.

told of the woe which his deceit had brought upon the servants and sanctuary of God, how keen must have been his anguish! But, besides the few words in 1 Samuel xxii. 22, 23, we have only one distinct reference to this event. Psalm lii., addressed to Doeg, burns and flashes with malediction and indignation, but does not reveal other feelings.

Saul, hearing that David was come to Keilah, called his warriors together and went down to besiege him. David once more experienced the fickleness of fortune, and the not less proverbial ingratitude of a populace. For, to avert the wrath of the king from their town, a conspiracy to murder David, or to deliver him up to Saul, was now hatching in Keilah. This, of course, could not be effected without first turning the people generally against him by circulating lying slanders, which naturally deepened public uneasiness and alarm. Seeing the fear on every side among his neighbors and acquaintance, David suspected what was going on, and became himself alarmed. He said, in his haste, that he was surely cut off from God's eyes; but soon faith came to his aid, and he said: "Thou art my God; my times are in thy hand." He called Abiathar, and consulted the Lord by the ephod. The oracle informed him that he could not rely upon the men of Keilah; for they, notwithstanding their obligations and fine professions, would surely deliver him up, as the men of Judah had formerly delivered up Samson.[1] There was no time to lose. The closing of the gates of the walled town would be sufficient to make him and all his men prisoners. A few hours more would perhaps ripen the plot, and draw the net they had laid privily for him. So David and his band hastily fled from Keilah, and dispersed over the hill country. He himself took refuge in the caves of a mountain in the wilderness of Ziph, between Hebron and the Dead Sea.[2]

Now safe in his stronghold, though alone, David felt that the Lord God of truth had redeemed him, notwithstanding his innate iniquity and ill desert; that considering his trouble, and knowing and approving his conduct amid his adversities, God did not shut him up in the town of his enemies, but had set his feet free in the wide wilderness. Yet he was stung by the desertion of his companions, who in the panic fled from him, and felt himself to be like a broken vessel; forgotten, as a dead man. Knowing that his troubles were

---
[1] Judges xv. 9-13.
[2] A rugged district southeast of Hebron. A rounded hill there still bears the name Tell Zif. (See authorities quoted on Keilah.)—*Denny.*

not over, that other nets were laying for him, having lost confidence in the help of man, seeing that the rock walls of a fortress such as Keilah, on which he had looked in complacent security, were no house of defense to save him, he is brought in his helplessness and abandonment to take home to his sad soul the lesson of God's providence, and say:

I

In thee, O LORD, do I put my trust;
Let me never be ashamed;
Deliver me in thy righteousness.
Bow down thine ear unto me,
Deliver me speedily.
Be thou my strong rock,
For an house of defense,
To save me.

II

For thou art my rock and my fortress;
Therefore for thy name's sake lead me and guide me.
Pluck me out of the net that they have laid privily for
For thou art my stronghold.   [me;
Into thine hand I commend my spirit;
Thou hast redeemed me, O LORD, thou God of truth.

NOTES.—*Strophe 1.* **Ashamed,** disappointed in my hopes, or shamed.

Strophe 2. Rock, cliff, steep rock, as well as "strong rock" of strophe 1.—**my spirit**: see remarks following the psalm, and Luke xxiii. 46.

III

I hate them that regard lying vanities;
But I trust in the LORD.
I will be glad and rejoice in thy mercy;
For thou hast seen my affliction,
Thou hast known my soul in adversities,
And hast not shut me up in the hand of the enemy;
Thou hast set my feet in a large place.

IV

Have mercy upon me, O LORD, for I am in distress;
Mine eye wasteth away with grief,
Yea, my soul and my body.
For my life is spent with sorrow,
And my years with sighing;
My strength faileth because of mine iniquity,
And my bones are wasted away.

Strophe 3. Regard, trust in.—lying vanities, idols.—known, approved the way of (*cf.* Psalm i. 6).—a large place, a wide, open region.

Strophe 4. Iniquity: here we have for the first time a deep consciousness of sin, and hence many commentators insist on a later date for this psalm. But the word rendered *iniquity* does not mean the guilt of evil deeds, but the innate depravity or perversity of the heart, an inward tendency to wrong-doing which may have been hitherto successfully resisted; as in Psalm xviii. 23, "I kept myself from mine iniquity." Surely David had by this time discovered and lamented his evil nature. If this is not satisfactory, then we may say that perhaps David was mourning the deceit by which he had imposed on

V

Because of all mine adversaries I am become a reproach,
Yea, unto my neighbors exceedingly,
And a fear to mine acquaintance;
They that did see me without fled from me.
I am forgotten as a dead man out of mind;
I am like a broken vessel.
For I have heard the defaming of many,
Terror was on every side;
While they took counsel together against me,
They devised to take away my life.

VI

But I trusted in thee, O LORD;
I said: "Thou art my God.
My times are in thy hand;
Deliver me from the hand of mine enemies,
And from them that persecute me.
Make thy face to shine upon thy servant;
Save me in thy loving-kindness."

---

the trustful priests at Nob, and that the heinousness of this sin was revealed by its dire consequences, recently made known to him. (See 1 Samuel xxii. 22.)

Strophe 5. **A broken vessel**, an earthen pot at best of little value, easily broken, and when broken worthless. A favorite figure with Jeremiah.

Strophe 6. A recall of a previous prayer (see strophe 9, last distich):—**my times**, all seasons of life.—**are in thy hand**, a declaration of trust in the special providence of God.

VII

Let me not be ashamed, O LORD;
For I have called upon thee.
Let the wicked be ashamed,
Let them be silent in the grave.
Let the lying lips be dumb,
Which speak against the righteous insolently,
With pride and contempt.

VIII

How great thy goodness,
Which thou hast laid up for them that fear thee,
Hast wrought for them that trust in thee,
Before the sons of men! [the plots of man;
In the covert of thy presence shalt thou hide them from
Thou shalt keep them secretly in a pavilion from the
[strife of tongues.

IX

Blessed be the LORD;
For he hath shewed me his marvelous loving-kindness
For I said in my haste, [in a strong city.
I am cut off from before thine eyes.
Nevertheless thou heardest the voice of my supplica-
When I cried unto thee. [tions,

Strophe 7. **Grave,** sheol, hades, the home of disembodied spirits.

Strophe 8. **Pavilion,** booth, a shelter or tent of boughs and leaves.

Strophe 9. **A strong city,** Keilah.

X

O love the LORD, all ye his saints;
For the LORD preserveth the faithful,
And plentifully rewardeth the proud doer.
Be of good courage,
And he shall strengthen your heart,
All ye that hope in the LORD.

The reference of this Psalm xxxi. to the situation above described is in accordance with the views of a majority of the early commentators. Many of the present day assign it to a later historic place, but, as they differ widely from each other, we may adhere to the old view of the Keilah Psalm, or "Fortress Hymn," as Stanley calls it, which is not without its advocates among recent authorities. The chief objection to this view is mentioned in the note on strophe 4.[1]

The psalm is a very precious one; whoever studies it must love it. There is a sweet elegiac softness, a languor and depression pervading it that reminds of Jeremiah. It is not difficult to think that it was a favorite with him. A number of his expressions appear to have been suggested by it, and, perhaps, in chapter xx. 10, he quotes from strophe 5, lines 7, 8. But there is even higher evidence of its worth. We all know that the human heart, in an hour of anxiety, of distress,

---

Strophe 10. The psalm begins with trust, and ends with hope.

[1] Ewald, in *Die Dichter des Alten Bundes*, has made an elaborate attempt to group all the psalms chronologically and historically, and no one has brought to the task more learning and acumen; but the result as a whole is generally considered a failure. Köster says that such attempts "cannot lead to any positive results; a fact sufficiently shown by the astounding divergences of hypotheses touching the age of the psalms."

or of great pain, forgets all things except those most dear to it, those which lie hidden in its inmost recesses, and when wrung by some fierce and final agony, it finds in these its solace. We remember that the last dying words of our Lord were taken from this psalm. May we not say he had studied it, and he loved it? That he had these words by heart, that they came to him in that hour, fills us, as we gaze on them, with reverential awe. The fact crowns the psalm with a halo of glory.[1] " He who had not the Spirit by measure, in whom were hidden all the treasures of wisdom and knowledge, and who spake as never man spake, yet chose to conclude his life, to solace himself in his greatest agony, and at last to breathe out his soul in the psalmist's form of words, rather than his own. No tongue of man or angel can convey a more exalted idea of their excellence."[2] And how is the psalmist honored that his very language impressed the memory of his Lord, and comforted his heart in the darkest hour that ever dawned on sinful earth! " But when the Holy One of God chose these words to express the solemn surrender of his life, he gave to them a new interpretation. The Jewish singer only meant by them that he put himself and all his hopes into the hand of God. Jesus meant that by his own act, of his own free will, he gave up his spirit, and therewith his life, to his Father. And many, who have died with their Lord, have died with the same words on their lips. These were the last words of Polycarp, of Basil, of Bernard, of Huss, of Jerome of Prague, of Luther, of Melanchthon, and of many others."[3]

---

[1] The same divine effulgence invests Psalm xxii.
[2] Bishop Horne, *On the Psalms;* *Introduction* by Irving.
[3] Perowne, *On the Psalms*, comment *ad loc.*

From the use made of it by our Lord, this psalm was considered by Augustine, Calvin, and others as directly Messianic. Luther says: "The psalm is spoken in the person of Christ and his saints who are plagued their life long, internally by trembling and alarm, externally by persecution, slander, and contempt, for the sake of the word of God, and yet are delivered by God from them all, and comforted." But in the strictly Messianic view, "iniquity" (strophe 4) and the hope and prayer for deliverance cannot be satisfactorily explained. So we prefer the view of Stier, adopted by Moll, which sees in the use of the words only an appropriation of an expression full of confidence, and concludes that neither this nor the psalm as a whole is properly prophetic.

§2. The scattered band came together to David in the forest of Ziph, and he found himself again in command of a large force, perhaps the whole six hundred men. It seems there was a town, Ziph, which gave its name to the neighboring forest. The citizens sent word to Saul to come down, that they might deliver David into his hand.[1] David heard of their intent, and offered the prayer recorded as Psalm liv., which by its title is referred to this event. The first strophe expresses his alarm; but in the second he becomes reassured, so fully that at last he speaks of his deliverance as already accomplished.

---

[1] 1 Samuel xxiii. 19, ff.

Jonathan, learning by the same means of David's whereabouts, came down to the wood, and comforted him in most beautiful and unselfish words.[1] After renewing their covenant, the friends part to meet no more. Jonathan retires to his own house, and henceforth remains painfully neutral between his father and his friend.

Saul, having sent a gracious reply to the message of the Ziphites, assembled his warriors, and came down. But David had removed farther south, to the wilderness of Maon, and sought refuge with his men on a mountain.[2] Perhaps it was a divine direction, "flee as a bird to your mountain."[3] Saul pursued, and surrounded this "Rock of Destiny"[4] with his large force. The net was complete, just ready to be drawn, when sudden news is brought of a Philistine invasion. The call is urgent, and Saul

---

[1] 1 Samuel xxiii. 16, ff.

[2] Tell Main is eight and a quarter miles south of Hebron. The wilderness of Maon is "the country to the east of Maon." (*Names and Places*, p. 123.) "Between Hebron and the wilderness there are nine miles by three of plateau, where the soil is almost free from stones, and the fair, red and green fields, broken by a few heathy mounds, might be a scene of upland agriculture in our own country. This is where Maon, Ziph, and the Judean Carmel lay with farms of Nabal." (Smith's *Historical Geography*, p. 306.)—*Denny*.

[3] Psalm xi. 1.   [4] Ewald, in *History of Israel, ad loc.*

hastily withdrew to encounter the national enemy. So David's prayer was answered by a special providence.

Immediately David marched his force up from Maon, and dwelt in the strongholds of the wilderness at Engedi.[1] This was about midway on the western shore of the Dead Sea. There a stream even now issues from a rock about four hundred feet above the level of the sea, and "rushes down the steep descent, fretted by many a rugged crag, and raining its spray over verdant borders of acacia, mimosa, and lotus." The cliffs of the neighborhood are full of caves, which

---

[1] "Engedi (=*fountain of the kid*), now *Ain Jidy*, is situated about halfway along the western shore of the Dead Sea. The precipitous cliffs recede from the water's edge, and enclose a sloping plain watered by the stream which gushes copiously from the limestone rock. Here in the days of Abraham stood the Amorite city of Hazazon-tamar (=*pruning of the palm*): see Genesis xiv. 7; 2 Chronicles xx. 2. It is still an oasis in the limestone desert, and though palm-trees and vineyards (Canticles i. 14) have vanished, the petrified leaves of the one and the terraces cut on the hills for the other attest its ancient fertility. On all sides the country is full of caverns which might serve as lurking places for David and his men, as they do for outlaws at the present day. See Robinson, *Biblical Researches*, i. 508 ff.; Tristram, *Land of Israel*, p. 277 ff.; Stanley, *Sinai and Palestine*, p. 295 ff., for descriptions of this remarkable spot." (Kirkpatrick on 1 Samuel, p. 195.)—*Denny.*

serve as lurking places for fugitives at the present day.

Saul again heard in what region David had taken refuge. So he mustered three thousand picked men, and went down to seek him.[1] This enormous disparity of force shows the determination of the king to search every nook and hollow and thicket, to beat the bushes, and turn the stones, if need be, to find his victim. Hunted like "a partridge in the mountains," David concealed himself and his men in the caves, and there for a time baffled his pursuer.

We must think of him now as lurking in one of these, a cave of Engedi, attended by a few chosen men. In some retired recess, whose friendly darkness reminds him of the shadow of God's wings, he cries to him in his evening prayer, before lying down to rest and sleep. He sees the twin guardian angels, Mercy and Truth, coming to his aid. He no longer fears his foes, though fierce as the lions of the surrounding wilderness, but can lie down in quietness and peace. The night which darkens the outer world, like that which darkens his life, will soon pass away. He will awaken the dawn of both with praise. In his steadfast heart he is confident that he shall yet praise the Lord before all peoples; for there is no

[1] 1 Samuel xxiv.

limit to his goodness whose mercy and truth are high as the heavens, to his power whose seat is above the heavens, and whose glory is above all the earth. Listen to his prayer and exultation:

I

Be merciful unto me, O God, be merciful unto me;
For my soul taketh refuge in thee;
Yea, in the shadow of thy wings will I take refuge;
Until these calamities be overpast.

Notes.—*Strophe 1.* **The shadow of thy wings**, a beautiful and favorite figure, suggested here, perhaps, by the darkness of the cave. (See also Psalms xvii. 8, xxxvi. 7, lxiii. 7.) Moses, in his "Song of the Rock" (Deuteronomy xxxii.) says of Jacob:

> "As an eagle stirreth up her nest,
> Fluttereth over her young,
> Spreadeth abroad her wings,
> Taketh them, beareth them on her wings;
> So the Lord alone did lead him."

We are reminded also of how the unknown author of Psalm xci. begins his "Ode of Special Providences:"

> "He that dwelleth in the secret place of the Most High,
> Shall abide under the shadow of the Almighty.
> He shall cover thee with his feathers,
> And under his wings shalt thou trust."

Did he have David in mind? Our Lord, influenced, perhaps, by these passages, uses a similar figure, but more tenderly, in the well-known lament over Jerusalem. (Matthew xxiii. 37.)

II

I will cry unto God Most High,
Unto God who performeth all things for me.
He shall send from heaven and save me,
   (Though he that would devour me revileth,)
God shall send forth his mercy and his truth.

III

My soul is in the midst of lions,
I lie down among them that breathe out flames,
Sons of men, whose teeth are spears and arrows,
And their tongue a sharp sword.

   Be thou exalted, O God, above the heavens;
   Let thy glory be above all the earth.

IV

They have prepared a net for my steps,
He hath bowed down my soul.
They have digged a pit before me,
Into the midst whereof they are fallen.

Strophe 2. **Performeth**, perfects his purposes concerning me. **—mercy and truth**, are personified. His compassion for me, and his fidelity to his promises.

Strophe 3. **Soul**, life.—**lie down**, to sleep without fear. The circumstances elucidate this highly figurative strophe. The battle array of spears, etc., are like the lion's row of teeth.

Strophe 4. **He**, his royal enemy.—**fallen**: his foes, by seeking his ruin, have insured their own.

V

My heart is fixed, O God, my heart is fixed;
I will sing, yea, I will sing praises.
Awake my glory, awake psaltery and harp;
I will awake the dawn.

VI

I will praise thee, O Lord, among the people;
I will sing praises unto thee among the nations.
For thy mercy is great unto the heavens,
And thy truth unto the clouds.

Be thou exalted, O God, above the heavens;
Let thy glory be above all the earth.

Strophe 5. A burst of rapture. The repetitions have a fine effect.—**my glory, my soul.**—**the dawn,** like the lark, *evocat Auroram.* I will arise from my couch before the morning light appears, and, with songs, will awake the dawn of day. So, too, will I anticipate with praise my sure deliverance from this night of troubles. This delicate jet of poetry is entirely lost in the common versions.

Strophe 6. "His song of praise is not to sound only in a narrow space, where it can scarcely be heard; he will appear as an evangelist of his deliverance and his deliverer, among the nations of the world; his calling extends beyond Israel, the experiences of his person are for the benefit of humanity. God's mercy and truth, towering up to heaven, is the motive, and shall be the theme. That they reach to heaven is the idea of their infinity." (*Delitzsch.*)

This is Psalm lvii.; let us call it the Engedi Psalm. The title says: "Michtam of David, when he fled from Saul in the cave." Truly it is as suitable to the situation as it is exquisite in sentiment. It begins with trembling trust and ends with hallelujah. The English Church reads it on Easter Sunday.

The construction is quite simple. The refrain here makes its first appearance, closing each of the two equal parts. The parenthesis in strophe 2, while it is a redundancy in structure, is far from being a blemish; the antithesis it introduces has fine rhetorical effect; we could not spare it. The emphatic repetitions of words, occurring in strophes 1 and 2, and especially in strophe 5, are peculiar to this psalm. In the Hebrew there are several obscure passages, and the Revised Version is questionable. It was necessary to remodel the parenthesis and the last line of strophe 5, which has been done in accord with good Hebraists. In some other places there are slight deviations in phraseology required by the admitted sense.

§3. Saul was encamped in the immediate neighborhood of David's hiding place. The story of their interview is familiar to every child, and needs no repetition.[1] The king's life was, for a moment, in David's power, but he would not lift up his hand against the Lord's anointed. In the subsequent interview, he asserts his innocence of the slanderous charges of his enemies, and appeals to Jeho-

---

[1] 1 Samuel xxiv. and xxvi. We adopt the view of many critics that these two chapters are a varied account of the same event.

vah to judge between them. The old impulsive affection of Saul burst the barriers of jealousy. David had called him "father," and with tears he responds, "Is this thy voice, my son David?" He confesses his injustice, and David's magnanimity in sparing his life; he acknowledges that divine decree had given the kingdom to him, and asks him to swear that he would not cut off his seed, nor destroy his name out of his father's house. "And David sware unto Saul. And Saul went home; but David and his men gat them up unto the hold." Prudent distrust! But they met no more, and, however much his feelings may have changed afterwards, Saul's last word to David was a benediction.

Psalm xxvii. may be referred to this occasion. Let us picture David standing on the high, rocky pedestal, which was his refuge, during the interview, waiting until Saul and his retiring army had disappeared, then waving his drawn sword triumphantly o'erhead, and exultingly declaiming:

I

The LORD is my light and my salvation,
    Whom shall I fear?
The LORD is the strength of my life,
    Of whom shall I be afraid?

NOTES.—*Strophe 1.* Light: it is said that this is the only in-

II

When evil-doers came upon me
    To eat up my flesh,
Mine adversaries and my foes,
    They stumbled and fell.

III

Though an host should encamp against me,
    My heart shall not fear;
Though war should rise against me,
    In this will I be confident.

IV

One thing have I asked of the LORD,
    That will I seek after:
That I may dwell in the house of the LORD
    All the days of my life,
To behold the beauty of the LORD,
    And to inquire in his temple.

---

stance in the Old Testament where God is called *light*, a figure made familiar to us by St. John. The rendering (English) of the first line is very fine; it sounds like drawing a sword from its sheath.—**strength**, stronghold.

Strophe 2. The Authorized Version is inaccurate, disordering the members.—**to eat**, reminds us of the lions in the Engedi Psalm.

Strophe 3. In this, relates to what he affirms in strophe 1.

Strophe 4. **Beauty**, graciousness.—**inquire**, meditate.—**temple**, not, of course, the Solomonic temple, but the palace of Jehovah, King of Israel; called above, *house;* below, *tabernacle.*

V

For in the day of trouble
    He shall keep me secretly in his pavilion,
    In the covert of his tabernacle shall hide me,
He shall lift me up upon a rock.

VI

And now shall my head be lifted up
Above mine enemies round about me;
    And I will offer in his tabernacle sacrifices of joy;
    I will sing, yea, I will sing praises unto the LORD.

This burst of triumph now changes suddenly to tremulous prayer. So long as his thoughts are on God's favors to him, he is full of joy and exultation; but, as soon as they revert to himself, the undeserving recipient, he comes to his knees with a plaintive cry:

VII

Hear, O LORD, when I cry with my voice;
Have mercy also upon me, and answer me.
My heart said unto thee—
    When thou saidst, Seek my face—
Thy face, LORD, will I seek.

Strophe 5. **Pavilion,** booth made of branches, as above in Psalm xxxi. strophe 7.—**rock,** on which he was standing high above his enemies, typical of his fortunes.

Strophe 7. "The cry is now for mercy, not for victory; the shadows are falling on David's heart."—**my heart said,** a sub-

VIII

Hide not thy face from me,
Put not thy servant away in anger;
  Thou hast been my help;
Cast me not off, neither forsake me,
  O God of my salvation.
(When my father and my mother forsake me,
  Then the LORD will take me up).

IX

Teach me thy way, O LORD,
And lead me in a plain path,
  Because of mine enemies.
Deliver me not over
  Unto the will of mine enemies;
For false witnesses are risen up against me,
  And such as breathe out cruelty.

---

jective dialogue. By an improper inversion of clauses, the usual versions lose the force of the original, making very good prose, but spoiling the poetry. The call and answer follow in immediate succession, indicating hearty promptness.

Strophe 8. The parenthesis is a reassuring thought, entering his mind during prayer; his faith is on the return. It does not mean that they have forsaken him, or would do so; but that even if he were so entirely abandoned, the Lord would not leave him, but come nearer. The sparkle of this gem was caught by Isaiah, when he said:

"Doubtless thou art our Father;
  Though Abraham be ignorant of us,
  And Israel acknowledge us not,
Thou, O Lord, art our Father, our Redeemer."
          (Isaiah lxiii. 16.)

THE DESERT

The prayer is ended; a soliloquy follows:

X

Unless I had believed that I should see
The goodness of the LORD
In the land of the living,—

XI

Wait on the LORD;
Be of good courage,
And stout of heart,
And—wait on the LORD.

And again, when he gives God's reply to Zion, who said:

"The Lord hath forsaken me,
And my Lord hath forgotten me.
Can a woman forget her sucking child
That she should not have compassion on the son of her
Yea, they may forget;   [womb?
Yet will not I forget thee." (Isaiah xlix. 14, 15.)

Strophe 10. We have ventured to indicate the aposiopesis by a dash. Both the Authorized and the Revised Version supply "*I had fainted*," which gives very good sense, but spoils the poetry. A feeling reader does not need this aid. The thought of the elided apodosis is far more forcible when unexpressed. (*Cf.* Genesis iii. 22.)—in the land of the living, not only during my lifetime, thus contrasting with Sheol; but, in contrast with his lonely cave life, when restored to free intercourse with the children of Israel. (See Psalm cxlii. 5.)

Strophe 11. He is talking to and exhorting himself. The third line differs from the Authorized Version, which gives the incorrect idea of an assurance conditioned on courage. Rather it is a parallel continuation of the self-exhortation. So Moses exhorts Joshua, "Be strong, and of a good courage." (Deuter-

§4. David soon removed with his force into the south region of Judah, and busied himself in protecting his people from the depredations of the Edomites, Amalekites, and Philistines. During this sojourn occurred the romantic episode of Abigail the Carmelitess.[1] It does not belong to our subject, but we are strongly tempted to turn aside and tell of the rich fool, he whom our Lord resketched in the parable. Especially are we tempted to analyze the plea of his charming wife, "a woman of a good understanding, and of a beautiful countenance," interceding with David for forbearance. All ye men who would learn how to plead, listen to the marvelous eloquence of her speech; study the circumstances, study its spirit, study its logic, study its rhetorical graces and power, study its exquisite delicacy, study its acute personalities, study its winning introduction, its superb climax, and, withal, study its simple, unaffected naturalness, and you will rise up wiser to sway the human heart; though, indeed, we find

---

onomy xxxi. 7.)—and wait, the repetition very simply but impressively implies that this is all that is needed. "Wait at his door with prayer; wait at his feet with humility; wait at his table with service; wait at his window with expectancy. He speeds best whose patron is in the skies." (*Spurgeon.*)

[1] 1 Samuel xxv.

running through it a thread of feminine adroitness such as may well cause the best of us to despair.

We cannot forbear to note one highly poetical passage, which for boldness of metaphor is almost unparalleled. Having presented her plea, she expresses her sympathy with David's fortunes, passionately and prophetically:

"Yet a man is risen to pursue thee,
And to seek thy soul;
But the soul of my lord   [thy God;
    Shall be bound in the bundle of life with Jehovah
And the souls of thine enemies,   [sling."
    Them shall he sling out, as from the middle of a

The strong antithesis, the rhetorical daring, the appropriateness of the imagery here, are very fine. "The bundle of life" probably refers to a quiver of arrows, suggested by those she sees hanging from the shoulders of the archers standing around David. She means that the cause of David and Jehovah are identical. The slinging out of souls (*soul* means *life* throughout the passage) is not only a powerful figure, but implies a covert compliment to David's prowess and early feat with the sling. We have placed the lines parallel, though probably it is not intentional poetry. But it seems that whenever the Hebrew mind became thoroughly aroused, and broke forth with passion, it expressed itself, more or less perfectly, in those natural forms which characterize its poetic literature.[1]

§5. Soon after his marriage with Abigail, the widow of the rich fool, whose soul had been required of him, David, hearing, probably, of new schemes to entrap him, concluded that he could do no better than to go into the land of the Philistines.[2] So he came to Gath, and offered his service to King Achish. He came this time as the leader of a hardy band of six hundred men, and was received more graciously than before. Achish gave him the town Ziklag for his residence and revenue, and this town ever thereafter pertained to the kings of Judah. Its exact locality is un-

---

[1] Another fine example of this is the lyrical burst of Moses, addressed to Joshua as they came down from Sinai. When they heard from a great distance the voice of the people shouting, the prosaic and military Joshua said, tersely, "A noise of war in the camp." The poetic and paternal Moses replied, fluently:

"Not the voice of a shout for mastery,
 Nor the voice of a cry for being overcome,
 But the voice of song do I hear."
 (Exodus xxxii. 18.)

[2] 1 Samuel xxvii.

known, but must have been somewhere near the border of Philistia, below the latitude of Hebron.[1] From this base, David made forages on the Amalekites and others, southward even as far as Egypt. These people were allies of the Philistines; but David deceived Achish, telling him that his expeditions were against southern Judah and its allies, the Kenites. This confirmed the confidence of the Philistine king that the breach between David and his people was irreconcilable, and, therefore, thought he, he shall be my servant forever.

War was renewed by the Philistines against Israel. Achish enrolled David and his band as his bodyguard, according to the politic custom, so common in all history, of placing a guard of foreign mercenaries next the person of the king. The Philistine army marched northward, proba-

---

[1] The work entitled *Names and Places in the Old and New Testament and Apocrypha, with Their Modern Identifications* (compiled by George Armstrong, and revised by Colonel Sir Charles W. Wilson and Major Conder: 1888), says of Ziklag: "Named between Hormah and Madmannah, a town of Simeon in Judah. The name 'Aslûj, applied to a heap of ruins south of Beersheba and seven miles to the east of Bered (Khalasah), was first discovered by Mr. Rowlands in 1842. (See Williams's *Holy City*, i. 463-468; Robinson's *Biblical Researches*, ii. 201.) The name is not very close to the Hebrew, but is a possible corruption." (*Denny*.)

bly along the seacoast, and pitched in Shunem, on the southern declivity of Little Hermon, in full view of Mount Gilboa to the southward, whereon the Israelites were encamped. The valley of Jezreel lay between. This was the great battleground of Palestine, on which not only Israel often contended with its enemies, but where the tides of Egyptian and Assyrian power met in conflict.[1]

David had made great professions of fidelity to Achish, and had won his entire confidence. But the Philistine generals distrusted him, and demanded his return, lest, when battle was joined, he should fight against them.[2] Achish defended him, but they persisted. So Achish called David,

---

[1] 1 Samuel xxviii. The Philistines encamped on the hill called, in later times, Little Hermon, on the north side of the deep valley which runs down from the plain of Jezreel to Bethshan and the Jordan; whilst Saul's army occupied the slopes of Gilboa, on the south of the valley. The battle was fought on nearly the same ground on which Gideon defeated the Midianites (Judges vii.), and a littte east of the scene of Sisera's defeat by Barak (Judges iv., v.), and of Josiah's by Pharaoh-necho (2 Kings xxiii. 29, 30). Thus the neighborhood of the plain of Jezreel, or Esdraelon, has always been, both in ancient times and subsequently in the times of the Crusades and of Napoleon, the great battlefield of Palestine; and it is referred to in Revelation xvi. 16, under the name Armageddon, as the scene of the great decisive battle of the future. (See Stanley's *Sinai and Palestine*, pp. 329–340.)

[2] 1 Samuel xxix.

and gently and most courteously told him of the disaffection, assured him of his own unshaken confidence, but requested his return. Next morning David led his band southward toward Ziklag. In all this Achish appears to great advantage, and proves himself a royal gentleman; whereas David, we are sorry to say, stands in dishonorable contrast, as a false betrayer of trust.

When David and his followers reached Ziklag, they found that the Amalekites had attacked and sacked and burned the town, and had carried off as captives their wives, their sons, and their daughters.[1] The men were frantic, and David greatly distressed. He inquired through Abiathar of the Lord by the ephod, was commanded to pursue, and told that he should recover all. We need not follow. His success was complete. On returning to Ziklag, he sent, of the spoil, presents to the elders of Judah and to their allies and to all his friends, widely scattered throughout Judah. Thus he showed that his interest was still with them, and, foreseeing, perhaps, the result of the battle of Gilboa, prepared the way for his return among them.

Very soon, a Bedouin runner came from the battlefield with the news.[2] He was probably a

---

[1] 1 Samuel xxx.   [2] 2 Samuel i.

mere camp-follower, who, after the battle, went out to strip the slain, and is said by Josephus to have been the son of Doeg, the executioner of the priests. He announced the death of Saul and Jonathan, and claimed to have given the king his deathblow. This was probably false, as his story seems irreconcilable with the narrative of the historian. However, he had got possession of Saul's crown and bracelet, which he laid at David's feet. We see how widely known and approved was David's claim to the succession. The miserable fellow, however, was not rewarded as he had hoped; for David said unto him: Thy blood be upon thy head, for thy mouth hath testified against thee, saying, I have slain the Lord's anointed. And he called one of the young men, and said: Go near, and fall upon him. And he smote him that he died. This was an act characteristic of the absolute oriental monarch. David was now a king.

§6. The thoroughly patriotic and unselfish character of David comes out clearly at this juncture. He looked upon the death of Saul and the defeat of Israel by a heathen foe with unmixed sorrow, though it opened to him, after long years of anxious waiting, the way to the throne. We read that: Then David took hold on his clothes, and rent them; and likewise all the men that were with him; and they mourned and wept and fasted until even, for Saul and for Jonathan his son, and for the people of the Lord, and for the house of Israel; because they were fallen by the sword.

That David's sorrow for Saul was sincere, and not mere decorum, is unquestionable. So, too, Alexander wept over Darius, Scipio over Carthage, Cæsar over Pompey, and Augustus over Antony. David also was a man of unbounded generosity, and thoroughly magnanimous. He remembered that Saul had lifted him with a free hand to the height of prosperity, and that he was the father of his princess bride, the wife of his youth. Moreover, he remembered that Saul was plagued by an evil spirit; and, therefore, he could the more easily pity and forgive his wild, vindictive conduct. Besides all this, there is evidence that Saul was endowed with those fascinating personal qualities that attract and attach men. He was certainly of extraordinary physical beauty and prowess. He was generous, and warmly impulsive. He was liberal in dividing the spoils of battle among his warriors, and many an Israelitish maiden rejoiced in jewels the royal hand had bestowed. Even his menial servants, as in the case of Shimei,[1] clung to his memory with loyal devotion. Samuel himself, after Saul had provoked his severest censure, after he had been distinctly rejected by Jehovah, clung to him with affection, and mourned for him until he himself incurred the divine rebuke.[2] This fact comes out curiously at the time of the anointing at Bethlehem. When his eye having first fallen on the tall and handsome Eliab, so like to Saul in outward appearance, Samuel thought, Surely the Lord hath chosen him. So, notwithstanding Saul was a tyrant, full of irregular impulses and unaccountable contradictions, we must believe that he possessed that strange personal magnetism which history so often exhibits as belonging to kings and successful generals, and that David, under its influence, felt for him an enthusiastic attachment, which all his wrongs could not efface.

But what shall we say of Jonathan? This was a character incomparable; almost the only one that Scripture history presents as faultless. Were it not Scripture, we might fairly pronounce the character a fiction; yet mere imagination could hardly depict one so truthfully vivid, so well balanced, so graceful, so pure. He first appears in the chival-

---

[1] 2 Samuel xvi. 5-8.   [2] 1 Samuel xvi. 1.

rous exploit at Michmash, an adventure so bold, and so thoroughly in the spirit of knight-errantry, that it would have shed luster on Tancred or Amadis de Gaul.[1] It was, however, most noble in this, that he acted in a spirit of true piety, trusting in the God of battles, saying, as he ventured himself against a host: It is all one to the Lord, to conquer by many or by few. A beautiful and a rare compound of piety, patriotism, and prowess.

He next appears giving his whole heart's affections to the shepherd lad who had killed the giant with a sling.[2] In token of his enthusiastic admiration, and as a pledge of his friendship, he bestows his armor on David, reminding us of Glaucus exchanging armor with Diomede, "a golden for a brazen, the value of a hundred oxen for the value of nine."[3] The duel with the giant outshone the exploit at Michmash, but there is no trace of the jealousy that possessed Saul, nothing but an heroic magnanimity that makes us think better of human nature on finding it capable of such lordly supremacy over its baser tendencies. In all his devoted friendship, Jonathan had nothing to gain, but lost and suffered much; it must have been purely unselfish; it was the sincere admiration of a nobly

---

[1] 1 Samuel xiv.   [2] 1 Samuel xviii. 1-4.   [3] *Iliad*, Bk. vi. 232.

chivalrous soul, its sympathy with its kind. He saw in David a near approach to that ideal of the truly heroic which inflamed his heart, and utterly forgetful of himself, he renders to him the homage of a love passing the love of women. David, in this relation, does not appear to so great advantage, for we cannot at first be sure that he was entirely unselfish, since he had something to gain, and did gain largely.

Jonathan's attachment was not a momentary impulse. His fidelity was sorely proved. He had very soon to choose between David and Saul; or, rather, so to conduct himself as to be true to his friend and yet not unfilial.[1] It was a severe and delicate trial, nobly sustained. Let us observe, also, that Jonathan, the heir apparent, soon became aware of David's expectation of the crown. His friend, then, was to be his supplanter. Did it change him, or shake him? Not a particle, not one instant. He rose above it majestically, as a noble ship surmounts a wave. The last interview of the two friends in the wilderness of Ziph is told in a few pathetic words.[2] Especially are we touched by the half-playful, half-sad way in which Jonathan acquiesces in their inverted fortunes, but not in their separation: Thou shalt be king in Is-

---

[1] 1 Samuel xix. 1–7; xx. 30–34.   [2] 1 Samuel xxiii. 15–18.

rael, and I shall be next to thee. We hear his name no more until his death on the battlefield of Gilboa.

§7. The heartfelt sorrow of David found utterance at last in an elegy celebrating the two heroes, and throbbing with grief at their fall. The father and son had lived and died together, and they were not divided in the lament of the generous poet. Theirs is the finest and most ancient of all dirges; one, too, which has inspired the noblest of all dirge music, Handel's Oratorio of Saul. The elegy is especially interesting as being the only specimen of David's secular poetry which has come down to us;[1] for, curiously enough, it contains no reference to the Deity, and not the least trace of religious sentiment. Its title is quite obscure, but probably means to name the poem The Bow, from Jonathan's favorite weapon.[2] In this name we can almost venture to find the fancy that the ode was intended to send arrows of grief into

---

[1] 2 Samuel i. 18, ff. The lament on the death of Abner (2 Samuel iii. 33, 34) can hardly be called another; it is very brief, and altogether informal.

[2] We find the bow referred to in strophe 3. Perhaps this suggested the name, just as the second Sura of the Koran was entitled "The Cow" from the incidental mention in it of the cow of Moses.

the hearts of the people; for the remainder of the title is: For the children of Judah to learn by heart. At least the intent was to commemorate and embalm the dead in poesy.

ELEGY OF THE BOW

Gazelle of Israel, slain on thine own mountains;
How are the heroes fallen!

I

Tell it not in Gath,
Proclaim it not in the streets of Askelon;
Lest the daughters of the Philistines rejoice,
Lest the daughters of the uncircumcised triumph.

II

Ye mountains of Gilboa, be no dew nor rain on you,
Nor fields of offerings;
For there is defiled the shield of the mighty,
The shield of Saul not anointed with oil.

NOTES.—*Proem*. On "gazelle," see remarks following the ode. The second line is a deep sigh.

Strophe 1. **Tell it not**: he did not know that the Philistines had obtained the bodies of the heroes; an evidence of the historic origin and immediate composition of the ode.—Gath, the royal city.—**Askelon**, the sacred city. The Athens and Eleusis or Delphi of Philistia. Being separated, east and west, by a considerable distance, they are put for the whole land. (*Cf.* " from Dan to Beersheba.")—triumph, as those of Israel did, meeting the victors with music and dance.

Strophe 2. **Nor fields of offerings**, a poetical malediction, invoking such complete barrenness that not even enough may

III

From the blood of the slain,
From the fat of the mighty,
The bow of Jonathan turned not back,
The sword of Saul returned not empty.

IV

Saul and Jonathan, loving and pleasant in life,
In their death undivided!
They were swifter than eagles;
They were stronger than lions.

V

Ye daughters of Israel,
Weep over Saul,
Who clothed you in scarlet with delight,
Who put ornaments of gold upon your apparel.

How are the heroes fallen in the midst of the battle!
O Jonathan, slain on thine own mountains!

---

grow on that bloody field for an "offering of first-fruits."—defiled, with dust, and the blood of him it had failed to protect; a great indignity. The helmet of Patroclus was rolled under the horses' feet, and soiled by dust and blood. (*Iliad*, xvi. 749.) —not anointed, as was usual before battle (see Isaiah xxi. 5), and after its successful issue, for cleansing and preservation; hence this implies utter and final defeat, and the death of both Saul and his armor-bearer.

Strophe 3. **Fat**, the best part.—**turned not back, empty.** The lines are alternately related. *Cf.* Deuteronomy xxxii. 42:

> "I will make mine arrows drunk with blood,
>   And my sword shall devour flesh."

Strophe 5. **With delight:** he delighted to do it. Bishop

VI

I am distressed for thee, my brother Jonathan;
Very pleasant hast thou been unto me;
Thy love to me was wonderful,
Passing the love of women.

How are the heroes fallen,
And perished the weapons of war!

We can hardly venture to remark on this exquisitely tender ode, lest, under a rude touch, its fragrance and bloom may disappear. It is, by unanimous consent of all critics, one of the most beautiful in the Bible, which is to say, one of the most beautiful in all literature. The common versions are incorrect in places, and we are compelled, in justice to truth, beauty, and love, to present a revised version. The structure is very simple, the strophes are quite obvious, and one would

---

Lowth says that this stanza "is most exquisite composition. The women of Israel are most happily introduced, and the subject of the encomium is most admirably adapted to the female character." They who had met Saul in his returns from victory, " with tabrets, with joy, and with instruments of music," receiving, in his royal bounty, presents from the spoil, are now called upon to weep over him. (*Cf.* Judges v. 29, 30.)

Strophe 6. Passing, the sweet, tender, devoted, enduring love with which women love. The passionate tenderness of this stanza has made it deservedly famous.

Epode. Weapons of war, the heroes themselves, as living weapons, or, by metonomy. Like a strain of music, it closes on the keynote.

think the parallelisms sufficiently so, had they not been so often missed by editors.

The gazelle, named in the proem, was so much admired by the Hebrews and Arabs that they even swore by it. (See Song of Solomon ii. 7, iii. 5.) Ewald conjectures that Jonathan was familiarly known to the soldiers of Israel as "the Gazelle," on account of his beauty and swiftness. Both he and Herder think that this first line refers to Jonathan alone; but Dr. Schaff and others think Saul was included. It seems to me that the variation of this refrain, as it recurs after strophe 5, is decisive in favor of the former view. It is also confirmed by the way in which the names alternate throughout, thus: Gazelle, Saul, Jonathan, Saul; then Saul and Jonathan (strophe 4); then Saul, Jonathan, Jonathan. The poet's thought turns in his grief restlessly from one to the other; a sort of trial of strength between generosity and love, and love wins. The first heart throb must have been for the dearest, as also is the last. Another rendering of the first phrase is: "Thy glory (or beauty), O Israel, is slain," etc. This has much weighty authority in its favor, but the one we have presented is as well authorized, is linguistically justifiable, and far more poetical. We will not give it up. Of the refrain, Bishop Lowth says: "This recurrence of the same idea is perfectly congenial to the nature of elegy, since grief is fond of dwelling upon the particular objects of the passion, and frequently repeating them. This intercalary period, or epode, is three times introduced, beautifully diversified in the order and diction."[1]

---

[1] In its last form the refrain is inscribed in Latin on the tomb of the Cid, near Burgos, Spain.

This monument to the dead, more beautiful and enduring than sculptured marble, is not less a witness of the poet's magnanimity. It clearly manifests that lofty spirit which long afterwards was formulated into "love your enemies." But it is remarkable that while in this purely secular poem we find only love and sorrow and forgiveness, there are many psalms, the religious poems, containing bitter accusations and fearful imprecations, which must refer to Saul. Why this strange contrast, this inconsistency the reverse of what we might expect? Is it merely the natural revulsion of a generous soul when his enemy is slain? Does it not rather point to the higher spiritual interpretation of the imprecatory psalms, which views them as expressing, not personal feeling, but the feeling of a representative who resents insult and injury as inflicted on the one he represents?

IV.—THE MOUNTAIN

§1. Soon after the death of the king, David, by divine direction, marched with all his adherents to Hebron. The tribe of Judah assembled, and through the elders, recognized him as its king. Amid public rejoicings, he, now thirty years of age, was again anointed. Hebron was the capital of the tribe, and here David reigned over Judah seven and a half years.[1]

The victory of the Philistines gave them possession of all the country north of Judah and Benjamin. Abner, Saul's uncle and commander in chief, survived him, and fled with the remnant of the royal family to Mahanaim, a city east of the Jordan. Here he proclaimed the second son of Saul, Ishbosheth, king of Israel, and set to work to repair the fallen fortunes of Saul's house. During the next five years, Abner succeeded in driving the Philistines, step by step, from the conquered territory, and he obtained from the elders of Israel an acknowledgment of Ishbosheth, a mere puppet in his hands, as their king. He then

---

[1] From 1056 to 1048 B.C. (*Usher*); 2 Samuel ii. 4; v. 5.

turned his attention to the southern kingdom of Judah, under David, and made ready to reduce it. The result was civil war, in which David waxed stronger and stronger, and the house of Saul weaker and weaker. Finally, Abner, disgusted with his puppet, and despairing of success, turned traitor and went over to David, but was immediately murdered by Joab, David's nephew and commander in chief. This act, which filled David with shame and horror, was ostensibly retaliation, Abner having killed in battle Joab's younger brother, Asahel. But Joab really wished to prevent interference with his own ambitious schemes. He could not brook a rival near the throne. Very soon afterwards, Ishbosheth was assassinated by some of his underlings, and there then remained no obstacle to the union of the kingdoms. So all the elders of Israel came to Hebron, and anointed David king over Israel.

We have now followed our warrior-poet from his deep humiliation in the cave of Adullam, and watched him mounting, step by step, toward the fulfillment of his high destiny. He is now king also of Israel, and about to enter on a career of royal dignity and power, but full of trouble and sorrow. Before we proceed, let us ask, During all the reign at Hebron was his harp silent? It is impossible to say.[1]. Yet we may be sure that in those untold years there was a fuller development of his character. His strong youth was maturing into strong manhood, and the ground was thus prepared for a new and extraordinary series of experiences whose echo should reverberate in resonant song.

Let us observe that two evils have now made their appearance, which subsequently infected as with canker the vitals of the king's power, happiness, and personal excellence. One was the ascendency which his nephews, Joab and Abishai, obtained over him, because they seemed necessary to him. To their arrogance he weakly yielded, allowing Joab especially to domineer over him, and to go unpunished for the murder of Abner. We feel mortified when we hear David's querulous whine: These men, the sons of Zeruiah, be too hard for me. The other canker was the harem.

---

[1] A number of his lyrics might be referred to this period, but no one by its title, or by internal marks, certainly belongs to it. At first glance, it seems that the several psalms which contribute to make up the liturgic ode in 1 Chronicles xvi. must have been composed during the reign at Hebron. But eminent critics, especially Hengstenberg, show clearly that this conclusion of nearly all early commentators is an error; that the interpretation of the context (favored by the Authorized Version), which concludes David to be the compiler, is uncritical and a mistake; and that the compilation in question is of much later date. So we are without ground for assigning any of David's poetry to this period.

The evils of polygamy need no other demonstration than is found in the domestic miseries which it brought upon this noble king. At Hebron were born to him of different wives all those children, excepting Solomon, who played so notable a part in his after history. This fact had great influence on the final development of David's character, and on the complexion of his later poetry.

§2. Having accepted the united crown, David, with statesmanlike wisdom, resolved to remove his capital nearer to the center of his realm, and that jealousies of other tribes might be prevented, outside his own tribal region. The stronghold of Jebus was yet in the hands of the Jebusites, a remnant of the ancient Canaanitish inhabitants, who had sustained a quasi-siege of more than four centuries. David displayed great military sagacity in selecting this town and citadel, whose history had proved its strength, for his new capital. It lay, too, only just beyond the border of Judah, and thus he does not remove out of reach of the prompt and effective support, should there be civil distractions, of his own loyal tribe. Moreover, it was excellent policy to inaugurate his new and greatly enlarged reign by a signal military exploit. Altogether, his idea was an admirable one, and history has vindicated his choice of the site; for it is the only city in western Asia which, age after age, even until now, has constantly maintained preëminence in its own region as the center of civil and military power. David led out his army of veterans, swelled now to a vast host by the armies of Israel, and took the "acra" (as Josephus characteristically calls it) by assault, Joab leading the way.[1] This was in the year 1046 B.C. (*Usher*); and now the City of David, Zion, Jerusalem, enters on its marvelous history of nearly thirty centuries.

The king's first care was to fortify. He then, by aid of Hiram, king of Tyre, built for himself a palace of cedar. Then, alas! he enlarged his seraglio. Then he had to defend himself against the whole power of the Philistines. Alarmed by the consolidation of the kingdom, by the fall of Jebus, by the rapid increase of David's royal power, they gathered an immense force to check the growing danger ere it should be too late. But it was already too late. In two decisive battles David so broke the Philistine power that thenceforth it acted only on the defensive, and ceased to play a prominent part in the history of Israel.

---

[1] 2 Samuel v.

§3. Now our hero-king, whom we have followed and loved from boyhood, has leisure to think of his internal administration. "Zion was his seat, but the new state had to be organized, and the great officers of state and of the household to be chosen. He was standing on the threshold of the most critical period of his life, and did not yet feel himself equal to the task which devolved upon him. Still, in the first period of his reign in Jerusalem, in the flush of victory, in the full splendor of his newly acquired domain, David is only the more earnest in looking to Jehovah, in striving to purify his own heart, and to form wise measures for the conduct of a strong and righteous rule, and in the resolution to keep far from him all that would bring reproach upon himself and a stain upon his court."[1] He has left us an exquisite little poetical summary of the principles by which he proposed to govern himself and select his ministers. We might almost think of it as a rhythmical memorandum, dropped from the notebook of the poet-king, of good resolutions respecting his own official conduct, and of the qualifications he deemed requisite in his ministers of state, and also of his determination to purify his domain of evil-doers. This

---

[1] Ewald, in *History of Israel*, ad loc.

Psalm ci. Luther calls the "Mirror of Rulers."
Let us contemplate its earnest, sincere, truth-loving, lofty, princely spirit:

I

I will sing of mercy and judgment;
   Unto thee, O LORD, will I sing.
I will behave myself wisely in a perfect way;
   Oh when wilt thou come unto me?

II

I will walk within mine house
   With a perfect heart.
I will set no base thing
   Before mine eyes.

III

I hate the work of them that turn aside;
   It shall not cleave unto me.
A froward heart shall depart from me;
   I will not know an evil person.

NOTES.—The psalm begins and ends with Jehovah. It expands from his own personal conduct (strophes 1 and 2) to that of his associates (strophes 3 and 4), then of his ministers (strophes 5 and 6), then of his subjects (strophe 7). Yet its unity is perfect; one general thought being variously applied.

Strophe 1. **Mercy and judgment**, attributes of God to be imitated by the king.—**Oh when**, asks either, When wilt thou assist me so to do? or, perhaps it alludes to his desire already formed, to bring the Ark to Zion. (The latter is the view of *Tholuck, Hammond, et al.*)

Strophe 3. **Turn aside, transgress.—know, approve, cherish.**

IV

Whoso privily slandereth his neighbor,
    Him will I destroy;
Him that hath a high look and a proud heart
    Will I not suffer.

V

Mine eyes shall be upon the faithful of the land,
    That they may dwell with me;
He that walketh in a perfect way,
    He shall minister unto me.

VI

He that worketh deceit
    Shall not dwell within my house;
He that speaketh falsehood
    Shall not be established before mine eyes.

VII

Early will I destroy
    All the wicked of the land;
To cut off all the workers of iniquity
    From the city of the LORD.

There seem to be frequent allusions to this psalm in the book of Proverbs, to which it is quite similar in tone. There are seven strophes, the sacred number. The structure is very simple and remark-

---

Strophe 7. **Early,** day by day, each morning continuously; is the repetitive force of the Hebrew.—**cut off,** drive out.—**the city of the Lord,** Zion. The theocratic king acknowledges himself a mere vicegerent.

ably regular, each strophe being a quatrain. Perowne says: "This psalm falls in admirably with the first part of David's reign, and the words are just what we might expect from one who came to the throne with a heart so true to his God." It is related that Duke Earnest, the Pious, sent a copy of it on one occasion to an unfaithful minister of his court, and that thereafter when any official was guilty of misconduct it was the custom to say: He will certainly soon have to read the prince's psalm.

§4. Now that David was firmly established king of Israel at Jerusalem, he began to look into the great future, and plan for the accomplishment of his heart's chief desire. A twofold work was appointed him: to establish the worship of Jehovah in the place he had chosen for his special abode, and to extend the kingdom of Israel to the bounds promised to the fathers. The first of these now impressed his thoughts. The Ark of God had rested in obscurity for twenty years past at Kirjath-jearim, a town whose locality is usually understood to have been at the eastern end of Wady Aly, about eight miles from Jerusalem on the road to Jaffa.[1] David had proposed to the

---

[1] The work entitled *Names and Places* says: "Kh. 'Erma (*) or Kuriet el 'E ab (?)." This line gives the modern name of the place, and the * means, due to the survey of Palestine conducted by the Palestine Exploration Fund. The book, *Names and Places*, continues: "Also called 'Baalah,' 'Kirjath-Baal,' 'Kir-

tribes who gathered at Hebron to bring it up, but wars had prevented. He was now in condition to carry out his project.

In order to appreciate the significance of this great movement, we must glance at the constitution of the Israelitish state. At Sinai, where the nation was organized, it accepted, through Moses, Jehovah as its temporal and eternal King, and entered into covenant with him as such. Jehovah enacted the code of laws—moral, ceremonial, civil. His visible presence accompanied the wanderings and the wars of conquest, dwelling in the midst of the camp in a royal tent, where he received the homage of his subjects. The Ark of the Covenant was his throne, whence he issued commands and pronounced judgments through

---

jath-Arin,' (?) 'Kirjath.' On the boundary line between Benjamin and Judah, a city belonging to the latter. Eusebius and Jerome (Onomasticon-'Cariathiarim') describe it as a village at the ninth or tenth mile between Jerusalem and Lydda. Kuriet el 'Enab, seven and a half miles from Jerusalem on the Jaffa road, was first proposed by Dr. Robinson (*Biblical Researches*, ii. 11), and has generally been the accepted site, till a ruin of the name of 'Erma' was found during the progress of the Western Survey, which Captain Conder proposes to identify with Jearim. Its position is four miles west of the hill overlooking Bethshemesh, and about twelve miles from Jerusalem." On the great map, scale one inch to the mile, the distance is eleven miles. (*Denny*.)

his ministers of state. Impersonated in the "Captain of the Lord's Host," he led the armies and fought the battles. After the conquest of the promised land, he continued to dwell in his tent, the tabernacle, and was still recognized as the supreme and peculiar ruler of this people. The nation for four centuries was without other ostensible head, the judges being only occasional deliverers, raised up from time to time to accomplish special ends, and were rulers in no other sense. Samuel, however, was both judge and prophet, and in this latter capacity communicated the will of the king to his people, and thus ruled the land as a commissioner. Such, in brief, was the essential element of the theocratic constitution and its history.

The rude people, now twelve generations removed from Sinai and the wonders of the wanderings, seemed to lose sight of this peculiar and glorious relation, and asked Samuel that they, like the surrounding nations, might have a king. Jehovah consented, not abdicating the throne, but appointing a vicegerent. Saul was chosen, but willfully refused or neglected to observe the relation, disobeyed the royal commands, and was rejected. David was now chosen. He seems to have had throughout a proper conception of his position as vicegerent. This appears repeatedly in his history, and comes to the surface in many expressions of the psalms—*e. g.*, his Psalm of Praise cxlv. begins: I will extol thee, my God, O King.

During the distractions of Saul's reign, and of David's until now, the theocratic element was not formally recognized. The Ark, Jehovah's symbol, was in exile, his priests had been slaughtered, his tent was neglected and almost in ruins, the homage of sacrifice had nearly ceased, and no one sought the King of Israel. But we should not say no one; for, since the day that Abiathar brought the ephod to Keilah, David had diligently inquired of the Lord, and ordered his ways by divine direction. Glorying in his relation of subordinate king, he longed for the day when he could make it manifest clearly to the eyes of the nation, and reëstablish the public worship and authority of the rightful, covenanted, and everlasting King. The unknown author of Psalm cxxxii., writing after this time, tells us of David's anxiety:

> How he sware unto Jehovah,
> And did vow unto the mighty one of Jacob:
> I will not enter into the tent of my house,
> I will not go up on the couch of my bed,
> I will not give sleep to mine eyes
> Nor slumber to mine eyelids,
> Until I shall find a place for Jehovah,
> A dwelling for the mighty one of Jacob.

The day had now come. With a select army of thirty thousand men as an escort for the Ark, he goes to Kirjath-jearim.[1] The Ark is placed on a new vehicle, and the march begun. Soon, however, there was a melancholy check—the death of Uzzah. David saw that something was wrong. So the Ark was left at a wayside house, the house of Obed-edom, and the king and his military array returned to Jerusalem.

After anxiously considering the matter, David concluded that though his King was the Lord of hosts, the God of Sabaoth, yet the exclusively military attendance was not acceptable to him. Moreover, the preparations for his reception at Jerusalem were not suitable nor sufficient. He therefore made large preparations. The old tabernacle at Shiloh, doubtless much impaired by age, he did not remove, but a new one was constructed and set up on Zion. He also arranged an elaborate musical ceremonial, a choral installation service for the occasion. He then assembled the three families of the house of Levi, with the sons of Aaron and the high priests of both branches—Zadok, of the house of Eleazar; and Abiathar, of the house of Ithamar. And he said unto them: Ye are the chief of the fathers of

---

[1] 2 Samuel vi,

the Levites; sanctify yourselves, both ye and your brethren, that ye may bring up the Ark of the Lord God of Israel unto the place that I have prepared for it. For because ye did it not at the first, the Lord our God made a breach upon us, for that we sought him not after the due order.[1]

Three months had passed since the first movement. Now the priestly array, attended subordinately by David and his chosen warriors and the elders of the tribes, repairs to the resting place of the Ark. The Levites, having taken it up, bear it in the due order upon their shoulders in the midst of the priestly procession. The first movement is watched by all with deep anxiety, lest Jehovah's displeasure should again appear; but especially by David, who thus invokes the favor of his King:

> Arise, O Lord, unto thy resting place,
> Thou and the Ark of thy strength.
> Let thy priests be clothed with righteousness,
> And let thy saints shout for joy.[2]

After the procession had advanced "six paces"[3] toward Jerusalem, a halt was made, and sacri-

---

[1] 1 Chronicles xv. 12, 13.   [2] Psalm cxxxii. 8, 9.
[3] This probably means something like six stadia, which would be about three-fourths of a mile.

fices offered of seven bullocks and seven rams. After joyful thanksgiving for assured favor and success, the stately march was resumed.

§ 6. We must try to imagine the scene. The road up to Jerusalem is thronged with thousands of glad people. The procession advances with the holy Ark borne on the shoulders of Levites. Before and behind and beside are ranks of priests in their rich sacerdotal robes. Farther forward are bands of music making a joyful noise with cornets and trumpets and cymbals and psalteries and harps. Next beyond are troops of maidens, dancing with timbrels. In the van are trained choirs chanting, in the intervals of instrumental music, the appointed anthems—a grand processional oratorio. Around about are distributed the veteran cohorts of Israel, in military splendor, guarding the holy throne of their Captain and King in its progress to his chosen capital. We observe here the marked features of a triumphal procession. The foes of Israel had been quelled after many hard-fought battles, and peace had been conquered. The Lord of hosts was with them, and they are bearing the symbol of his presence to Zion. Accordingly, we find a note of victory and triumph, otherwise inexplicable, sounding through all the odes connected with this great festival.

There is an open space in the august procession immediately in front of the sacred Ark. Here we see alone the warrior-chief who had led the armies of Israel to their victories, but now without armor, without weapons. We see him, the representative king of Israel, but now without royal robes, without crown, without scepter. All these have been humbly laid aside as baubles in that holy, supreme presence, and, clothed only in a linen ephod, the simple robe of a priestly worshiper, with head and feet bare, and with a harp of praise in his hand, David sounds the trembling chords, and sings in joyful strains, and dances before the Lord. What a picture! No wonder the great painters have so often striven to depict its striking contrasts and thrilling significance. And when does David appear nobler, more exalted, more true, more admirable than in this burst of holy enthusiasm, this full, emphatic recognition and public symbolic expression of his own nothingness in the presence of Jehovah, who had honored him as his instrument and representative? When he thus uncovered himself in the eyes of the people before the Lord, he reached the climax of his life.

But the eye of inspiration, glancing upward, sees something higher than this terrestrial array. There is a triumph in the skies. Jehovah, with ten thousand of his saints and an innumerable company of cherubic warriors in myriad chariots of fire, is advancing amid hallelujahs to the mount of God. The march below is but an emblem of the progress of the heavenly host, and both are prophetic of that culminating triumph, the return of the ascending Redeemer, who, having spoiled principalities and powers, and leading captivity captive, made a show of them openly, triumphing over them in it. Hosanna to the Son of David! Blessed is he that cometh in the name of the Lord! The conception, in its richness and sublimity, is unparalleled, too vast and holy for human words.

With this scene before our eyes, let us listen to the anthem of the Levite choirs, and try to catch its spirit, follow its soarings, and comprehend something of its mysteries. The ode, so grand, so archaic, so alone like a pyramid, must, notwithstanding its length and obscurities, detain our attentive ear. Conceive the chanting to begin after the sacrifices, as the Ark is lifted and the march resumed. The opening words awaken the most precious memories of Israel by repeating the ancient watchword which Moses designated to be used in the wanderings when the Ark was lifted for an onward march:

I

Let God arise,
Let his enemies be scattered,
Let them that hate him flee before him.
As smoke is driven away,
　So drive them away;
As wax melteth before the fire,
　So let the wicked perish at the presence of God.
But let the righteous be glad,
Let them exult before God;
Yea, let them rejoice with gladness.

II

Sing unto God,
Sing praises to his name;
Cast up a highway for him that rideth through the
　　His name is JAH; [deserts,
And exult ye before him.

NOTES.—*Strophe 1.* The first three lines are quoted from Numbers x. 35. The address is directed rather to the Shekinah than to the Ark. The figures of smoke and fire in the next stanza, Herder insists, were suggested by the pillar of cloud and fire that rested on the Ark. (*Cf.* Leviticus x. 2: "And there went a fire from the Lord, and devoured them, and they died before the Lord.") History, however, does not mention the Shekinah from the time of entering Canaan until the dedication of the temple, and it is questionable whether in this interval it was apparent only on special occasions, like the present, or not at all.

Strophe 2. **Cast up a highway,** the customary preparation by

III

A father of the fatherless,
And a judge of the widows,
  Is God in his holy habitation.

God maketh the solitary to dwell in families;
He bringeth out the prisoners into prosperity;
  Only the rebellious dwell in a parched land.

The choirs having thus, perhaps responsively, extolled God's might and mercy, now celebrate his miraculous wonders and providence during the wanderings:

IV

O God, when thou wentest forth before thy people,
When thou didst march through the wilderness,
The earth trembled,
Yea, the heavens also dropped
  At the presence of God;
Even that Sinai
  At the presence of God,
  The God of Israel.

---

pioneers for the march of an eastern monarch and his armies over pathless wastes. (*Cf.* Isaiah xl. 3, 4, where the prophet adopts this figure, which was afterwards applied to John the Baptist—Matthew iii. 3.)—**Jah,** the abbreviated form of Jehovah, familiar to us in the last syllable of the word hallelujah. It is frequent in the psalms, and first occurs in the Song of Moses. (Exodus xv. 2.)

Strophe 4. **The heavens dropped, a storm of rain.** The entire strophe is a quotation, adapted and abbreviated, from the

V

With plentiful rain, O God,
Thou didst confirm thine heritage,
And when it was weary
Thou didst raise it up.
Thy congregation dwelt therein;
Thou, O God, didst provide of thy goodness for the
[poor.

Now are celebrated God's victories over the foes of his people:

VI

The Lord giveth the word;
The women that publish the tidings are a great host.
Kings of armies flee, they flee;
And she that tarrieth at home divideth the spoil.

---

triumphant Song of Deborah. (Judges v. 4, 5.) This was a national ode, doubtless familiar to the people in the time of David, and the present use of it was well calculated to fan the fires of patriotism. By referring to it we find that the heavens dropped water and Sinai melted.

Strophe 5. Plentiful rain, of manna, which is expressly called rain in Exodus xvi. 4. It includes the general bestowal of gifts which come down from heaven freely and richly.—thine heritage, thy people.—dwelt therein, in the abundant shower of gifts and blessings.—the poor, the needy and toil-worn wanderer.

Strophe 6. **Giveth the word,** of authority or command, the blast of the trumpet, the signal for the onset.—**women**: the psalmist is still thinking of Deborah; also, perhaps, of Miriam

VII

Will ye lie among the sheepfolds?
    It is as the wings of the dove covered with silver,
    And her pinions with yellow gold.

When the Almighty scattered kings therein,
    It was snow-white on Salmon.

The moving procession has now come within sight of Mount Zion, and the choirs exult in God's choice of it for a perpetual dwelling, and in his taking possession of it with power, attended by an innumerable train:

---

and her chorus (Exodus xv. 20), and of those who met Saul and himself returning in triumph (1 Samuel xviii. 6).—**kings of armies**, of hosts, in ironical contrast with the God of Sabaoth, *cf.* Judges v. 19.—**she that tarrieth**; *cf.* Song of Deborah Judges v. 28–30.

Strophe 7. **Will ye,** a sharp remonstrance against tame inaction. So Deborah:

    Why abodest thou among the sheepfolds?
    To hear the bleatings of the flocks?
                          (Judges v. 16.)

The meaning of the two following lines is very obscure. We accept the view adopted by Moll, that the rapid flight of the enemy is symbolized, and the glistening richness of the booty is pointed out to inflame Israel in the pursuit. The last line, "It was snow-white on Salmon," is also an enigma. We have adopted Conant's rendering; his explanation is: "Salmon, an eminence probably in the vicinity of Shechem, snow-white with the bones of the slain."

VIII

A mountain of God is the mountain of Bashan;
A mountain of summits is the mountain of Bashan.
Why look ye with envy, ye many mountain peaks,
At the mountain where God hath chosen to dwell?
Yea, here will JEHOVAH forever abide.

IX

The chariots of God are myriad-fold,
Thousands upon thousands;
The Lord is among them.
A Sinai in sanctity!

X

Thou hast ascended on high,
Thou hast led away captives,
Thou hast received gifts of men, and even of rebels,
In order that JAH, God, may dwell there.

Strophe 8. **A mountain of God—Bashan**; this was the region of basaltic rocks east of Galilee, and south of Damascus, very broken, mountainous, and abounding in conical peaks. The district was conquered by Moses, and hence its mountains, as well as Sinai, were mountains of God. But God did not choose them for a dwelling; hence these peaks are represented as looking down, as from the outer world, with envy on the lowly hill of Zion. What superb poetry! "The joyous, exulting, triumphant air of the original here can hardly be imitated in any rendering." (*Dean of Wells.*)

Strophe 9. A procession in the skies.—**chariots**, the symbol of sovereign power and of triumphant victory. God came to Sinai with ten thousands of saints. (Deuteronomy xxxiii. 2; Acts vii. 53; Galatians iii. 19.) Jehovah is now manifest on Zion, as once on Sinai.

Israel is now assured of support, and of the ruin of God's enemies:

XI

Blessed be the LORD, day by day!
Are we burdened? he, God, is our help.
God is unto us a God of deliverances,   [death.
And to JEHOVAH the Lord belongeth escape from

XII

Surely God will crush the head of his enemies,
The hairy crown of him that goeth on in his trespasses.
The Lord hath said: From Bashan will I bring back,
I will bring them again from the depths of the sea;
That thou mayest bathe thy foot in blood,   [mies.
The tongue of thy dogs have its portion of thine ene-

Strophe 10. **Hast led,** in the train of the victor. So Deborah: "Arise, Barak, and lead thy captivity captive." (Judges v. 12.) In the title of this psalm in the LXX. we read, "When the house was built after the captivity." Hence this may refer primarily to the captivity of the Ark in Philistia. (*Cf.* Psalm lxxviii. 61.)—**gifts of men,** consisting of men. St. Paul, in Ephesians iv. 8, quotes the words thus: "And gave gifts unto men." The Hebrew will not bear this rendering. "Yet from the standpoint of its fulfillment in the victorious march of the triumphant Redeemer (Colossians ii. 15), it is applied in such a way that the thought comes out that the conqueror has taken to himself these gifts, which constitute his spoils, not for his own enrichment, but for the benefit of man." (*Moll.*)

Strophe 11. **Escape;** the expression is so comprehensive that it can mean the escape from death to eternal life. (*Moll.*)

The order of the march is now described:

XIII

They have seen thy processions, O God,
Even the processions of my God,
   Of my King, in the sanctuary.

Before went the singers,
The minstrels followed after,
In the midst, maidens beating on timbrels.
They bless God in companies,
The Lord, they that are of the fountain of Israel.
   There is little Benjamin, their ruler,
   Princes of Judah, their multitude,
   Princes of Zebulun,
   Princes of Naphtali.

There is an expression of the highest triumph in the rhymes [?] at the ends of the verses in the Hebrew. (*Böttcher.*)

Strophe 12. **Hairy crown**, luxuriant hair, the sign of youth and strength—*e. g.*, Absalom, Samson. What follows may be paraphrased thus: The Lord hath said, Though my scattered foes hide amid the hills of Bashan, or in the depths of the Dead Sea, yet will I capture and bring them back, that ye may take vengeance on them.

Strophe 13. **They have seen**, all men, friends and foes.—**my King**, is emphatic in the Hebrew. It recognizes the theocratic relation.—**the fountain of Israel**—*i. e.*, stock of Israel. Quite similarly in Isaiah xlviii. 1:

    Hear ye this, O house of Jacob,
    Which are called by the name of Israel,
    And are come forth out of the waters of Judah.

(*Cf.* also Isaiah li. 1.)—**little Benjamin**, the youngest son; or,

Future conquests are anticipated, and the subjection of the whole world predicted. All kingdoms are summoned to praise God, and to acknowledge his power:

XIV

Thy God hath commanded thy strength;
Strengthen, O God, what thou hast wrought for us.
Because of thy temple at Jerusalem,
Kings shall bring presents unto thee.

Rebuke the wild beast of the reeds,
    The bulls, with the calves of the peoples
    Prostrating themselves with pieces of silver.
Scatter the peoples that delight in war.

Princes shall come out of Egypt;
Ethiopia shall eagerly stretch out her hands unto God.

---

in allusion to the small number of the tribe, as Saul said: Am I not a Benjamite, of the smallest of the tribes of Israel? (1 Samuel ix. 21.)—**their ruler;** this is quite obscure; it may mean the leader of the procession; it may mean the conqueror of the heathen, in allusion to Saul. The two royal tribes are named. We should remember that Zion was in Benjamin. Benjamin and Judah were the two southern tribes, while Zebulun and Naphtali were on the extreme north; hence the four may stand for all. The two latter are named in the Song of Deborah. (Judges v. 18.)—**their multitude,** is still more obscure. It possibly is intended to indicate the strength of Judah; or, possibly, the great throng of Judahites present in the procession.

Strophe 14. **Commanded thy strength,** ordained thy dominion.—**strengthen,** confirm and enlarge.—**because of,** out of re-

XV

Sing unto God, ye kingdoms of the earth,
Sing praises unto the Lord,
To him that rideth upon the ancient heaven of heavens;
Lo, he uttereth his voice, a mighty voice.

Ascribe ye strength unto God;
   Over Israel is his majesty,
   And his strength is in the skies.
Terrible art thou, O God, from thy holy places.
   The God of Israel,
He giveth strength and peace unto his people.
   Blessed be God.

---

spect for.—**thy temple**, not, of course, the Solomonic temple, but thy palace, the tabernacle being so called as the home of royalty. It is elsewhere called so in the psalms, and also in 1 Samuel i. 10. But, as we are now looking into the future, may not the Solomonic temple be referred to by anticipation?—**beasts of the reeds**, crocodile or hippopotamus, symbolic of Egypt. (*Cf.* Job xl. 21; Isaiah xxx. 6, and xxxiv. 7.)—**bulls**—**calves**, the princes and the common people. May this not symbolize Assyria? Or is the reference still to Egypt and to her national gods? The next line is very obscure. More literally it is: *Stamping along with pieces of silver*. *Stamping* agrees better with *bulls* and *calves* than *prostrating*. We have, however, adopted Conant's rendering, whose explanation is: Rendering homage with tribute money.—**princes shall come**, to do homage.

Strophe 15. **Lo, he uttereth his voice**; the poet hears the mighty voice of Jehovah as it thunders along the ancient heavens, commanding the triumphal march of his cherubic hosts.—

Most of the early interpreters (also Stier *et al.*) refer this Psalm lxviii. to the historic connection we have indicated. It seems eminently suitable thereto, but it may be viewed as a general festival hymn to be used on occasions of victory, either accomplished or anticipated. In the modern Jewish ritual it is used at Pentecost, the thanksgiving for harvest.

It is a Titan, says Hitzig. It is the most glowing, the boldest, and most powerful hymn of the Psalter, says Hupfeld. A psalm in the style of Deborah, advancing to the highest pinnacle of hymnic invention and representation, says Delitzsch. The authorities also agree that it is one of the most ancient monuments of Hebrew poetry, involving the highest originality in its imagery. " The fundamental thought is as clear as the arrangement and rhythmical organizations, namely: The celebration of the entrance of Jehovah into his sanctuary on Zion after victories; and his rule over the world extending itself from thence." (*Moll.*)

The structure is quite irregular, having that dithyrambic form which is generally adopted in the processional odes of classical poets. It is probably antiphonal, and one can readily fancy which are the themes and which the responses, guided by the frequent and abrupt changes of subject.

The Authorized Version is very defective, and

---

thy holy places, the earthly and the heavenly sanctuaries. (*Hitzig.*)

N. B. Or the sacred names, Elohim (God) occurs most frequently. Adonai (Lord), Shaddai (Almighty), Jehovah and Jah also occur. Each of the two latter names occurs twice.

the Revised Version not altogether satisfactory. Hence we have given a different rendering in several places, supported by the authority of various translators. The obscurities of the text are thereby diminished, but not entirely eliminated. The general tenor of the psalm, however, is quite transparent, and it is evidently in free imitation of the great national war song of Israel, the Song of Deborah. (Judges v.)

The ode, or anthem, has marked prophetic features, and moreover, is capable throughout of a typical and spiritual interpretation. Probably, however, it is not directly Messianic, but only has a Messianic meaning and application, as indicated by the use made of strophe 10 in Ephesians iv. 8. To apply it to Christian times, adding Christian meditations, has been the chief aim of many commentators, and is not difficult. Such treatment is, however, quite foreign to our purpose here, and would draw attention away from its æsthetic features. It impresses us, when we think of it, as a product of poetic genius, very much as we are impressed by a grand colossal statue of antiquity. Time has marred and obscured some of its features, but not its majestic outlines. We may fail to fix its true origin, and its symbolic significance, but we are none the less fascinated by its archaic dignity, its mystery, its granitic mass and superhuman proportions.

§7. The procession has now reached the foot of the declivity on which the citadel of Zion stands. The ramparts are lined with a multitude, shouting joyous welcome in response to the clangor of musical instruments. The great embattled gates, toward which the procession is wending upward, are closed, and on the tower that guards them stands the warder.

At the beginning of the ascent the shoutings cease, the instruments are silent, or merely accompany a new anthem which is now chanted by the Levitical choirs. First, in full chorus it declares, an echo from the ode just sung, that to the King now resuming his throne the whole earth belongs, for he made it. Second, the vicegerent king, in solo chant, asks who is worthy to go up as attendant to his palace. Third, the high priest gives oracular response: He only who is outwardly and inwardly pure. Fourth, the full chorus responds: Such shall be blessed, and such is the character of redeemed Israel.

Now the closed gates are reached. A semichorus of Levites commands them to open to the King; not commanding the warder, but the dead matter of the portals themselves, which surely must be conscious in such a presence, and obedient. The warder, from the tower, issues his challenge: Who is this King of glory? A choral burst from the whole multitude of Levite singers responds: Jehovah! By another semi-chorus the demand for entrance is repeated; so also the challenge and reply. The gates are then thrown open. Here are the words of this sublime oratorio:

I

The earth is the LORD's and the fullness thereof,
The world and they that dwell therein;
For he hath founded it upon the seas,
And established it upon the floods.

II

Who shall ascend into the hill of the LORD?
And who shall stand in his holy place?

III

He that hath clean hands,
  And a pure heart;
Who hath not lifted up his soul unto vanity,
  Nor sworn deceitfully.

NOTES.—*Strophe 1*. The declaration of the universal sovereignty of Jehovah, about to be enthroned on Zion, forcibly expresses the eminent distinction of Israel, with whom he condescends to make his abode.—fullness, denotes the inhabitants, parallel to "they that dwell." It is applied by St. Paul in 1 Corinthians x. 26 to include the flesh to be eaten.—he: the Hebrew is emphatic.—founded upon: the ancient notion of the earth as a plain, surrounded by and resting upon the ocean. The Bible was not written to teach cosmology, and always speaks of nature in the popular language of its own day. The expression probably alludes to Genesis i. 9. The same notion appears elsewhere—*e. g.*, "The fountains of the great deep were broken up" (Genesis vii. 11); "The waters under the earth" (Exodus xx. 4); *et al*. Here the thought is to be taken in a

IV

He shall receive a blessing from the LORD,
And righteousness from the God of his salvation.
This is the generation of them that seek after him,
That seek thy face, even Jacob.—Selah.

---

poetical sense, with the added idea of firm establishment upon so unstable a foundation.

Strophe 3. **He that hath:** four cardinal points of character are named, two internal and two external, two positive and two negative. The first probably refers to the unclean hands of Uzzah. (2 Samuel vi. 6, 7.) *The lifting up of the soul unto vanity* is fixing the desires on what is wrong and false—those internal strivings which issue in the outward practice of deceit. The whole is thoroughly evangelical, and wonderfully comprehensive.

Strophe 4. In the arrangement of strophes we have given to this two distichs. The first of these, "He shall receive," etc., is frequently thrown into the second strophe as a part of the answer to the previous question. We prefer the present arrangement, because, first, the oracular response attributed to the high priest is complete and perfect without this distich, which would add words without adding meaning; for all that is said in the distich is already fully and clearly implied in the previous words of reply. Second, when transferred to strophe 4, and attributed to the people, they gain significance, since they are then an explication and endorsement of the oracle by the people. Third, the symmetry of the construction is promoted by this division.—**the blessing**, probably refers to that which the presence of the Ark brought on the house of Obed-edom, though not of Israel. (2 Samuel vi. 11.)—**righteousness**, imputed to him. (*Cf.* Genesis xv. 6.)—**this is the generation**, this is the race of people who now seek to stand

V.

Lift up your heads, O ye gates,
And be ye lift up, ye everlasting doors,
And the King of glory shall come in.
Who is this King of glory?
The LORD, strong and mighty,
The LORD, mighty in battle.

before God, and their historic name is Israel. "This" is emphatic in the Hebrew.—**even Jacob**: this race that seek him is Jacob, is the true Israel of clean hands and pure hearts, Israelites not in name only, but in spirit. Here is our only deviation from the Authorized Version. We have adopted Conant's phrase, as in the margin of the Revised Version, and preferred by the American Old Testament Revision Company. The construction has been much discussed, many preferring to read, with the Revised Version, "O God of Jacob." This dulls the point of the second distich, losing the profession or claim involved in the rendering "even Jacob," by which rendering "Jacob" becomes the sum of the preceding predicates. The Authorized Version rendering, "O Jacob," must be rejected; for why God should be called Jacob is far to seek.

Strophe 5. **Lift up**, arouse yourselves, behold his presence and give way. The gates are boldly personified, and called upon to arouse, as if from lethargy, and look up. This seems a simple, sufficient, and obvious explanation; but many others have been given, some of which are quite startling.—**everlasting doors**, so called because, as typical of the gates of celestial glory which opened to receive our ascending Lord, **he**, the Eternal One, shall dwell within forever. Stanley refers the phrase to the antiquity of the citadel of Jebus (!).—**strong**, is an essential attribute, and **mighty** is its manifestation in action; not

VI

Lift up your heads, O ye gates,
Even lift them up, ye everlasting doors,
   And the King of glory shall come in.

Who is this King of glory?

The LORD of hosts,
He is the King of glory.—Selah.

    This hymn of entrance into Zion is David's Psalm xxiv. The structure is quite obvious, owing to the abrupt changes of sentiment. It divides into two nearly equal parts, marked by the *Selah*, which has, therefore, in this case been retained. The repetition of strophe 5 with slight and elegant variations is very beautiful. With one exception, considered in the notes, the phraseology of the Authorized Version and Revised Version has been adhered to.

    That the bringing up of the Ark is the historic occasion of this psalm is generally admitted, and also that it is antiphonal. We have ventured to indicate a way in which it may have been rendered (substantially the view adopted by Delitzsch), on which, however, we do not insist; though that there are distinct themes, questions, and responses will hardly be questioned. This character makes

---

hendiadys—the words do not merely repeat the idea.—Who is this: Delitzsch regards this question as the speech of the gates themselves, making the whole representation ideal. Since it is here viewed as an actual ceremony, we assign the question to the warder.

   Strophe 6. **The Lord of hosts, Jehovah Sabaoth.**

it suitable for liturgic use, and it is noticeable that, according to Talmudic tradition, which is confirmed by the title in the LXX., it was chanted every Sabbath morning in the temple. It is appointed by the Anglican Church to be read on Ascension Sunday. Certainly, the psalm is eminently applicable to the ascension of our Lord, but is not to be reckoned among the psalms directly Messianic. Its poetic beauty, originality, and vivid coloring have been themes of universal admiration.

§ 8. The gates are thrown open. A great burst of instrumental music gladdens the air, the shoutings again ascend, and the festive procession and the Ark of God pass through the everlasting doors, pass joyously through the thronged streets to the new tabernacle on the summit of Zion. There Jehovah is installed King forever.

> For the LORD hath chosen Zion,
> He hath desired it for his habitation:
> This is my rest forever,
> Here will I dwell,
> For I have desired it.
>
> I will abundantly bless her provision,
> I will satisfy her poor with bread,
> And her priests will I clothe with salvation,
> And her saints shall shout aloud for joy.

There will I make the horn of David to bud,
I have ordained a lamp for mine anointed.
His enemies will I clothe with shame,
But upon himself shall his crown flourish.[1]

Other anthems no doubt were chanted, the smoke of sacrifice ascends and fills the firmament, and the multitude bow themselves in glad homage.

We must insert here one other of David's psalms as belonging to this occasion. We will think of him as standing between the high priests Abiathar and Zadok, before the blazing altar, before the Ark of the Presence, to inquire of the Lord.

---

[1] The closing verses of Psalm cxxxii. These, together with the quotations at the close of §4 and §5, constitute nearly all the psalm. It is a very beautiful composition, attributed by some critics to David, and referred to this historic occasion, to which it is in sentiment eminently applicable, and to which it probably alludes. We have not included it directly in our account, because it is almost beyond doubt the production of some other poet. There is a great variety of opinion respecting it among the critics. The most satisfactory view seems to be that an unknown poet, soon after the establishment of the worship of Jehovah on Zion, gives a lyrical account of David's anxious wish to accomplish this great work, of the finding and bringing up of the Ark, of God's everlasting covenant with David, and of his blessing on Zion. "At all events," says Delitzsch, "it proceeded from an age when the throne of David still remained, and the holy Ark was not yet irrecoverably lost."

When coming up the hill, he had asked: Who shall ascend and stand in the holy places? Now he asks: Who shall here abide as the guest of Jehovah? The holy oracle responds in plain, direct, and searching words, answerable for all time.

I

LORD, who shall abide in thy tabernacle?
Who shall dwell in thy holy hill?

II

He that walketh uprightly,
And worketh righteousness,
And speaketh truth in his heart.

NOTES.—*Strophe 1*. Abide, sojourn as a guest, involving the idea of friendship and protection. "Modern interpreters have weakened this technical expression, taken from the concrete relations of life, into a merely figurative designation of communion with God in general."—dwell, permanently reside. "The difference of the two ideas is this: that the one from a wandering life means the finding of a permanent place; the other, from the idea of membership in the family, denotes the possession of a permanent place." (*Delitzsch*.)

Strophe 2. The expressions progress positively from outward inoffensiveness, on through deeds of charity, to the innermost nature of the man.—in his heart, not merely with his tongue. "Our heart must be the sanctuary and refuge of truth, should it be banished from all the world beside, and hunted from among men. At all risks we must entertain the angel of truth, for truth is God's daughter." (*Spurgeon*.)

III

He that slandereth not with his tongue,
Nor doeth evil to his friend,
Nor taketh up a reproach against his neighbor.

IV

In whose eyes a vile person is contemned;
But he honoreth them that fear the LORD.

V

He that sweareth to his own hurt and changeth not.
He that putteth not out his money to usury,
Nor taketh reward against the innocent.

VI

He that doeth these things shall never be moved.

Strophe 3. This is the negative of the above perfect walk.—*with his tongue;* literally, *on his tongue;* a forcible Hebrew idiom representing the slanderous lie as a store of venom ready to be discharged. (*Cook.*)—**taketh up a reproach,** taking up from the ground and circulating a lie. (*Calvin.*) Delitzsch, Hengstenberg, and Hitzig give it the meaning of bringing or loading disgrace on anyone.

Strophe 4. Positive and antithetic.—**a vile person,** a reprobate.—**contemned,** abhorred. Such is the common interpretation. But the old Jewish view is more in accord with other Scriptures, and is now accepted by the ablest critics: He that in his own eyes is despised and worthy of rejection. So the Prayer Book version: He that setteth not by himself, but is lowly in his own eyes. This view is much more forcible, and accords exactly with that humility which David exhibits

Hitzig, Wordsworth, Alexander, and many other authorities, refer this Psalm xv. to the time of the removal of the Ark, and all bear witness to the severe dignity and power of the style. The construction is simple, but not perfectly symmetrical. The symmetry is broken by strophe 4, which is a distich, while the three other descriptive strophes

---

on this very occasion; see his own words in 2 Samuel vi. 22. Blessed are the poor in spirit.

Strophe 5. Positive.—**to his own hurt**, to his injury, as he finds after the oath has been taken. The Rabbis explain thus: Vows to do himself an injury by fasting or other mortification, is too ascetic. Rosemüller, and many since, translate: Sweareth to the wicked. The LXX., Syriac, and Luther have: To his neighbors. The Prayer Book version combines the LXX. and the Authorized Version: He that sweareth unto his neighbor, and disappointeth him not, though it were to his own hindrance. Hupfeld, Hitzig, Delitzsch, Moll, Cook, and Kay give the meaning which we have adopted, and they refer to Leviticus v. 4 ff, and xxvii. 10 ff. The Law permits no change if it hurt himself only; but if it involves injury to others it provides a trespass offering.—**usury**, prohibited among the Israelites. (Exodus xxii. 25.) The same principle forbids the abuse of usury in all ages; proved too by its natural consequences—*e. g.*, it ruined agriculture in Italy under the Roman Empire.—**reward**, a bribe; applies to magistrates in their judicial and executive functions. "Thou shalt take no gift; for a gift blindeth them that have sight, and perverteth the cause of the righteous." (Exodus xxiii. 8.)

Strophe 6. Summary.—**never be moved**, from God's dwelling place, but shall "abide" and "dwell" there throughout eternity. The whole in marked contrast with the ceremonial and inquisitional service of Psalm xxiv.

are tristichs. This strophe 4 is of doubtful translation, but being essentially antithetic in sentiment, it is without question a distich. This breaks monotony. Eleven particulars are enumerated by which the approved character is defined. Hence, in the German it is said that David comprised the six hundred and thirteen commands of the Law given on Sinai in eleven, but that Habakkuk summed them in one: The just shall live by his faith (Habakkuk ii. 4, Romans i. 17).—*Perowne*. The four descriptive strophes are alternately positive and negative. The horizon continually enlarges, and in the summary monostich at the close it expands to infinity.

The words of the psalm are in harmonious concord with those of Psalm ci. (§ 3), and sound like a prolonged echo of strophe 3 in Psalm xxiv., just quoted. This oracle speaks "in forms of expression heard in the Law, but passes over beyond the limits of the Old Testament, and describes, in evangelical and prophetic spirit, the man whom God will accept as his guest and his friend. It does not demand nor even allude to the observance of rites and ceremonies. The entire spirit is in the sphere of morals, and not of the Law." (*Moll.*)

"Such is the figure of stainless honor drawn by the pen of a Jewish poet. Christian chivalry has not dreamed of a brighter. We have need often and seriously to ponder it. For it shows us that faith in God and spotless integrity may not be sundered; that religion does not veil or excuse petty dishonesties; that love to God is only worthy of the name when it is the life and bond of every social virtue. Each line is a touchstone to which we should bring ourselves." (*Perowne.*)

§ 9. And when David had made an end of offering the burnt offering and the peace offerings, he blessed the people in the name of the Lord of hosts. And he dealt among all the people, even among the whole multitude of Israel, both to men and women, to every one a cake of bread, and a portion of wine, and a cake of raisins. So all the people departed, every one to his own house.[1]

It was the greatest and most joyful day of his life. Poet, Musician, Conqueror, Prophet, Priest, and King, in one. With a heart full of gratitude and love to all, he returns to his own house to bless his household. And Michal, his wife, Saul's proud daughter, reproached him for uncovering himself in the eyes of all the people. Witness his reply: "It was before Jehovah, which chose me to appoint me ruler over his people, over Israel; therefore will I play before the Lord. And I will yet be more vile than thus, and will be base in mine own sight." Blessed are the meek.

---
[1] 2 Samuel vi. 18, ff.

V.—THE VALLEY

§1. The second work assigned by Providence to David was the extension of the kingdom of Israel to the limits assigned in prophecy. As preparatory, he systematizes and confirms the present rule. This is done by a complete reorganization of the military establishment; by instituting social and civil regulations, including agricultural, municipal, and financial interests; by enlarging the judicial code; and by organizing the royal court and council. This being accomplished, he then proceeds to the enlargement of the kingdom to the bounds of empire.[1] He carried his arms first against the Philistines on the west, and completely subdued them. He then smote the Moabites on the east so that they became his servants and paid tribute. Then he marched against Syria on the north, overcame it, and garrisoned Damascus. Lastly, he put garrisons throughout Edom on the south, and all they of Edom became his servants.[2] And so it was that from the snows of Lebanon and Hermon to the burning deserts of Paran, from the

---
[1] 2 Samuel viii.   [2] Psalm lx.

rivers of Babylon even to the uttermost sea, the empire of Israel stretched forth her spear and shield according to the prophetic word.[1]

Now the ruler of Israel ranks with the great potentates of the world. He is an imperial conqueror, and the promise is fulfilled: I have made thee a great name like unto the name of the great men that are in the earth. The chief interest in this extension of the kingdom arises from its typical significance, and its influence on the subsequent religious development of the nation. "For as on the one hand the external relations of life, and the great incidents of war and conquest, receive an elevation by their contact with the religious history, so the religious history swells into larger and broader dimensions from its contact with the course of the outer world. The enlargement of territory, the amplification of power and state, leads to a corresponding enlargement and amplification of ideas, of imagery, of sympathies; and thus, humanly speaking, the magnificent forebodings of a wider dispensation in the prophetic writings first became possible through the court and empire of David." (*Stanley*.)

In the peaceful quiet that followed, David composed Psalm xviii., a triumphant Pæan of Thanks-

---

[1] Genesis xv. 18–21; Deuteronomy xi. 24; Psalm lxxii. 8.

giving in the retrospect of God's favor throughout his life, culminating in his present exalted state.[1] It is the longest, and, in some respects, the most remarkable of his compositions. It was written evidently before his great sin had thrown a dark shadow over his spirit. It contains no indication of remorse for special guilt, and no allusion to domestic enemies. All his foes are subdued, and confident in God's salvation, he looks forward to a peaceful and glorious future for himself and his posterity. The spirit of the king, as head of the theocracy, pervades the poem, and it exhausts the experience of his early manhood. Its style evinces the maturity of his genius, being remarkable for vigor, grace, regal dignity, and archaic sublimity. Especially the passage from verse 5 to verse 20 is famous for its unsurpassed grandeur. It describes a theophany. Natural phenomena supply the imagery, and are described with minute and graphic accuracy. There is an earthquake, followed by dense smoke, an outburst of flame and showers of burning coals, then

---

[1] This psalm is found also in 2 Samuel xxii., but out of its chronological place, which is immediately after chapter viii. Hitzig and other critics, upon a careful examination of the differences of the two texts, conclude that they are independent recensions, neither of which gives the original text in its purity, and that the form in the Psalter is to be preferred.

heavy clouds, thick darkness, a sound as of chariot wheels sped by rushing winds, black thunderclouds rifted by sudden flashes, the crash of thunder, then Jehovah's voice. To this Milton refers in the well-known passage:

"How oft amidst
Thick clouds and dark doth Heaven's all-ruling Sire
Choose to reside, his glory unobscured,
And with the majesty of darkness round
Covers his throne, from whence deep thunders roar,
Mustering their rage, and Heaven resembles Hell!"
(*Paradise Lost*, II. 263, ff.)

§2. Had David's life ended here, how beautiful and finished its record! But his was a destiny higher than the throne of Israel, something nobler than to fill a niche in the history of emperors. It was for him to make the songs of all people for all time. His own personal experiences, comprehending all phases of man's doing and suffering, must furnish the themes. For there is no power in poetry without pathos, and there is no true pathos that is not wrung out by a crushing force from a suffering heart.

From his present height, his kingly work perfected, we must follow David through a new range of experiences, in a far deeper descent than before, alas! into the depths of crime, and through all the horrors and agonies that attended it, and were inevitably consequent upon it. Then we may see his return to righteousness, and learn how, out from the horrible pit, to look upward, and at last regain foothold on the rock.

We will pass with merely a reference to the facts of David's double crime of adultery and murder, narrated with all their shocking and disgusting details in 2 Samuel xi. and xii. We need only remark that the taking of Rabboth-Ammon, and the terrible cruelties practiced on its captured citizens, occurred after his crimes but before his penitence, before the interview with Nathan, though this is previously narrated. This view, in which commentators generally agree, partially explains—without, of course, justifying—David's savagery. He was suffering the tortures of remorse, but his heart was still hard in impenitence. The recollection of Uriah's death under the walls of the city, though of his own devising, yet by the hands of these Ammonites, would naturally irritate him to the utmost. We say naturally, for it is one of the many contradictions in human nature that a principal should seek a sort of self-justification and expiation by wreaking vengeance on his tools.

In this impenitent and remorseful mood David

continued probably for a year or more. Then came the message of Nathan, couched after a fashion thoroughly oriental, in the exquisite parable of the poor man and his lamb.[1] Before Nathan finished his story, David broke forth impetuously, and with characteristic generosity, swore that the man that had done this thing should surely die. Thou art the man, says the prophet, and proceeds to charge home his crimes upon him. David listens in abashed, convicted silence to the fearful harangue which so perfectly harmonizes with the accusations of his conscience, and at the close, exclaims from the depths of his crushed heart: I have sinned against the Lord. This confession from a broken and a contrite heart is not despised, but is instantly followed by the divine forgiveness: The Lord hath put away thy sin; thou shalt not die. What a lesson for us! Afterwards, perhaps long afterwards, he records in Psalm xxxii. this remarkable fact of his instant forgiveness, in these memorable and instructive words:

---

[1] This incident is justly regarded as one of the most charming in the Old Testament. All modern literatures abound with allusions to it, but we especially note Lessing's imitation in his noble drama, *Nathan der Weise*. The scene is laid in the same place, Jerusalem, and another Nathan tells Saladin the beautiful symbolic story of The Three Rings.

I acknowledged my sin unto thee,
And mine iniquity I did not hide;
I said, I will confess my transgressions unto the Lord;
And thou forgavest the iniquity of my sin.

But David, as so often with ourselves, could not at once realize his pardon. In the meantime, he suffered the profoundest humiliation, the fierce agonies of repentance, and the fearful thought of being shut out forever from God's favor. This terrible interval gave birth to Psalm li., one of the most familiar and most precious in the Psalter. In studying it we should keep clearly before us the unhappy condition of the penitent as he pours out his soul in an impassioned prayer that has no parallel in all the recorded heart-histories of all time:

I

Have mercy upon me, O God;
   According to thy loving-kindness,
   According to the multitude of thy tender mercies,
Blot out my transgressions,
Wash me thoroughly from mine iniquity,
And cleanse me from my sin.

NOTES.—*Strophe 1.* The prayer reposes wholly on grace—unmerited favor. Observe the beautiful amplification of loving-kindness in the third line.—**blot out, wash, cleanse,** denote more than justification. He longs for a restoration to purity. —**transgressions,** observe the plural: adultery, treachery, murder, cruelty. The plural is also consistently preserved in other

II

For I acknowledge my transgressions,
And my sin is ever before me;
Against thee, thee only, have I sinned,
And done that which is evil in thy sight;
That thou mayest be justified when thou speakest,
And be clear when thou judgest.

---

psalms belonging to this period (*e. g.*, Psalm xxxii.), though often overlooked by readers and commentators. Moll, however, thinks the plural is not to be explained historically, but psychologically. Two other words are used—iniquity, sin—which are not synonymous in the Hebrew. Transgression is a violation of God's law by overt act Sin is the consequent personal defilement, a leprosy. Iniquity is the inherent depravity of human nature. See also the discriminated use of these terms in Psalms xxxii., xxxviii., xxxix., and xl. David never confesses *wickedness*, nor is it anywhere attributed to a recognized servant of God.

Strophe 2. David has nothing to plead but confession. Moll renders the first line more accurately, "For my transgressions I know." Still, confession is implied, and comes out in the context.—**thee only**: had he not sinned against himself, his neighbor, his country, mankind? Yes, surely; but sin as such is primarily against God; or, we may say that Hebrew idiom constantly represents secondary objects as absolutely nothing in comparison with the highest. The second distich is best regarded as parenthetical, and the third connected by that with the first distich, the confession, rather than with the second, the commission. He confesses unreservedly, in order that the justice of God's sentence, whatever it may be, being already fully admitted, may stand without question.—**be clear**, of question or dispute.

III

Behold I was shapen in iniquity,
And in sin did my mother conceive me.
Behold thou desirest truth in the inward parts,
And in the hidden part thou shalt make me to know
[wisdom.

IV

Purge me with hyssop, and I shall be clean,
Wash me, and I shall be whiter than snow.
Make me to hear joy and gladness,
That the bones which thou hast broken may rejoice.

V

Hide thy face from my sins,
    And blot out all mine iniquities.
Create in me a clean heart, O God,
    And renew a right spirit within me.

Strophe 3. An acknowledgment of inherent and inherited sinfulness, not named in excuse, but as the origin of misdeeds. —**shapen**, brought forth. His mother was sinful (not adulterous) before him, so that his own sinfulness was inborn.—**inward parts**, the innermost consciousness.

Strophe 4. The purification for leprosy. (Leviticus xiv. 4-6.) Quoted by Isaiah, i. 18.—**broken**, by stroke after stroke of an accusing and avenging conscience. A more accurate and significant rendering of the second distich is:

    Thou wilt make me to hear joy and gladness;
    The bones which thou hast broken shall rejoice.

Strophe 5. **Create**, the doctrine of a new birth. Our Lord expresses surprise that the teacher of Israel knew not this es-

Cast me not away from thy presence,
And take not thy holy spirit from me.
Restore unto me the joy of thy salvation,
And uphold me with a free spirit.
Then will I teach transgressors thy ways,
And sinners shall be converted unto thee.

VI

Deliver me from bloodguiltiness, O God, thou God of [my salvation,
And my tongue shall sing aloud of thy righteous-
O Lord, open thou my lips, [ness.
And my mouth shall shew forth thy praise.

---

sential thing. (John iii. 10.) How could he miss it with this well-known text before him.—a right spirit, a steadfast spirit. (See Isaiah xxvi. 3.)—thy holy spirit, the spirit of the Lord that had departed from Saul, and which came upon David at the first anointing. (1 Samuel xvi. 13.) But the meaning is deeper and broader than this; it is personal rather than official.—a free spirit, the Authorized Version has "thy free spirit," the word *thy* being supplied by the translators. It means rather a free, willing spirit or disposition of his own heart, generous and noble motives that shall lead to righteous conduct.—converted, not from unbelief, but from error; it refers to the return of backsliders from straying. This longing has been abundantly fulfilled; David ever since that day has been a teacher of transgressors. Such a desire is one of the surest signs of true penitence. (*Cf.* Psalm xxxii. 8.)

Strophe 6. The ability to offer praise is the gift of God. The beauty and depth of the second distich is universally admitted. No Scripture phrase is more familiar in devotion.

VII

For thou delightest not in sacrifice, else would I give it,
Thou hast no pleasure in burnt offering.
The sacrifices of God are a broken spirit;
A broken and a contrite heart, O God, thou wilt not
[despise.

VIII

Do good in thy good pleasure unto Zion,
Build thou the walls of Jerusalem.
Then shalt thou delight in the sacrifices of righteous-
In burnt offering, and whole burnt offering;   [ness,
Then shall they offer bullocks upon thine altar.

Strophe 7. Ceremonial observance of itself is nothing. The acceptable sacrifices are those which arise from a broken spirit. Samuel had said:

"Behold, to obey is better than sacrifice;
And to hearken, than the fat of rams."
(1 Samuel xv. 22.)

God, through Asaph, rejects the burnt offerings, and says:

"Offer unto God thanksgiving." (Psalm l. 14.)

And then the present psalm, next following, complements the duties of obedience and gratitude with penitence. These are the inner principles which sanctify all sacrifice. How could the Jews fall into ritualism, or fail to see the harmony of the law and the prophets with the gospel?

Strophe 8. If this be a part of the original psalm, **build** refers primarily to the fortifications progressing under David's direction, but has a higher spiritual significance.—**sacrifices of righteousness**, obedience, gratitude, and penitence, accompanied by burnt offering, which was not rejected except when it stood alone.—**bullocks**, the finest and choicest victims.

Dr. Van Ess tells us that Voltaire once undertook to write a travesty of this psalm, but when studying it to catch the vein, it went to his heart like a barbed arrow, and he fell back upon his couch in an agony of remorse. We can easily believe it. Let us study it with reverential awe, and make its spirit our own.

The structure is simple and irregular. It is too passionate for artistic symmetry. Observe the four parallel distichs in strophe 5. Four general divisions may be noted: First, an ardent prayer for mercy and forgiveness, founded on confession and the acknowledgment of God's justice (strophes 1, 2, 3). Second, entreaty for restoration to favor and renewal of spirit (strophes 4, 5). Third, vows of spiritual sacrifice as those only acceptable to God (strophes 6, 7). Fourth, a prayer for Zion (strophe 8).

The psalm was evidently a favorite with Isaiah, if we may judge by the frequency with which he alludes to it. And to how many thousand times ten thousand transgressors has it taught the way of return to God, and who has yet exhausted its depths or compassed its illimitable bounds? Luther says: "It has been used by the Church in song and prayer oftener than any other in the Psalter." The Anglican Church appoints it for Ash Wednesday, and inserts portions of it in her most solemn services. It is one of the seven Penitential Psalms (see Chap. II. §5, note). Luther was once asked which are the best of all the psalms. In reply he named four of the Penitential Psalms, xxxii., li., cxxx., and cxliii. The last has already been quoted (Chap. II. §5). Because of their evangelical tone, he called these the Pauline Psalms. Perhaps of the four this, the fifty-first, is the chiefest. Its spirit is thoroughly in anticipation of the gospel teachings. It makes allusion to legal forms only to renounce them as being of themselves unacceptable, and insufficient in procuring salvation.

The remark, however, is not true of strophe 8, which contradicts the first portion of strophe 7; and this fact inclines us strongly to the view of those critics who, on various and seemingly conclusive grounds, consider that strophe an addition of later days. They surmise that it was annexed after the Captivity, when the walls of Jerusalem were rebuilding, in order to adapt the psalm to liturgical use. (*Tholuck, Köster, Perowne, et al.*) It certainly seems that this strophe does not accord entirely with the evangelical tone of those preceding it, and that the self-forgetfulness it manifests does not correspond with the intensely unipersonal bearing of every other word of the psalm. Moreover, the cadence of strophe 7 forms a complete, harmonious, and beautiful close.

In the Psalter this psalm begins a series of fifteen psalms, all ascribed to David by their titles, and remarkable for the prevalent, though not exclusive, use of the divine name, Elohim (rendered God), rather than Jehovah, whence they are sometimes called the Elohistic Psalms. It is certainly worthy of note that in the one before us the name Jehovah does not occur.[1] Its absence may in this case be accounted for by David's feeling that his transgressions had at least suspended for him the privileges assured to God's people by the covenant name. Elsewhere he is frequent and fond in the phrase Jehovah our God, but in his present frame he did not dare to claim this nearness, and there-

---

[1] In strophe 6 the word rendered Lord is Adonai, not Jehovah, though many uncritical editions of the Authorized Version (improperly) print it in small capitals.

fore addresses him only from the lower common ground of sinful humanity.

When David came to realize his state before God, his restoration to divine favor, he gave vent to his joy and gratitude in Psalm xxxii.:

Blessed is he whose transgression is forgiven,
  Whose sin is covered;
Blessed is the man unto whom the Lord imputeth not
  And in whose spirit there is no guile. [iniquity,

This psalm, already referred to, is one of David's noblest works, and should be studied in connection with Psalm li., of which it is the sequel. It is marred in the Authorized Version by a bad translation of the ninth verse.

§3. Perhaps it is needful to notice the oft-repeated question: How could David, who was guilty of such heinous crimes, be " a man after God's own heart?" The expression occurs but twice in Scripture: first, in 1 Samuel xiii. 14. This was early in David's life, and at that time he might, perhaps as much as any man that has lived, have been the object of his Maker's complacency. But the phrase does not indicate complacency. In Hebrew usage the reins were the seat of the feelings and affections, and the heart quite generally the seat of the will, choice, volition. Certainly in this case the word has no other significance. The phrase merely means the man whom God has chosen to take the place of the rejected Saul, and it conveys no approbation more than is necessarily implied in the choice. The other occurrence of the expression is in Acts xiii. 22, where the former passage is quoted in the same sense.

The essential difficulty is not, however, hereby removed; for it is unquestionable that God did regard David with special favor and approbation, as many passages plainly state—*e. g.*, 1 Kings xv. 3-5. But, we should remember that if God approves any one of our race, it must be in spite of sins and sinfulness. God looks at the heart, and who of us that knows anything of his own heart can say that he is better or purer than was David? or if pressed by similar temptations, would not fall as low? Had the best and purest man that we know been brought up under an eastern sun, and endowed with a sensitive and passionate nature, with that poetic temperament so susceptible to impressions from without, and so quickly inflamed to enthusiasm, to love, hate, and resentment, so deeply stirred by shame and public disgrace, and by the pangs of remorse; were he then raised to the throne of an absolute oriental monarchy, with all its freedom from responsibility and customary indulgence of every caprice; then were he tempted as David was—can we be sure he would not fall? One false step taken, the descent to Avernus is proverbially easy.

Neither these considerations, nor any others, can excuse or palliate crime, but may well make us pause before passing harsh comparative judgment. Some Rabbis of former times, and in later times Bayle and sneering critics of his sort, have exaggerated to the utmost the dark features in David's career. In their best aspect these are dark enough, but it is only a partial, superficial view if one look not within. God looks within, and though he hates sin, and will surely punish it, either in the sinner or in his substitute, yet he has so ordered in his infinite wisdom and love that he can hide his face from sins and blot out iniquities. All he demands is a broken and a contrite heart. And where can we find clearer evidence of this hearty penitence than in David, who from the time of his transgression went mourning all through the remnant of his days?

Moreover, throughout his life David's eyes were ever toward the Lord. He stumbled and fell, but his cry was to his helper. Whenever cast down by the adversary, his heart rebounded Godward. His life had eddies like a river, and his great sin was a whirlpool, but the main current was constantly onward. His whole course was a fearful and never-ceasing struggle, and this it is that our God looks upon with approval and complacency.

I cannot refrain from quoting the oft-quoted, and now classical, passage from "Heroes and Hero Worship," by the cynical, and sometimes savage, Carlyle, a sort of literary iconoclast, wielding at will a sledge-hammer, a rapier, or a dissecting knife, and who does not redeem his habitual severity by being an indulgent critic of sacred characters. Yet hear him in this case: "Faults," says he, "the greatest of faults I should say, is to be conscious of none. Readers of the Bible, above all, one would think, might know better. Who is called there the man according to God's own heart? David, the Hebrew king, had fallen into sins enough; blackest crimes; there was no want of sins. And thereupon unbelievers sneer, and ask: Is this your man according to God's heart? The sneer, I must say, seems to me but a shallow one. What are faults? what are the outward details of a life, if the inner secret of it, the remorse, temptations, the often baffled, never-ending struggle of it, be forgotten? It is not in man that walketh to direct his steps. Of all acts, is not, for a man, repentance the most divine? The deadliest sin, I say, were that same supercilious consciousness of no sin. That is death. The heart so conscious is divorced from sincerity, humility; in fact is dead. It is pure, as dead, dry sand is pure.

David's life and history, as written for us in those psalms of his, I consider to be the truest emblem ever given of a man's moral progress and warfare here below. All earnest souls will ever discern in it the faithful struggle of an earnest human soul toward what is good and best. Struggle, often baffled sore, baffled down into entire wreck, yet a struggle never ended; ever with tears, repentance, true, unconquerable purpose begun anew. Poor human nature! Is not a man's walking in truth always that—a succession of falls? Man can do no other. In this wild element of a life he has to struggle upward; now fallen, now abased; and ever with tears, repentance, and bleeding heart he has to rise again, struggle again, still onward. That his struggle be a faithful, unconquerable one, that is the question of questions."

§4. Nathan had said unto David: Thou shalt not die; howbeit, because by this deed thou hast given great occasion to the enemies of the Lord to blaspheme, the child that is born unto thee shall surely die. He was not to be exempt from chastisement. It was manifest that, though forgiven, he needed discipline; and in this bereavement, which greatly distressed the tender-hearted father, and in the long and painful series of afflictions that occupied subsequent years, the trial of his faith, though tried with fire, was found unto praise and honor and glory. So the enemies of the Lord, though they seize this occasion to blaspheme, yet are estopped from saying that God sanctioned guilt or cleared the guilty.

It is worthy of note here that the bereavement is the only one of these retributive afflictions named by Nathan. Why so? Perhaps because the rest were the natural consequences of the sin, their connection with it was obvious, and needed not to be specified. We say natural consequence, because there is a chain of cause and effect in the moral as well as in the physical sphere. The two are often interlinked, but even where apparently independent, it is true that moral effects follow moral causes just as inevitably and with the same absolute inherent necessity as physical effects follow physical causes. Our calculus does not solve that problem; nevertheless, in the accumulated experience of mankind, in the lessons of history, we do not hesitate to trace moral causation, and in our personal relations we do not hesitate to predict moral effects. Now forgiveness of sin does not imply the rupture of this chain. God does not work a miracle counteracting his natural laws when he pardons. Were one, standing on the pinnacle of the temple, to cast himself down, expecting safety by God's intervention, we should say he were guilty of presumptuous folly. The same folly is his who hopes to escape the natural consequences of his misdeeds, although by repentance he may be already restored to God's favor, and although in them all it is a merciful Father that deals with him, and not an impersonal destiny.

So the inexorable consequences of David's guilt came upon him and his in dire calamities. The father's example led his children into incest and fratricide.[1] Then came the banishment of Absalom, then his nearly successful rebellion and meditated parricide, then his death, then years afterwards the rebellion of Adonijah. There is no end of evil. Thus David passed from mature manhood to old age amid the bitterest distresses.

§5. Five years after the murder of Ammon by Absalom, David kissed him. Very soon began the plot for dethronement.[2] When the conspiracy was nearly ripe, David was laid low by disease. Of this affliction we have perhaps not even an intimation in the narrative, but we have a thrilling record of it in certain psalms composed upon the couch of suffering. His physical pain was

---
[1] 2 Samuel xiii. [2] 2 Samuel xv.

aggravated by mental anguish. For David evidently suspected the machinations of the conspirators, and found himself powerless to thwart them. Ahithophel, his prime counselor and his own familiar friend, with whom he had often knelt before the altar of God, was lending countenance to Absalom's schemes, and in some way excited David's distrust. His words were softer than oil, yet were they drawn swords.[1] The court and the people were slandering the king for crimes unknown to him; also they pronounced him hopelessly diseased and an imbecile.[2] The conspirators fomented these slanders to justify their procedures, and his name became a common scoff. Says he:

> They that sit in the gate speak against me;
> And I, the song of the drunkards![3]

Besides the bodily pain and this mental distress, the sufferer's sin was ever before him. He recognizes in his prostration the rebuke of God. He cries: Chasten me not in thy hot displeasure;—

> For thine arrows stick fast in me,
> And thy hand presseth me sore.
> No soundness in my flesh,
>   Because of thine anger;
> Neither rest in my bones,
>   Because of my sin.[4]

---

[1]Psalm lv. 21.   [2]Psalm xli. 5-9.   [3]Psalm lxix. 12.
[4]Psalm xxxviii. 2, 3.

He complains that his lovers and friends stand aloof, and his kinsmen afar off, that his enemies are lively and strong; and he cries aloud:

> Forsake me not, O LORD,
> O my God, be not far from me.
> Make haste to help me,
> O Lord of my salvation.[1]

There are five psalms directly referable to this occasion, vi. and xxxviii.–xli. The four latter are consecutively placed in the Psalter, probably in the order of composition.[2] The fortieth seems to have been written in an interval of comparative tranquillity, and in the hope of speedy recovery, but the forty-first indicates a relapse and a renewal of all his troubles. These psalms are inestimably precious to the sick, and to those distressed by the estrangement of friends and kindred. In many a darkened chamber they have come like a beam of benign light upon the soul drawing nigh unto death. They come, too, with a soft and soothing sympathy in times of isolation and abandonment, and lift up the sinking heart to God. How from the crushed leaf drops the healing balm! David had himself a similar consolation. He remembered the afflictions of Job, and these his sad

---

[1] Psalm xxxviii. 21, 22.   [2] Psalm cii. is in a similar vein, but is probably a psalm of the Captivity.

elegies are full of reminiscences and allusions to the great poem of sorrow, and also to the dirge-like Psalm of Moses (Psalm xc.), both which, no doubt, he studied with profoundest emotion. We may imagine that Seraiah, his secretary, often read favorite passages to him, just as these psalms of his are now read at the bedside of suffering.

While he lay helpless, waiting patiently for the Lord, the conspirators sought to entrap him in his words, that they might justify their schemes. He was in danger of giving them ground to accuse him and denounce him as a reprobate. He says:

> They also that seek after my life lay snares for me;
> And they that seek my hurt speak mischievous things,
>   And imagine deceits all the day long.

He resolves to be silent, and to trust in God:

> But I, as a deaf man, heard not,
>   And as a dumb man, opened not my mouth.
> Thus was I as a man that heareth not,
>   And in whose mouth are no reproofs.
> For in thee, O LORD, do I hope;
>   Thou wilt answer, O Lord my God.
> Lest when my foot slippeth,
>   They magnify themselves against me.[1]

This silence brought no comfort. Turning his

---
[1] Psalm xxxviii. 12-16.

thoughts away from the outer world, his heart grew hot as he began to reflect upon his own condition, and his sad musings found utterance in irrepressible words. Perhaps he dictated to Seraiah Psalm xxxix., on the Brevity and Vanity of Life. It begins in a narrative or descriptive tone, but soon passes over into plaintive prayer and meditation.

I

I said, I will take heed to my ways,
    That I sin not with my tongue;
I will keep my mouth with a bridle,
    While the wicked is before me.

II

I was dumb with silence,
    I held my peace even from good,
        And my sorrow was stirred.
My heart was hot within me,
    While I was musing the fire kindled;
        Then spake I with my tongue:

NOTES.—*Strophe 1.* **A bridle,** rather a muzzle. In Psalm cxli. 3 he prays:
    Set a watch, O Lord, before my mouth,
    Keep the door of my lips.
Compare also James iii. 2, ff; and Job ii. 10.

Strophe 2. **With silence,** with silent submission.—**even from good;** literally, away from prosperity. This is very obscure. It does not mean, as commonly supposed: Refrained from speaking even good, sound, safe, righteous words. Probably it means: Silence brought no relief, no comfort. (*Hupfeld.*)

III

Lord, make me to know mine end,
 And the measure of my days, what it is,
  Let me know how frail I am.
Behold, thou hast made my days as hand-breadths,
 And mine age is as nothing before thee,
  Surely every man at his best state is altogether
                                    [vanity.—Selah.

IV

Surely every man walketh in a vain show,
 Surely they are disquieted in vain;
  He heapeth up riches, and knoweth not who shall
                                          [gather them.

My heart; this describes a mental struggle. Silence became impossible. The flame bursts forth in prayer. (*Cf.* Job xxxii. 18-20.)

Strophe 3. As in Psalm xc. 12:
   So teach us to number our days,
   That we may get us an heart of wisdom.
Surely; the text of the Preacher, in Ecclesiastes.—vanity; Heb., a breath.

Strophe 4. **Surely,** he says to himself, it is true. Every man walketh as a shadow—literally, as an image.
   He cometh forth like a flower, and is cut down;
   He fleeth also as a shadow, and continueth not. (Job xiv. 2.)
"*Pulvis et umbra sumus.*" (*Horace.*) *Cf.* also Psalm cxliv. 4.— **disquieted in vain;** more accurately, mere empty sounds, *vana voces.* Σκιᾶς ὄναρ ἄνθρωποι. (*Pindar.*) **Riches;** a word supplied by the translators; *sheaves* would better correspond with *gather.* We think of the Rich Fool. (Luke xii. 16-21.) *Cf.* Psalm xlix. 6-10. David had been heaping up materials for the Temple, but knew not who should build.

V

And now, Lord, what wait I for?
My hope is in thee.
Deliver me from all my transgressions;
Make me not the reproach of the foolish.

VI

I was dumb,
I opened not my mouth
 Because thou didst it.
Remove thy stroke away from me;
I am consumed by the blow of thy hand.

VII

When thou with rebukes dost correct man for iniquity,
 Thou makest his beauty to consume away like a moth;
 Surely every man is vanity.—Selah.

Strophe 5. "He turns away, as it were, with a sense of relief from the sad contemplation of man's fleeting, transitory life, to fix the eye of his heart on Him who abideth forever. We seem almost to hear the deep sigh with which the words are uttered." (*Perowne.*)—**My** hope. The Heb. here is so similar to Job xiii. 15 that it looks like a quotation of: Though he slay me, yet will I trust in him.—**Deliver;** this is his first need.—**reproach,** the scorn of fools.

Strophe 6. **Dumb,** not murmuring. (*Cf.* 2 Samuel xii. 20-23 and Job xl. 5.)—**consumed.** (*Cf.* Psalm xc. 7.):
 We are consumed by thine anger,
 And by thy wrath are we troubled.

Strophe 7. **With rebukes.** (*Cf.* Psalm xc. 8, 9.)—**his beauty,** disappears as if eaten by moths, as in Job xiii. 28:
 And he as a rotten thing consumeth,
 As a garment that is moth-eaten.

VIII

Hear my prayer, O LORD,
And give ear unto my cry;
   Hold not thy peace at my tears.
For I am a stranger with thee,
A sojourner, as all my fathers were.

IX

O spare me,
That I may recover strength,
Before I go hence,
And be no more.

For a beauty that is imperishable, see Psalm xc. 17. The last line is a refrain; see strophe 3.

Strophe 8. **A stranger,** rather a guest.—**A sojourner.** In 1 Chronicles xxix. 15, David says: For we are strangers before thee, and sojourners, as were all our fathers. (*Cf.* Hebrews xi. 13, and Ephesians ii. 19.)

Strophe 9. Again reminiscent of Job.—**O spare me;** literally, Look away from me—*i. e.,* Turn away thy wrathful countenance. Turn from him that he may rest. (Job xiv. 6.) **Recover strength;** literally, that I may shine—as light dawning from darkness. See the following beautiful passage from Job x. 20-22, where the expression rendered *take comfort* is the same as that here rendered *recover strength:*

    Are not my days few?
    Cease then and let me alone,
    That I may take comfort a little
    Before I go whence I shall not return,
    Even to the land of darkness, and the shadow of death;
    A land of thick darkness, as darkness itself,
    And of the shadow of death, without any order,
    And where the light is as darkness.

And be no more; Enoch was not (same Heb. word), for God

Ewald pronounces this "the most beautiful of all the elegies in the Psalter." It is intimately associated in our minds with the ninetieth Psalm, the two forming a part of every burial service.

The above arrangement seems to be justified by obvious parallelisms and by pauses in the sense. There are two general divisions: The first, of four strophes, includes an explanatory introduction (strophes 1, 2); a prayer (strophe 3); and a soliloquy or meditation (strophe 4). In form this part is characterized, after the first quatrain, by tristichs; those of strophes 2 and 3 are double, the tristichs being parallel to each other. The refrain and *Selah*, in the last line of strophe 3, close the prayer. In this prayer he asks, Make me to know so that the truth may go home to my heart. He wants to realize deeply the fact of the brevity and uncertainty of life. The second tristich begins, Behold! an exclamation of wonder, as if, in prompt answer, a sudden conviction, deeper and more practical than heretofore, had come upon him. Here the *Selah* with the refrain marks an unquestionable pause; how, then, are we to explain the next tristich, strophe 4? This has been done variously. It would seem simple and satisfactory to regard it as a soliloquy, endorsing and emphasizing the answer, declaring it to harmonize with common observation. Then the prayer is resumed.

The second general division renews the prayer, which continues to the close. It is subdivided into two parts by the refrain and *Selah*, strophe 7.

---

took him. (Genesis v. 24.) Job vii. 8 is another parallel passage:

>The eye of him that seeth me
> Shall behold me no more;
>Thine eyes shall be upon me,
> But I shall not be.

The symmetry of the introverted structure of this second part is sufficiently obvious to the eye. The tristich, strophe 7, which lies in the middle, is an echo of the tristich structure of the first portion of the ode, and especially of the second tristich of strophe 3, to which it is parallel. Strophe 9 is the short panting of a fainting spirit.

§ 6. The incidents of the rebellion of Absalom should be studied by everyone who would understand the psalms to which it gave occasion. It seems to have occurred immediately on the recovery of the king. The circumstances are minutely detailed, with graphic vividness, and often with rare pathos.[1] The mustering of the rebels at Hebron, the defection of Ahithophel, the march on Jerusalem, the flight of the king, the faithful adherence of his bodyguard under the noble Ittai, the commission of the priests and of Hushai, the artifice of Ziba, the insults of Cushai (Shimei), the encampment of the fugitives near Jericho—all pass before our eyes as an historic panorama.

For the night spent near Jericho and for the next morning were probably composed the sweet evening and morning hymns, Psalms iv. and v.

---

[1] 2 Samuel xv.–xvii. Dryden uses this narrative as a frame for his poem, the noted political satire of the times of Charles II., "Absalom and Achitophel," by which names he alludes to Monmouth and Lord Shaftesbury.

David's youthful habit of daily devotion probably continued with him throughout life. Delitzsch gives us this pretty legend from the Talmud: "A cither hung at all times over David's bed, and when the midnight came, the north wind blew upon the strings, so that it sounded of itself; he arose at once, and occupied himself with the law until the pillars of the dawn arose." To this custom he alludes, say the Rabbis, in Psalm lvii. 8: Awake, my soul; awake, psaltery and harp; and I will awake the dawn. Our fancy can easily adapt this story to the writing of the morning hymn. During this next day, perhaps the Sabbath, while waiting in the wilderness of Judah for news from Jerusalem, David probably wrote Psalm lxiii. (see its title), in which he longs for the services of the sanctuary. "This," says Perowne, "is unquestionably one of the most beautiful and touching psalms in the whole Psalter." And Donne says: "It is one of the imperial psalms, that command all affections, and spread themselves over all occasions; catholic, universal psalms, that apply to all necessities." And again: "The spirit and soul of the whole Psalter is contracted into this psalm."

When the news came, David crossed the Jordan, and finally took up his post at Mahanaim, a strongly fortified and friendly city, probably on the river Jabbok. Jacob had given the spot this name, meaning, The two camps, because there, in a time of danger, he had seen in a vision the Lord's host on his right hand and on his left.

The angel of the Lord encampeth around about them
And delivereth them.[1]   [that fear him,

"Now for about three months,"[2] says Dean Stanley, "the whole interest is transferred, for the only time in the history of Israel, to the trans-Jordanic territory." David occupied himself with assembling and organizing an army to encounter the impending attack of Israel under Absalom and Amasa. We may be very sure that he did not cease often to pour out his soul, a libation before God, in psalmody. To him it was given to sing. It was the constraint of his nature. A change of fortune only changed the key of his melodies, varying from the triumphant major of the Tehillah, the Song of Praise, to the plaintive minor of the Tephillah, the Prayer of Loving Trust.[3]

---

[1] Psalm xxxiv. 7.

[2] This is Ewald's estimate of the time, now generally accepted. Jewish tradition, given by Jerome, makes it six months.

[3] Commonly referred to this time are Psalms xxviii., lv., lxi., lxix., lxx., and some others which are not inappropriate to his present exiled condition.

We will quote Psalms xlii., xliii., as vividly expressing his feelings at this time. The two are one composition, and should never be separated. It was not, however, written by David, though popularly ascribed to him because of its entire, suitableness to his condition, and because it is in the exact style, and breathes the spirit of the royal psalmist. It was written for him by one of his faithful followers, one of the sons of Korah (so biblical scholars generally agree), who had been devoted to the musical services of the sanctuary— by one who was in complete sympathy with the exiled king, and had caught his poetic fervor. The genius displayed in this composition is so unsurpassed, that it is hard to give up the belief that it came from the sweet singer himself. Ewald thinks it superior to all others in artistic form, and that "the imagery also in all its details is in the highest degree tender and poetical."

In reading this exquisite elegy we must not forget the painful circumstances of David, in whose name we may at least assume that the psalmist speaks. During his three months of exile he felt keenly the loss of the services of the tabernacle; and especially when the Sabbaths came round in their priestly procession did he long to go up to the courts of the Lord. His tears could not quench this spiritual thirst. His soul sinks within him when gazing on the unfamiliar and unloved scenery east of the Jordan, on Hermon and Mizar clad in armor of ice. When he hears in the stillness of night the roar of distant mountain cataracts, he fancies that in the abyss wherein he is plunged the boisterous waves and billows, striving to overwhelm him, are shouting encouragement to each other. He complains that God has forgotten him, and that he is made the scorn of fools, who ask: Where is thy God? But he confides his cause to God; the trust inspires hope that he may yet bow before his altars, and satisfy his heart's deepest desire:

I

As the hart panteth after the water brooks,
So panteth my soul after thee, O God.
My soul thirsteth for God, for the living God;
When shall I come and appear before God?
My tears have been my meat day and night,
While they continually say unto me, Where is thy God?

NOTES.—*Strophe 1.* The hart, the wild gazelle of that region. —my meat, my food. " *Cura dolorque animi, lacrimæque alimenta fuere.*" (*Ovid.*)

> For I have eaten ashes like bread,
> And mingled my drink with weeping.
> (Psalm cii. 9.)

II

These things I remember,
And pour out my soul within me;
How I went with the throng,
And led them to the house of God,
With the voice of joy and praise,
A multitude keeping holyday.

III

Why art thou cast down, O my soul?
And why art thou disquieted within me?
Hope thou in God; for I shall yet praise him
For the help of his countenance.

IV

O my God, my soul is cast down within me;
Therefore do I remember thee
From the land of Jordan, and the Hermons,
From the hill Mizar.
Deep calleth unto deep at the noise of thy waterspouts;
All thy waves and thy billows are gone over me.

Strophe 2. A festive procession.

Strophe 3. In the refrain, he turns from prayer to address his own soul, a natural and beautiful reversion. "*Castigat suam mollitiem.*" (*Calvin.*) Many Hebraists consider the first words of strophe 4, "O my God," to belong to the close of this refrain. If so, a correct translation would make the language of the refrain, in its three cases, identical. It is questionable whether this would be a rhetorical gain. The law of the refrain does not require identity.

Strophe 4. **Hermons;** this is best explained by considering

V

Yet the LORD will command his loving-kindness in the
And in the night his song shall be with me, [daytime,
Even a prayer unto the God of my life.
I will say unto God my rock:
Why hast thou forgotten me? [enemy?
Why go I mourning because of the oppression of the
As with a sword in my bones, mine adversaries re-
[proach me,
While they continually say unto me, Where is thy God?

VI

Why art thou cast down, O my soul?
And why art thou disquieted within me?
Hope thou in God; for I shall yet praise him
Who is the help of my countenance, and my God.

---

that Mount Hermon was characteristic of the trans-Jordanic, as Mount Tabor was of the cis-Jordanic territory. Conant explains the plural as "the three summits." Hermon was visible as far south as the Dead Sea.—**Mizar,** is unknown. The word means *small*, and may be a mere appellative used by way of contrast.—**waterspouts;** some object to understanding cataracts and insist on literal waterspouts. Dr. Thomson says: "In the neighborhood of Hermon I witnessed waterspouts repeatedly, and was caught in one last year which in five minutes flooded the whole mountain side, and carried off whatever the tumultuous torrents encountered, as they leaped madly down in noisy cascades." Lynch described similar phenomena.—**all thy waves;** very appropriately quoted by Jonah, ii. 3.

Strophe 5. **His song.** "God my maker, who giveth songs in the night." (Job xxxv. 10.)—**my rock,** a steep cliff, inaccessible

VII

Judge me, O God,
And plead my cause against an ungodly nation;
O deliver me from the deceitful and unjust man.
For thou art the God of my strength;
Why hast thou cast me off? [enemy?
Why go I mourning because of the oppression of the

VIII

O send out thy light and thy truth;
Let them lead me, let them bring me
Unto thy holy hill, and to thy tabernacles.
Then will I go unto the altar of God,
Unto God my exceeding joy;
And upon the harp will I praise thee, O God, my God.

IX

Why art thou cast down, O my soul?
And why art thou disquieted within me?
Hope thou in God; for I shall yet praise him
Who is the help of my countenance, and my God.

---

to foes. "The Lord is my rock and my fortress." (Psalm xviii. 2.)—with a sword in my bones; rather, with a breaking (or crushing) my bones.

Strophe 7. An ungodly nation, his rebellious subjects.— unjust man, probably Ahithophel, whose suicide was yet unknown. Prayer answered by anticipation. (See Isaiah lxv. 24.)

Strophe 8. Thy light and thy truth. "Instead of the more usual loving-kindness and truth, these shall be to him, so he hopes, as angels of God, who shall lead him by the hand until

THE VALLEY 195

In the title the expression rendered "for the sons of Korah" is held by biblical scholars to indicate authorship, and cannot be justifiably set aside. We have assumed, however, that the psalmist speaks in David's name. The text is that of the Revised Version. At several points the translation might be improved, but the words have become household words, and it would be a sort of sacrilege to change them. The structure is symmetrical and simple; three nearly equal parts, indicated by the refrain. The separation of the third part in the Psalter, as a distinct psalm, was made probably in adapting it to liturgical use, as it has none of the local references of the second part. The only irregularity is found in strophe 5, it having eight lines, instead of six, like the others. It consists of two tristichs and a distich. The other strophes consist in some cases of three distichs, in others of two tristichs. The last distich of strophe 5 is parallel to the last of strophe 1. The second tristich of strophe 7 is parallel to the second of strophe 5. The second and third lines of strophe 8 are a peculiar variation of parallelism, equivalent to the usual form:

> Let them lead me unto thy holy hill,
> Let them bring me to thy tabernacles.

The fundamental thought is a longing to share in the services of the tabernacle. The first part expresses Desire; the second, Complaint; the third, Confidence. "There are two voices, despondency and trust, which at the beginning stand

---

they bring him to the holy mountain. Possibly there may be an allusion to the Urim and Thummim." (*Perowne.*) The psalm begins in a very despondent tone, but, in this eighth strophe, rises to almost joyous confidence.

out in entire discord and almost harsh antagonism. They are at the last brought into loving harmony, so that emotion and insight, excitement and thoughtfulness, are wholly reconciled and intimately blended. All this is without affectation or constraint; the true expression of the struggles between two contending forces in a spirit at once susceptible of tenderest feeling, yet upon reflection full of strength." (*Ewald.*)

In a vein entirely similar to this psalm is Psalm lxxxiv., possibly by the same writer:

How amiable are thy tabernacles, O LORD of hosts!
My soul longeth, yea, even fainteth for the courts of the
 [Lord,
My heart and my flesh crieth out for the living God.

§ 6. The issue of the rebellion of Absalom need not be narrated here. The restoration of David, after the defeat and death of his son, to the throne at Jerusalem, was marred by the rebellion of Sheba. When this had been crushed by Joab's energy, public affairs resumed their course, and the prospects of the kingdom were bright again.[1] A census, unwarranted by Israel's supreme King, brought down his judgment upon his vicar and the nation. A three-days' pestilence swept many thousands from the land, and only when David interceded in the spirit of Moses, and of One higher

[1] To this time may perhaps be referred Psalm cxliv. If not a florilege, it is certainly reminiscent of Psalms viii., xviii., and some others. It admirably suits the present situation.

than either, that the punishment might fall upon him alone, was the plague stayed. The angel hovering over the summit of Moriah, with his drawn sword extended over Zion to destroy the dwellers thereon, sheathed the flaming weapon, and health and peace came once again upon the land.[1] At this point in the narrative the books of Samuel close. It is resumed in Kings with the conspiracy of Adonijah.

There was probably a long and peaceful interval. David was growing old, and in these years of matured wisdom was gathering up the fruits of experience, the teachings of an eventful and stormy life. The calm sunlight of a peaceful evening was now shining on his way, and enabled him thoughtfully to review the long vista of troubles that had beset his journey. With devout gratitude he acknowledges God's goodness to

---

[1] 2 Samuel xviii.–xxiv. The incidents narrated in chapter xxi. are out of their chronological place, belonging to an early time in the reign at Jerusalem. We have already made a similar remark about chapter xxii., containing the eighteenth Psalm. Chapter xxiii., from the eighth verse through, is also to be referred to an earlier date; it occurs in duplicate in 1 Chronicles xi., in immediate connection with David's accession to the throne of Israel. One who would read consecutively the history of David from the time of his flight, should omit these three chapters.

him as he passed through the valley, in blotting out his transgressions, in restoring his health, in delivering him from the dangers of conspiracy and rebellion, and then crowning his life with the present peaceful enjoyment of ripened years, a crown more precious than his royal diadem. In the deepening twilight we can almost hear his harp and voice enumerating these, in this self-communing Even-Song:

Bless the LORD, O my soul,
And all that is within me, bless his holy name.
Bless the LORD, O my soul,
And forget not all his benefits,
Who forgiveth all thine iniquities,
Who healeth all thy diseases,
Who redeemeth thy life from destruction,
Who crowneth thee with loving-kindness and tender
Who satisfieth thy mouth with good things, [mercies,
So that thy youth is renewed like the eagle's.[1]

Especially in Psalm xxxvii. did David compress the practical wisdom of mature reflection. It is purely didactic, giving counsel, good at all times for all men everywhere:

Fret not thyself because of evil-doers.

This is the keynote of instruction from a sage of the highest authority. There is no passion, the

---
[1] Psalm ciii.

tone is calm and grave, and nothing personal, save where he enforces his authority by the claim of experience:

> I have been young, and now am old.

"It is the teaching of the early dispensation, which nowhere stands out more distinct, more complete, or in a nobler and more attractive form." (*Cook.*) It declares in hortatory phrase that the peace, prosperity, and salvation of the righteous are certain, and find a complete antithesis in the destiny of the wicked.

> Depart from evil and do good,
>   And dwell for evermore;
> For the Lord loveth judgment,
>   And forsaketh not his saints.
> They are preserved forever;
> But the seed of the wicked shall be cut off.
> Mark the perfect man, and behold the upright,
> For the end of that man is peace.

That "the meek shall inherit the earth" is five times asserted in this psalm, and was adopted by our Lord in the third Beatitude.

We can only mention Psalm lxv., which from its serene dignity we think must be referred to David's old age. It is remarkable for its strong realization of Jehovah's presence in nature and history, and in the noblest poetical vein celebrates his bounteous harvests. Psalm cxlv., David's noble "Psalm of Praise," which has given title, in the Hebrew, to the Psalter, must not be unnamed. It certainly belongs to a late period of his life, and by some is esteemed his most excellent composition. The Jews thought so highly of it that they were accustomed to say that no one could fail of salvation who would repeat this psalm three times daily.

But one psalm of David's old age we cannot forbear to quote at length, Psalm cxxxix. Aben Ezra pronounces it "the crown of psalm poetry." We can hardly deem this extravagant when we reflect upon the depth of religious feeling, the weight of thought, and the force and beauty of expression by which it is characterized. Its wonderful spirit, originality, and majesty show that the author must have been gifted above all the sons of men with poetic genius, as well as with divinely inspired insight. We approach it with a feeling of unusual awe. Well may one shrink from an attempt to illustrate it, since the great genius Herder, at once a poet, a philosopher, and a theologian, has said: " Language utterly fails me in the exposition of this psalm. Let anyone read it and he will see that, after the fullest explanation of every verse, and of the purport of the whole, it is at each reading new, each word suggestive perpetually of new thoughts."[1]

The psalm consists of four clearly marked divisions, each handling a different topic; and it is a nearer approach to a systematic theology than anything elsewhere found in the Bible. For these divisions treat successively of God's Omniscience, of his Omnipresence, of his Omnipotence, and the last part exhibits the spirit which a contemplation of these awful attributes should inspire. There is, however, a great difference between the mode of discussion here and in our systematic theologies. They generally proceed abstractly, in a philosophic spirit, while this proceeds concretely, in a practical spirit; they divorce themselves from homiletics, not proposing to persuade, while this is quite in the homiletic vein, indirectly making a powerful appeal to the heart and conscience; they are quite impersonal in their disquisitions, while this is intensely personal throughout. Would it not be well if some of our theologies were remodeled on this inspired plan?

The concrete and personal character of the psalm are worthy of particular note. There is hardly a word in it that can fairly be called an abstract term, there is no nebulosity, no rare atmos-

[1] *Vom Geist hebräischer Poesie.*

phere hard to breathe as the difficult air of the iced mountain top. This is in accord with the genius of Hebrew thought, which makes the particular stand for the general; for here we have the loftiest and largest conceptions with which the human mind can deal, expressed definitely and fully in narrow and specific terms. This does not follow because the treatment is poetical; Aryan poetry, both Teutonic and Indian, abounds in wide and vague abstractions. It is rather that spirit of the thinker which ever keeps in view the immediate practical application of the matter to his own person. So is human nature that such handling, and such alone, can reach the heart. He that made us also made for us Christianity and Christ identical.

Of this psalm Perowne says: "Nowhere are the great attributes of God set forth so strikingly as they are in this magnificent ode. Nowhere is there a more overwhelming sense of the fact that man is beset and compassed about by God, pervaded by his Spirit, and unable to take a step without his control; and yet nowhere is there a more emphatic assertion of the personality of man as distinct from, not absorbed in, the Deity. This is no pantheistic speculation. Man is here the workmanship of God, and stands in the presence and under the eye of Him who is his Judge. The power of conscience, the sense of sin and responsibility, are felt and acknowledged, and prayer is offered to One who is not only the Judge, but the Friend; One who is feared as none else are feared; One who is loved as none else are loved."

I

O LORD, thou hast searched me, and known me;

Thou knowest my downsitting and mine uprising,
Thou understandest my thought from afar,
Thou winnowest my path and my bed,
And art acquainted with all my ways.

For there is not a word in my tongue,
But, lo, O LORD, thou knowest it altogether.
Thou hast beset me behind and before,
And laid thine hand upon me.

Knowledge too wonderful for me!
It is high, I cannot attain unto it.

NOTES.—*Strophe 1.* God's Omniscience.— from afar, when on high.

> Is not God in the height of heaven?
> And behold the height of the stars, how high they are!
> And thou sayest: What doth God know?
> Can he judge through the thick darkness?
> Thick clouds are a covering to him, that he seeth not;
> And he walketh in the circuit of heaven. (Job xxii. 12, 14.)

—acquainted, intimately.—For; the argument is *a fortiori.*

II

Whither shall I go from thy spirit?
Whither shall I flee from thy presence?

If I ascend up into heaven, thou art there;
If I make my bed in Sheol, lo, thou art there.
If I take the wings of the morning,
And dwell in the uttermost part of the sea;
Even there shall thy hand lead me,
And thy right hand shall hold me.

If I say: Only let darkness cover me,
And the light about me shall be night;
Even the darkness hideth not from thee,
But the night shineth as the day;
Darkness is as light to thee.

Strophe 2. God's Omnipresence.—**Whither shall I go,** not in terror, but in awe.—**Sheol,** not hell (A. V.), but the underworld, Hades, the realm of disembodied spirits.—**take the wings,** and fly as quickly as the light of dawn flits across the sky to the west.—**and dwell,** he is already there.—**sea,** beyond the horizon of the Mediterranean.—**shall hold me,** I cannot escape.—**the light;** this line is more accurate and more poetical than the Authorized Version, which in this second line conveys the same idea that is found in the fourth line of the stanza.

Strophe 3. God's Omnipotence.—**reins,** were with the Hebrews poetically the seat of emotions, as the heart with us.—**weave,** as a texture or fabric of interlacing bones, sinews, veins, and nerves.—**fearfully made.** Nothing more highly displays the power and skill of the Creator than the human frame, his last work; and no man can rightly contemplate the mechanism of his own body and not be filled with awe.—**in se-**

III

For thou, thou didst form my reins,
Thou didst weave me in my mother's womb.
I will praise thee, for I am fearfully, wonderfully made;
Marvelous are thy works, my soul knoweth it well.

My frame was not hidden from thee,
  When I was made in secret,
  Curiously wrought in the depths of the earth.
Thine eyes did see my unformed substance,
  And in thy book were all written,
  The days that were ordained when there were none.

How precious unto me are thy thoughts, O God!
How great is the sum of them!
If I would recount them, they are more in number than
I awake, and I am still with thee.   [the sand;

---

cret, in the womb. (*Cf.* Ecclesiastes xi. 5.)—**curiously wrought**, as an embroidered garment diversified with colors. — **the depths**, a region of darkness and mystery, thus representing the womb.—**unformed substance**; undeveloped life, not yet unrolled. The figure is passing over to the skein of life, in which the threads that are to form the web of human existence and destiny are not yet unrolled. (*Hupfeld.*)—**How precious**; how dear to me are thy wondrous thoughts expressed in these miracles of creation, how great their sum! I recount them all the day long until sleep overtakes me; I sleep, and awake, and am still with thee, still recounting the endless number of thy thoughts, of thy wonderful designs of art, wisdom, and love. Said Kepler, the astronomer: I am thinking thy thoughts, O God, after thee.

IV

O that thou wouldest slay the wicked, O God!
Depart from me, ye men of blood,
For they speak against thee wickedly,
Thine enemies, they act against thee vainly.

Should not I hate thy haters, O Lord?
Should not I abhor thine adversaries?
I hate them with perfect hatred,
I count them mine enemies.

Search me, O God, and know my heart,
Try me, and know my thoughts,
And see if in me there be any offending way,
And lead me in the way everlasting.

Strophe 4. Exhibits the spirit which such contemplations properly excite. "The exquisite meditations upon God's attributes may have been suggested by sharp trial caused by the enemies of God, of the nature of which no hint is given, but which gave tone to the fourth part." (*Dean of Wells.*) Some critics deem this part to be unworthy of the rest of the psalm, and judge it to have been added by another hand. But Luther, Delitzsch, *et al.*, feel that the psalm would be incomplete without it, and that it tends to this point from the beginning. "Hatred and abhorrence of impiety is the inevitable result of that intense realization of God's perfections which the psalm discovers, and the prayer to him who knows the heart is so natural and appropriate that no fitter conclusion could be imagined." (*Dean of Wells.*) Chrysostom remarks: "Now a higher philosophy is required than then; for they are ordered to hate not only impiety, but impious persons, lest their friendship should be an occasion to them of going astray." Let us rather

The rendering of the Authorized Version is so inaccurate that we have ventured to present a revision, in which the Revised Version and various other versions have given assistance. The structure is simple and calls for no remark. Most of the German commentators question the Davidic authorship on account of certain Aramaisms in the text; but the English commentators generally hold to it.

§ 7. Now King David was old and stricken in years. And in the remnant of his days there was for him yet one sore trouble. Adonijah, the eldest of his surviving sons, exalted himself, saying: I will be king. He sought to accomplish his purpose much as Absalom had done, and only at the last moment—indeed not until the people were already shouting: God save King Adonijah—was his purpose thwarted. This was accomplished through the interference of Nathan and Queen Bathsheba. Solomon, her son, was, by the order of King

---

remember that the Hebrew does not deal in abstractions. A Greek might hate wickedness, but a Hebrew hates wicked men. Hengstenberg suggests: "The psalmist speaks of wicked men as such, not of his own personal enemies."—Search me; an harmonious echo of strophe 1, not in self-confidence, but in the conviction that God knows his heart better than he does himself, and with the earnest desire to have it cleansed of secret faults, secret to him, but known to God. It is a touching repetition of the prayer of his early youth closing the nineteenth psalm, his Morning Hymn.

David, promptly anointed and crowned, and the scheme of Adonijah came to naught.[1]

Then the days of David drew nigh that he should die, and he gave a dying charge to Solomon his son. Probably, after it was delivered, he had its substance recorded as his last psalm. This psalm is not found in the Psalter, but only in 2 Samuel xxiii., which is not its chronological place. It should be carefully compared with the charge found in 1 Kings ii. We quote it because of the interest attaching to it as the dying song of the greatest of poets, and for its intrinsic excellence. The rendering of the Authorized Version being defective, we present a revised version. The scribe introduces it with a stanza of his own, perhaps unconsciously poetical, inspired by the forecast of what he is about to record:

> Now these be the last words of David.
> Saith David the son of Jesse,
> Saith the man raised up on high,
> The anointed of the God of Jacob,
> And the sweet psalmist of Israel:

---

[1] 1 Kings i.

NOTES.—There are many obscurities in this ode, owing to its extreme conciseness. Our somewhat free rendering gives the generally accepted meaning. In the introductory stanza, the anointed = the Messiah. Bunsen renders the last line thus: "The darling of the songs of Israel"—*i. e.*, he was their theme.

I

The spirit of the LORD spake by me,
And his word was in my tongue.
The God of Israel said,
The rock of Israel spake to me:

II

He that ruleth over men must be just,
Ruling in the fear of God.

And he shall be as morning light when the sun ariseth,
    A morning without clouds;
As tender grass out of the earth,
    From sunshine and from rain.

III

Is not my house so with God,
That he hath made with me an everlasting covenant,
    Ordered in all things and sure?
For all my salvation,
And all my desire,
    Will he not cause it to spring up?

Strophe 1. Spirit; it was the *breath* of Jehovah that passed through his frame.—spake; a *divine outpouring* is the sense of the Hebrew. The repetitions in this strophe are very effective, suspending progress, and thus emphasizing the idea.

Strophe 2. The oracle. This and strophe 4 should be compared with Psalm i., which is so closely parallel as to appear like an imitation. The first line is sometimes rendered, "The Just One shall rule over men," and understood as prophetic of Christ; but this seems forced. The general thought is rather, "the ideal of a just reign, whether as looking back upon his

IV

But all the sons of Belial shall be as thorns thrust away;
Because they cannot be taken with hands;
But the man that would touch them,
Must be fenced with iron,
And the staff of a spear;
And they shall be utterly burned with fire in its place.

---

own, or forward to that of Solomon." (*Stanley*.) The second stanza illustrates the prosperity of the just ruler, his brilliant glory, and its delectable fruit.

Strophe 3. An assurance of prosperity of the kingdom of Solomon, who was typical of David's greater Son.—everlasting covenant. See Isaiah lv. 3. *Cf.* also Isaiah xi. 1, 4:—

> There shall come forth a shoot out of the stock of Jesse,
> And a branch out of his roots shall bear fruit.
> With righteousness shall he judge the poor,
> And reprove with equity for the meek of the earth.
> He shall smite the earth with the rod of his mouth,
> And with the breath of his lips shall he slay the wicked.

Strophe 4. Contrasts with the others the destruction of the wicked, referring primarily to Joab and Shimei. (See the "Charge," 1 Kings ii.)—thorns, in contrast with the "tender grass" of royal prosperity. They can be subdued only with long pruning-hooks. So the sons of Belial must be "thrust away" by men clad in iron armor, wielding the spear. To root out and burn this evil growth of the court is the duty of a just ruler, as much as the fostering of the good.—in its place probably means: In the very place where the thorns are, there shall they be burned. The structure of this strophe is peculiar and worthy of note. The first and last lines are parallel.

This is a melancholy strain to close a song which begins so full of brightness and joy. But it is a true picture of the checkered life of David. Such a rugged, four-faced monument is a fitting memorial of the man who was at once a prophet and a king, a penitent and a saint.

The words of David, the son of Jesse, are ended.

Adieu! thou sweet psalmist; thou royal prophet; thou tempted, tried, stricken, erring, yet in the main, true-hearted servant of God. We shall know thee better when we meet above, now that we have traced thy heart-history here.

> So David slept with his fathers,
> And was buried in the city of David.

"He set as sets the morning star,
  Which goes not down beyond the darkened west,
  But melts away into the light of heaven."

VI.—VERSES

§1. THE general subject must now receive more direct consideration. Quite a number of Hebrew lyrics have been presented and discussed, in the hope that the reader should have his heart aglow with love and admiration before entering on the cold analytical details now before us. Very many points have necessarily been anticipated, but we shall not hesitate to repeat these, as a strictly systematic or scientific development of the subject is not intended. We proceed to an analysis of the structure of Hebrew poetry, and to point out those æsthetic elements which entitle it to rank with the best classical poetry, and the distinctive marks which set it apart and give it a place all its own.

Let it be remembered that while we hold this to be sacred poetry, and the poet inspired by the Holy Spirit of God; while we do not disregard its teachings, nor fail to gaze with reverence into its spiritual depths, nor neglect to welcome its blessed influences on our hearts; yet our present purpose is not to consider these points, though by far of highest importance—an importance that is inestimable. But we propose to illustrate features which, though of vastly less value and interest, are nevertheless true features, and have an importance of their own. We descend to the low plain common to all literatures, and view Hebrew poetry simply as poetry, studying its forms and characters, comparing and contrasting it with others, and making acquaintance with its peculiar modes of expression. Although this poetry be inspired, yet no sound theory of inspiration will ascribe to the Holy Spirit its many rhetorical excellences; nor, on the other hand, its literary imperfections, if any there be. The writers were used as instruments, and expressed themselves each according to his own genius, without help or hindrance as to form and manner. Hence on this ground they stand as merely human authors, and it is admissible to descant, in these respects, upon their accomplishments as belonging to themselves, and to institute comparisons between Hebrew and heathen classic literature. The only advantage that may be attributed to Hebrew writers, and indeed it is a great one, is that they had the light of truth, and hence their productions attained a dignity and power surpassing the noblest ideals of other ancient literatures.

Sometimes it has been thought that to speak of

Holy Scripture as poetry is an irreverent disparagement of it; and yet the simple fact is that more than one-third of the Bible is poetry. The mistake arises from a misconception of the real origin and nature of poetry, and from greatly underrating the power of its influence.

Poetry is not an invention of man. The psalmists and prophets did not take herein a human contrivance and bend it to their service. Rather they took a noble gift of God, and used it for the noble purposes for which it was ordained. His Maker fashioned man for poetic utterance that his praises might burn with eloquence, and his prayers rise with the fragrance of incense. But the best gifts of God are liable to the worst abuse; and from its abuse has arisen the notion, under the high sanction of both Plato and Aristotle, that poetry is essentially fictitious, and antagonistic to truth. Rather is it the festive, Sabbath-day robe of truth, a veil to soften her awful severity and the dazzling flash of her eyes. Poetry is the perfection of expression, and the noblest vehicle of thought. "Let no one, then," says Bishop Lowth, " speak of this art as light and trifling in itself, or regard it as profane and impious; this art which has been conceded to man by his Creator, and for the most sacred purposes; this art consecrated by the authority of God himself, and by his example in his most august ministrations."

The influence which poetry, even when not fulfilling its highest offices, exerts on the human race is incalculable. The childhood of all nations has been spent in singing. The richest treasures of every literature are its poems; and, says Fletcher, one who can make the songs of a people need not care who makes the laws. Of all those departments of thought into which mind has expanded, we may doubt whether any one has had more influence in determining the destinies of mankind than that which embodies the creations of imagination, and gives enduring form and expression to human feeling. Was Raphael wrong when, in the chamber of sciences of the Vatican, he gave in his frescoes the same rank to poetry as to philosophy, jurisprudence, and theology?

But while making this high claim for poetry in general, we make a higher special claim for sacred poetry. None is comparable to the Hebrew poetry in the effects it has wrought; and the sway of the Hebrew bard surpasses the sway of all others. For who is king among men? Is it not he that rules? On the Parnassus, Raphael assigns to Homer the highest place. Was he right? Yes, if Greek poetry, or even European poetry, be intended. But if Raphael would represent the poetry of the world; if he would distinguish its highest seat, and that poet who has been most potent in molding the hearts, thoughts, and conduct of men through a hundred generations, he should paint Zion higher than Parnassus, and the sweet singer of Israel seated thereon; not in royal robes, with crown and scepter, but in the linen ephod, and with a harp in hand. From the hour when his songs exorcised the evil spirit in Saul, throughout his wanderings and his long reign, until the words of the son of Jesse were ended:

> "They softened men of iron mold,
>   They gave them virtues not their own;
> No ear so dull, no heart so cold,
>   That felt not, fired not at the tone,
> Till David's lyre grew mightier than his throne."

His visible kingdom did not long survive him, but his dominion over the hearts of men was established forever.

§2. In attempting to catch a glimpse of the characteristics of true poetry, we first distinguish its essence from its form. Of the essence we can say very little. But is it not truth, beauty, and goodness—the Platonic triad—becoming a trinity?

We may have an expression of truth alone, but this is not poetry. We may have truth and goodness combined, but yet not poetry. We may have beauty alone, transcendent beauty, expressed in perfect poetical form, but, specious and false, this is not true poetry. Like the brilliant glare of the aurora, it gives no warmth, quickens no life. But when truth, goodness, and beauty unite, is not this essentially poetry, whatever be the form? It seems to me that these three are great archangels belonging to God's throne, but sent on a mission to every open heart, and spreading a halo of heaven's own glory all around our way.

The form of poetry is more palpable. Yet we cannot fix it. It is protean. If we were to grasp in one statement all the forms that have yet appeared, the next original poet that is born, if there is ever to be another, would violate our rule, and give us a new form. We propose here to consider only one external mark, one which seems to attend beauty wherever it appears, whether in poetry or other arts, or in nature. The somewhat musty definition of beauty, unity amid variety, seems at once too wide and too narrow, yet it involves the mark to which we allude, and which is here emphasized, since it is especially prominent in Hebrew poetry. Let us call this mark Repetition.

In the beautiful objects of nature we find a constant repetition. We see it in the eyes and lips of the human face, in the petals of the flower, in the stars of the sky. We hear it in the trilling song of birds, and in the echo. In art we see it in the columns of the Parthenon, the statues of the Agora, repeating the human form, and in the paintings of Stoa Pœcile, repeating memorable scenes. In music there is frequent repetition. To each of Mozart's model melodies, and of Beethoven's tone poems, there is a theme, of perhaps not more than one or two measures, which is worked out with numerous variations and frequent reappearances, and which, never being entirely lost, preserves that unity essential to a true work of art.

In modern poetry we have a repetition of sound in rhyme. This is a device to increase the poetical effect by a purely sensuous impression.[1] It is not found in classical Latin, but appears in the later Latin of the mediæval hymns; nor does it occur in classical Greek, except traces here and there in comedy, but has been adopted by modern Greek versifiers. It has not been found in early Hebrew poetry, though searched for with great assiduity; but rhyme and, soon after, meter,

---

[1] We cite especially Southey's *Lodore*, the sole merit of which consists in the sensuous effect of skillful rhyming.

makes its appearance here also, first in the seventh century, in some poetical attempts of rabbinical scholars. The lack of syllabic accent makes rhyme necessary in French poetry; in other modern tongues it is unnecessary, and marks decadence of poetical taste and power. We hold to what Milton says in his preface to *Paradise Lost* (ed. 1660): "Rhime is no necessary adjunct or true ornament of poem or good verse, in longer works especially, but the invention of a barbarous age, to set off wretched matter and lame metre; graced indeed since by the use of some famous modern poets, carried away by custom, but much to their own vexation, hindrance, and constraint to express many things otherwise, and for the most part worse than else they would have expressed them. Poets of prime note have rejected Rhime as a thing of itself, to all judicious ears, trivial and of no true musical delight; which consists not in the jingling sound of like endings, a fault avoided by the learned ancients both in poetry and all good oratory."

It is needless to detail the various ways in which the principle of repetition gives form to poetry. It is the very ground of all meter, whether by modern accent or ancient quantity. It is the very essence of all rhythm, even of that obscure rhythm which is felt rather than seen in graceful prose; for, as Augustine, in *De Musica*, says, "all meter is rhythm, but not all rhythm is meter." The delicate and pleasing effect of the refrain is due to repetition. Besides these, we frequently find in good poetry the effect greatly heightened, though by a sensuous rather than an intellectual appeal, through the repetition of words and phrases.[1]

§3. Before showing that this principle of repetition is the prominent characteristic of Hebrew poetry, we must refer to the investigations of eminent scholars into this matter. The influence of European classical literature has led Hebraists to search thoroughly the Hebrew poetry to ascertain the quantity of its syllables and its metrical laws, and not until of late have they abandoned the conviction that there must be some poetic system corresponding to the Greek and Latin prosody. Josephus roundly asserts that the Song of Moses is in hexameters. Philo Judæus, in his life of Moses, gravely states that he was the inventor "of numbers and geometry, the theory of rhythm, har-

---

[1] We cite as familiar examples, Tennyson's Charge of the Light Brigade, and Milton's Address of Eve (*Paradise Lost*, iv. 634-658), one of the most tender and exquisite passages of the great epic.

mony, and meter, and the whole science of music, practical and theoretical." Both these writers of the first century endeavored to show that the Greeks had been anticipated by the Hebrews in literature and philosophy. Eusebius in the fourth century said that the Song of Moses and Psalm cxix. were in heroic measure, and that other verses were trimeters; this was denied by Julian the Apostate. Jerome of the fifth century compares the psalms to the odes of Horace, Pindar, Alceus, and Sappho, their meters now running in iambics, now ringing with alcaics, now swelling with Sapphics. Gregory of Nyssa, of the fourth century, expressly denied that the Hebrew poems were composed in classical meter; but the great philologist and universal scholar, Joseph Scaliger, of the sixteenth century, first explicitly denounced the error, and declared that Hebrew poetry was not bound by any known metrical laws; yet even he found traces of rhythm which he compared to the classical.

Many scholars have maintained that the Hebrew poetry has an independent metrical system of its own, and have expended great labor and exhibited great ingenuity in attempting to discover it, but without agreed result; among others, Gomarus Anton, Bishop Hare, and Sir William Jones, the great orientalist. The latter, in his *Poesos Asiaticæ*, attempted to apply the rules of Arabic meter to the Hebrew. Merx finds in the Book of Job a regular syllabic and strophic structure, eight syllables in each stich, and an equal number of stichs in each strophe; but he is obliged to resort to arbitrary conjectures of lacunæ and interpolations of the masoretic text. Another class of scholars, while affirming the existence of a metrical system, abandon all hope of recovering it; among these are Lowth, Jahn, Buxtorf, Bauer, and to some extent, Herder and also Dr. Wright. Ewald discusses the matter at great length and learnedly, but his views have not been generally accepted. Sommer claims to have found intentional rhyme in many places, but Ewald ascribes such appearances to mere accident. Scholars of to-day very generally disbelieve the existence of any metric system, of any prosody corresponding in any sense to that of classical and modern languages, and this negative result, so slowly and laboriously reached, is now hardly questionable.

Robert Lowth, professor of poetry at Oxford, and afterwards Bishop of London (died 1787), published in 1753 his *De Sacri Poësi Hebræorum, Prælectiones Academicæ*. This publication marks an era in the literature of the subject. It was edited, with learned annotations, by J. D. Michaelis, professor in Göttingen, and has been translated and republished in numerous editions. Bishop Jebb, of Limerick, followed the views of Lowth, and enlarged upon them in his *Sacra Literaria*, and the substantial correctness of Lowth's principle has been generally admitted by scholars, both English and continental. Other classifications, based on the same principle, have been proposed, one especially acute and scientific by De Wette, one by Ewald, and others, but none have been so generally adopted.

Before stating the positive results of Lowth's analysis, we must observe that he had been anticipated. A number of Rabbis had asserted that in Hebrew poetry there is only a rhythm of sentences, and not of syllables, and that the rhythmical quantity is originally and essentially determined by the content; partly by the repetition of the same thought in similar or allied expression, and partly by the prominence which is imparted to it by antithetic or synthetic terms of expression. This, as will be seen, is substantially Lowth's analysis. Rabbi Azariah de Rossi states it with great clearness. The anticipation was yet more complete by Schöttingen in his *Horæ Hebraicæ*. With none of these, however, does Lowth seem to have been acquainted, and the system is generally attributed to him.[1]

§ 4. The basis of this system is Parallelism. This is the name adopted for the correspondence of one line, or stich,[2] with another—word answering to word, or phrase to phrase, or thought to thought, or the construction of one line to the construction of another. This may be more fully stated, adopting Lowth's phraseology, thus: Lines parallel are characterized by a relation and proportion which arise from a correspondence of terms, and from a singular syntatic construction. From this arises a rhythmus of propositions, an harmonious cadence of sentences, so that generally periods coincide with stanzas, members of periods with lines, and the pauses in one line with those in the other, the words and phrases answering to one another. Frequently, however, the forms of expression are insufficiently balanced to enable us by them to determine the parallels. We are then driven wholly to the thought, to the sentiment conveyed, and may often by it alone trace that dupli-

---

[1] It has been, after Jebb, more fully developed by Herder, Gesenius, De Wette, Köster, Ewald, and Hupfeld.

[2] The word *verse* would be a correct and a better term but for its common loose usage, especially in reference to the subdivisions of the biblical text.

cation which characterizes the parallelism. Thus the parallelism is oftentimes so evident as to strike the most careless reader, but sometimes so subtle and obscure as to require considerable practice and familiarity with the system to develop the different members in their probable order and connection. The relation of lines, thus described by Lowth, is happily defined by Aben Ezra: *Duplicatio sententiæ, verbis variatis.* We present at once some examples of the obvious sort:

The heavens	declare	the glory of God,
The firmament	sheweth	his handiwork;
Day unto day	uttereth	speech,
Night unto night	sheweth	knowledge.

(Psalm xix. 1, 2.)

| Hear | the word of the Lord, | ye rulers | of Sodom; |
| Give ear unto the law | of our God, | ye people | of Gomorrah. |

(Isaiah i. 10.)

One is conscious on reading the simplest passage of this sort that it is not prose. The unusual animation of the style arouses attention. There is no life without movement, and the movement characteristic of life is pulsation. In this throbbing of thought is plainly manifest the principle of repetition on which we have laid stress. Parallelism is repetition. It is so especially prominent in all Hebrew poetry as to constitute its chief, almost its sole characteristic, becoming specific by virtue of its persistent prominence.

This mode of poetical expression in parallel, duplicate, balanced sentiments seems entirely natural, as natural as the heaving and sinking of an agitated heart, as the breathing the air of heaven. We find a tendency to it in prose whenever style becomes animated and elevated. Passion tends to express itself lyrically, and in the Old Testament especially the style oftentimes rises with the feeling from plain prose by imperceptible degrees into one highly poetical, involving parallelisms.

That this form of poetry is entirely natural is evidenced by the fact that it is the earliest of all. In confirmation of this, and also because it exhibits in great perfection the principle of parallelism, we will present the most ancient poem extant, coming to us from the antediluvian age. It is the brief lyric of Lamech, a descendant of Cain, the father of Jubal the inventor of musical instruments, the prototype of Apollo and Orpheus, and also the father of Tubal Cain the smith, the prototype of Vulcan the armorer. This song of the wild old chief, addressed to his wives, is found in Genesis iv. 23, 24. Its obscure and enigmatical character is admitted as a mark of remote antiquity, and it has exercised the skill of translators and interpreters of all times. Herder pronounces it " a sword song "—*i. e.*, a song of triumph; Lamech rejoicing and confidently boasting in the enlarged power he now has by virtue of the new weapon, fabricated by his son and placed in his hands. We give the following version:

> And Lamech said unto his wives:
> Adah and Zillah, hear my voice,
> Ye wives of Lamech, give ear to my speech;
> For I slay a man if he woundeth me,
> Even a young man if he hurteth me.
> Lo! Cain would be avenged seven-fold,
> But Lamech, seventy and seven-fold.

The second distich would be more literally rendered by the past tense, " For I have slain a man who wounded me," etc.; and this is explained as being the most arrogant form of boasting, in which, like the sure word of prophecy, the future is represented as having all the certainty of the past. Herder's interpretation of it as a sword song is preferred to the view that it is a lament for some deed of violence which Lamech had committed; to which view, however, the perfect tense gives weight. In reference to its naturalness and passionate earnestness, Ewald calls the song, "A daughter of the moment, of swift-rising, powerful feelings, of deep stirrings and fiery emotions of the heart." We call attention to the perfection of the parallelisms.

The natural tendency of warm feeling to run into parallel expressions is exhibited in many places in the Greek of the New Testament, which, outside of the first two chapters of Luke, contains no intentional poetry except quotations. The Beatitudes (Matthew v. 3-12) are strictly parallel, and remind us forcibly of the first psalm and of Psalm xix. 7-9. Other parts of the Sermon on the Mount exhibit the same form, particularly the close, which is presented by Bishop Jebb thus:

Whosoever heareth my words and doeth them,
I will liken him to a prudent man,
Who built his house upon the rock:
    And the rain descended,
    And the floods came,
    And the winds blew,
    And fell upon that house;
And it fell not; for it was founded upon the rock.

And every one hearing my words, and doing them not,
Shall be likened to a foolish man,
Who built his house upon the sand:
    And the rain descended,
    And the floods came,
    And the winds blew,
    And struck upon that house;
And it fell; and the fall thereof was great.

In the following instance, from Matthew viii. 20, observe the swell in sentiment:

> The foxes have holes,
> The birds of the air have nests,
> But the Son of man hath not where to lay his head.

In this next, from John xv. 10, the lines are alternately parallel:

> If ye keep my commandments,
>   Ye shall abide in my love;
> Even as I have kept my Father's commandments,
>   And abide in his love.

This final example, from 2 Timothy ii. 11, is more complex:

> For if we died with him,
>   We shall also live with him;
> If we endure, we shall also reign with him.
>   If we shall deny him,
>   He also will deny us;
> If we are faithless, he remains faithful;
>   For he cannot deny himself.

Here is Hebrew poetry, flowing unconsciously from the Hebrew mind, though thinking and expressing itself in the Greek language.

§5. The naturalness of parallel expression is further shown by the fact that it is found in other ancient poetic literature besides the Semitic.

From Lefèvre we obtain a few lines of an ancient Egyptian hymn, which, literally rendered into English, is as follows:

> God prefers purity to millions of riches,
> And to hundreds of thousands of gold;
> He feeds on truth which satisfies him,
> His heart watches over sin.

The Hymn to the Nile, dating from the Ramesian period, is also characterized by frequent parallelisms. The following are the closing lines:

> Shine forth, shine, O Nile, shine forth,
>   Giving life to men by his oxen,
>   Giving life to his oxen by the pastures;
> Shine forth in glory, O Nile.[1]

We find them, too, in the ancient Aryan tongues. The following is from Buddha's *Drammapada*, or, Path of Virtue, translated by Max Müller, which was incorporated into the Buddhist canon about 246 B.C., but has undoubtedly a much earlier origin:

Let us live happily then, not hating those that hate us,
Let us dwell free from hatred among those that hate.
Let us live happily then, free from sin among the sinning,
Let us dwell free from sin among men who sin.
Let us live happily then, though we call nothing our own,
We shall be like the bright gods, feeding on happiness.

---

[1] See Birch's *Records of the Past*, Vol. IV., p. 114.

There is no fire like passion,
  There is no unlucky die like hatred;
There is no pain like the body,
  There is no happiness like rest.
Health is the greatest of gifts,
  Contentedness the best riches;
Trust is the best of relatives,
  Nirvana the highest happiness.

I open my Vergil, which comes first to hand, and find:

Quem sequimur? quove ire jubes? ubi ponere sedes?
Da, Pater, augurium, atque animis inlabere nostris!
(*Æneid*, iii. 88.)

Nam quid dissimulo aut quæ me ad majora reservo?
Num fletu ingemuit nostro? num lumina flexit?
Num lacrymas victus dedit, aut miseratus amantem est?
(*Æneid*, iv. 368.)

Examples in classical literature are not, however, frequent, but are to be looked for in passages expressing warm passion.

In modern poetry parallelism is quite common, although, of course, not intentional. The melancholy Jaques—

> Found tongues in trees,
> Books in the running brooks,
> Sermons in stones,
> And good in everything.

Byron, describing the destruction of Sennacherib's army, says:

> Like the leaves of the forest when summer is green,
> That host with their banners at sunset were seen;
> Like the leaves of the forest when autumn hath blown,
> That host on the morrow lay wither'd and strown.

Mrs. Browning, in the Cry of the Children, has this stanza:

> The old tree is leafless in the forest,
>   The old year is ending in the frost,
> The old wound, if stricken, is the sorest,
>   The old hope is hardest to be lost.

From Keble's Christian Year, Sunday after Ascension, we take:

> Largely thou givest, gracious Lord,
> Largely thy gifts should be restored,
> Truly thou givest, and thy word
>   Is: Freely give.
> He only who forgets to hoard,
>   Has learned to live.

Schiller's Mary Stuart says, in her indignation:

> Fahr' hin lammherzige Gelassenheit!
> Zum himmel fliehe, leidende Geduld!

Goethe's Faust hears the choir of Easter angels singing:

> Thätig ihn preisenden,
> Liebe beweisenden,
> Brüderlich speisenden,
> Predigend reisenden,
> Wonne verheissenden,
> Euch ist der Meister nah,
> Euch ist er da!

§ 6. In an analysis of Parallelism as the fundamental form of Hebrew poetry, the first requisite is to determine what constitutes a line. Proceeding from this we may be able to restore and exhibit to the eye that artistic structure so important to the full understanding of a poem, and to its impression on us. We cannot rely on the masoretic division generally followed in the verses of the Authorized Version, for in many cases it is clearly incorrect. The Masorites used in the poetical books a peculiar system of accentuation, indicating both the divisions of stichs and of strophes. It is older than the vowel pointings, but rests merely on the tradition of the synagogue; and that it is unreliable is shown by the fact that they almost always apply this poetic accentuation to those prose passages which occasionally occur in the poetic sections. Nor do the ancient Hebrew manuscripts furnish any ground by their arrangement of lines for determining the poetic line. They usually break the lines quite arbitrarily without regard to sense or rhythm. Primary recourse must be had to the alphabetic Psalms cxi. and cxii., in which the initial letters of the lines taken in order form the Hebrew alphabet, thus definitely fixing the lines according to the intent of the writer. In these psalms the stichs are quite short and nearly equal in length, consisting mostly of three Hebrew words each. We then turn to Psalms xxv., xxxiv., and cxlv., wherein the initial letters of the distichs are those of the alphabet. Here we can study not only what constitutes a line, but also what constitutes the parallelism of two lines. We find, in general, a correspondence in length between lines parallel, which lines, however, sometimes extend to eight or ten syllables. But in looking beyond these psalms we find the exceptions so numerous that we cannot ground a rule on these facts; for the second line often swells with the sentiment to much greater length than its parallel, and on the other hand it sometimes contracts to a condensed expression, apparently for the sake of emphasis. But we find that a line generally contains a complete sentence or a clause, so that the pause in the progress of thought fixes the point at which the line must end. This is our safest guide.

In endeavoring to form a conception of a line sufficiently clear, we need to observe that lines are often bi-membral, and the subordinate parts parallel to each other. This is manifest in the following line, which indeed may be taken as embodying in itself the whole principle of Hebrew poetry:

Hear, O heavens, and give ear, O earth. (Isaiah i. 2.)

In the following the lines are bi-membral, but without parallelism between the hemistichs of the same line:

God is in the midst of her, she shall not be moved;
God shall help her, and that right early.
The heathen raged, the kingdoms were moved;
He uttered his voice, the earth melted.
(Psalm xlvi. 5, 6.)

The pause occurring in the midst may be compared to the cæsura. Thereby is added to the style the arsis and thesis, the rise and fall, the flow and ebb, so effective in classic verse. When these hemistichs are long clauses, it is often hard to say why each should not be regarded as a complete line, producing a quatrain—*i. e.*, a stanza of four lines alternately parallel. For example, the last distich above may be thrown into this form:

> The heathen raged,
> > The kingdoms were moved:
> He uttered his voice,
> > The earth melted.

We have no rule by which to decide such cases; but generally when the length of the subordinate members does not determine a case, we may be guided by the structure of the context. Since the lines often cannot be satisfactorily thus arranged, the fact of frequent bi-membral structure of lines remains, and in rare cases we find them tri-membral.

§ 7. From the study of the line, we may proceed to the parallelism more specifically. Various classifications have been proposed; but that generally adopted is substantially Lowth's. Though not rigidly scientific, it is perhaps as nearly so as the nature of the subject admits, and sufficiently so for all practical purposes. We will now distinguish and illustrate three species.

I. Synonymous Parallelism.[1] Parallel lines that

---

[1] Bishop Jebb objects to the term Synonymous, and suggests the term Cognate as more accurately describing this species of parallelism. Gradational Parallelism has also been sug-

are synonymous correspond to each other by expressing a similar sense in different but equivalent terms—*e. g..*

> What is man that thou art mindful of him?
> Or the son of man that thou visitest him?
> (Psalm viii. 4.)

This might be taken as a kind of extended hendiadys, were it not that, as Bishop Jebb observes, "the second line very often diversifies the preceding one, and generally so as to rise above it, forming a sort of climax in the sense." Lowth observes this in his fourth Prelection where he says: "*Idem, iterant, variant, augent;*" thus marking the cumulative force, the swell in sense, which so commonly attends this species of parallelism. The following examples illustrate this characteristic increase of intensity:

> Purge me with hyssop, and I shall be clean;
> Wash me, and I shall be whiter than snow.
> (Psalm li. 7.)

gested as a preferable phrase, having reference to the usual swell in sense. Each of these happily expresses the character in question, but if we take Lowth's term Synonymous in its wide sense, it answers well enough. To the term Gradational we object that the swell only frequently, not always, occurs; and besides, we need to reserve this term to designate the peculiar structure found in the Songs of Degrees.

And the Gentiles shall come to thy light,
And kings to the brightness of thy rising.

(Isaiah lx. 3.)

There is hardly a page of the poetical books that does not furnish numerous examples, for the great majority of parallel distichs are to be referred to this class, and hence others need not be gathered here.

If thus much were all, we might expect monotony. But from this fault Hebrew poetry is especially free. It is avoided by the elasticity of the principle admitting many variations. By way of illustration, we note some of these.

First, the cumulative force of the second line may be accomplished by an added clause—*e. g.:*

The wilderness and the solitary place shall be glad;
And the desert shall rejoice, and blossom as the rose.

(Isaiah xxxv. 1.)

The parallelism here would be complete without the last clause, which, however, adds much beauty, as well as increase of thought. We may also observe that "The wilderness and the solitary place" are condensed into the parallel "desert," as if to make rhythmical room for the added clause.

A second variation is the omission of a phrase answering to one part of the first stich—*c. g.:*

When I behold thy heavens, the work of thy fingers,
— — — — — — — the moon and the stars, which thou
[hast ordained.
(Psalm viii. 3.)

Make us glad according to the days wherein thou hast
[afflicted us,
— — — — — — and the years wherein we have seen evil.
(Psalm xc. 15.)

The glory of Lebanon shall be given to it,
The excellency of Carmel and Sharon.
(Isaiah xxxv. 2.)

A third variation is the exact repetition of a phrase, a sort of anadiplosis—*e. g.*:

It is better to trust in the Lord than to put confidence
[in man,
It is better to trust in the Lord than to put confidence
[in princes.
(Psalm cxviii. 8, 9.)

This Psalm cxviii., written probably for the feast of Purim, and having a Messianic application, is remarkable for numerous cases of such repetitions, highly expressive of rapturous joy. The example cited is an extreme case, but minor exact repetitions, introduced for emphasis or iterative effect, are quite common in the poetical books.

A fourth notable variation is the inversion of the members of the second line—*e. g.:*

O Lord God of hosts, hear my prayer;
Give ear, O God of Jacob. (Psalm lxxxiv. 8.)

For we are consumed by thine anger,
And by thy wrath are we troubled. (Psalm xc. 7.)

In the following examples mark also the cumulative force:

Thou shalt tread upon the lion and adder,
The young lion and the dragon shalt thou trample under
[feet.
(Psalm xci. 13.)
Bless the Lord, O my soul;
And all that is within me, bless his holy name.
(Psalm ciii. 1.)
She is more precious than rubies,
And all the things thou canst desire, are not to be com-
[pared to her.
(Proverbs iii. 15.)

Behold thou shalt call a nation that thou knowest not,
And nations that knew not thee shall run unto thee.
(Isaiah lv. 5.)

Such inversions as found in the Authorized Version are sometimes the work of the translators (*e. g.*, Psalm li. 3), but many are original.

It is sufficiently manifest from these cited variations that Synonymous Parallelism is susceptible of great diversity. The enumeration, however, is far from being exhaustive. There are many other variations which it would be hard and useless to classify.

II. Antithetic Parallelism. This species occurs when two lines exhibit an opposition of terms and sentiments; when the second is contrasted with the first, sometimes in expression, sometimes in sense only. The antithesis may be complete or partial, and is not confined to any particular form, but is subject to all the variations above enumerated. The following are examples:

A wise son maketh a glad father;
But a foolish son is the heaviness of his mother.
(Proverbs x. 1.)

Here every phrase has its antithesis, the terms "father" and "mother" being correlatively opposite. Again:

The memory of the just is blessed;
But the name of the wicked shall rot. (Proverbs x. 7.)

In this instance the antithesis is partial only, the terms "memory" and "name" being synonymous. In the following the order is inverted:

The Lord knoweth the way of the righteous;
But the way of the wicked shall perish. (Psalm i. 6.)

The following illustration, from the Indian *Dram-*

mapada, has the adjacent lines antithetic, the alternate ones synonymous:

Reflection is the path of immortality,
   Thoughtlessness the path of death.
Those who reflect do not die,
   Those who are thoughtless are as if dead already.

This species of parallelism is peculiarly suited to gnomic literature, giving point to aphorisms, adages, and detached sentences, looking at the subject in hand on both sides. Much of the elegance, acuteness, and force of the proverbs of Solomon arise from this form of expression, in which they most generally appear, cutting both ways like a two-edged sword. Thought is the sword of the magistrate rather than of the warrior. Antithesis is generally a figure of a cool nature, the product of reflection rather than passion, and hence more frequent in didactic composition. Seneca abounds in antithesis to excess. It is the favorite form in Arabic literature. Hebrew poetry of all kinds furnishes illustrations, but they are especially numerous in the gnomic and didactic poems. One has only to glance at any page of the book of Proverbs, after the ninth chapter, to be impressed with their frequency. The following examples are taken from poems not didactic, and exhibit some of the many variations and combinations. The first shows antithesis between the hemistichs only, the lines being synonymously parallel:

The Lord killeth, and maketh alive,
He bringeth down to the grave, and bringeth up.
The Lord maketh poor, and maketh rich,
He bringeth low, and lifteth up. (1 Samuel ii. 6, 7.)

In the following there is a partial inversion of opposed terms:

> In the morning it flourisheth and groweth up,
> In the evening it is cut down and withereth.
> (Psalm xc. 6.)

The following stanza exhibits antithesis between the alternate lines:

> If ye be willing and obedient,
>   Ye shall eat of the good of the land;
> If ye refuse and rebel,
>   Ye shall be devoured with the sword.
> (Isaiah i. 19, 20.)

The following pentastich consists of a quatrain and an added line. The alternate lines of the quatrain are synonymously parallel, while the lines of each distich are antithetic, as in the above quotation from the *Drammapada:*

For a small moment have I forsaken thee,
  But with great mercies will I gather thee;
In a little wrath I hid my face from thee for a moment,
  But with everlasting kindness will I have mercy
                                              [on thee,
Saith the Lord, thy Redeemer.   (Isaiah liv. 7, 8.)

The following stanza exhibits a more elaborate variation, also combining both species of parallelism:

Therefore thus saith the Lord God:
  Behold my servants shall eat,
    But ye shall be hungry;
  Behold my servants shall drink,
    But ye shall be thirsty;
  Behold my servants shall rejoice,
    But ye shall be ashamed;
  Behold my servants shall sing for joy of heart,
    But ye shall cry for sorrow of heart,
    And shall howl for vexation of spirit.
                              (Isaiah lxv. 13, 14.)

Of the two kinds of parallelism now described, Bishop Jebb says: " The Antithetic Parallelism serves to mark the broad distinction between truth and falsehood, between good and evil; the Cognate [Synonymous] Parallelism discharges the more difficult and more critical function of discriminating (by its gradational structure) between different degrees of truth and good on the one hand, and of falsehood and evil on the other."[1]

III. Synthetic Parallelism. Lowth describes this species as "consisting only in the similar form of construction; in which word does not answer to word, and sentence to sentence as equivalent or opposite; but there is a correspondence and equality between different propositions in respect of the shape and turn of the whole sentence, and of the constructive parts, such as noun answering to noun, verb to verb, member to member, negative to negative, interrogative to interrogative." If this statement be accepted, it were better to call it Grammatical or Syntatic Parallelism; but the statement is too narrow, since, if strictly adhered to, it would include no very great number of cases, and necessitate at least one other class for the large remainder. Nordheimer describes it better as the species wherein "an idea is neither repeated nor followed by its opposite, but is kept in view by the writer while he proceeds to develop and enforce his meaning by accessory ideas and modifications." This is quite wide enough, but is very general and vague. It hardly indicates more than that parallelism in thoughts (*parallelismus sen-*

---

[1] *Sacra Literaria*, p. 39.

tentiarum), that logical but not necessarily formal correspondence, which Herder insists upon as being the basis of the original and essential rhythm of poetry in general. In De Wette's classification there is a species not unlike the present, which he calls Rhythmical Parallelism; and perhaps this phrase would express the character of the parallelism now under consideration better than the one in use. It may not be possible to define synthetic or constructive parallelism very clearly and distinctly; and we shall not go far wrong in considering it an indefinite or negative class, to which may conveniently be referred those forms not clearly referable to either of the two other classes, but which show by rhythmical or other correspondence, or by mere association, that they are without doubt poetical. The following example is quoted by Gesenius:

> One thing have I desired of the Lord,
>   That will I seek after,
> That I may dwell in the house of the Lord,
>   All the days of my life,
> To behold the beauty of the Lord,
>   And to inquire in his temple.
>
>   (Psalm xxvii. 4.)

Here we see that a certain rhythm is secured by the similar length of lines. Sometimes this may be observed when there is little else in the form to distinguish it from prose. But in all the examples here given there are synonymous phrases, with only an obscure, irregular, and partial correspondence between the lines. In some cases the synonyms are so numerous and regular that we hardly can decide whether the parallelism belongs to the first or the third class. The following we class as synthetic:

With plentiful rain, O God,
    Thou didst sprinkle thine heritage,
And when fainting
    Thou didst raise it up.
Thy congregation hath dwelt therein;
Thou, O God, didst provide in thy goodness for the poor.
Ascribe ye strength unto God;
    Over Israel is his majesty,
    And his strength in the clouds.
Fearful art thou, O God, from thy holy places,
    Mighty one of Israel,
He that gives strength and peace to the people.
    Blessed be God. (Psalm lxviii. 9, 10; 34, 35.)

The standard example, cited by Lowth, is this·

    The Lord Jehovah hath opened my ear,
    And I was not rebellious,
    Neither did I withdraw myself backward.
    I gave my back to the smiters,
    And my cheeks to them that plucked off the hair;
    My face I hid not from shame and spitting.
                                 (Isaiah l. 5, 6.)

Finally, we merely refer to the notable Psalm cx. as throughout only constructive or synthetic in its parallelisms.

In addition to the three kinds of parallelism now described, others have frequently been proposed. All are here rejected, either as useless or erroneous. Those suggested by Bishop Jebb and by Zöckler will be considered in the sequel.

It is obvious that these three species may be so combined among themselves as greatly to diversify and enliven the expression. Hence whatever be the nature of the sentiment, it can find among these plastic forms that which is adequate to convey its full impression. The law of parallelism, at once vigorous and flexible, adapts itself readily to the movements of the spirit. There is a complete subordination of outer form to the inward sense— "the thought lords it over the form"—so that the law for the poet is a law of liberty. He rises on its alternate wings, exulting in a freedom from metrical bonds unknown to poets in modern or classical tongues. Some critics regard parallelism as an early stage in the development of full artistic form; others, more justly, as the result of the native constitution of mind which clings to and reviews the object of passion.

§ 8. This parallelism in one form or the other most happily takes the place of meter and rhyme, as being more consonant to nature, and less fettered by artificial rules. There is no meter in Hebrew poetry, but there is rhythm, more impressive, flexible, and free by its separation from meter. There are no sensuous rhymes, that jingling sound of like-word endings, but in the parallel expressions and sentiments there are thought-rhymes of far more dignity and power.

Let us dwell for a moment on one consequence of this fact. Suppose the poetry of the Bible had been metrical, what would have been the result? One-half the Old Testament would have been to the Gentiles a fountain sealed. There are literal translations of Homer and Horace into fair English prose, but they convey no adequate idea of the originals. *Paradise Lost* turned into German prose would be Paradise lost, indeed. Had the prophecies of Isaiah or the Psalter been composed in classical meters or with modern rhymes, they would have fared as ill at the hands of translators. They would have remained unknown in their highest power to move the heart, until some man of genius should give us a metrical version, which would be but a paraphrase after all. Something must unavoidably be sacrificed to the importunities of metrical necessity, and sense and substance could not maintain its predominance over sound and form. Such versions would be like Pope's *Iliad* and Dryden's *Æneid*, which are not Homer's and Vergil's, but Pope's and Dryden's.

But as the case stands, there being no word-rhymes, but only rhymes in thought; there being no meter, but only that rhythmic movement which arises from the rhythm of sentiments, it is perfectly possible to preserve both the form and spirit of Hebrew poetry when translated into any language whatever. Only let the scholarly pen be literal, and, so far as the genius of its language will permit, let it preserve the original order of words, then it will reproduce for the Gentile reader about all that the Hebrew text can give to the best Jewish Hebraists of our day.[1] It is, however, true that to convey the full poetic effect, a translation should be rhythmical, but it need not be metrical. The metrical versions, so often attempted, are failures. Dr. Tayler Lewis has brought to the task great labor, learning, and skill, and in his versions of Job and Ecclesiastes has adopted a

---

[1] Bishop Jebb, *Sacra Literaria*. We may add that for this reason it is possible, in this discussion, to exhibit the principles of Hebrew prosody, with very little reference to the original language.

meter of great freedom, so that he is still quite literal, and one sufficiently smooth; yet we do not hesitate to say that the result is on the whole a loss, rather than a gain, and that his versions are not likely to be adopted by Bible readers. After preserving the parallelisms, we need no more than what the original has—rhythm; indeed, anything more becomes rather offensive to taste and devotional feeling. Our common English version is generally rhythmical, and needs only perfecting in this respect and in accurate translation to make it a complete and admirable representative of the original.

The Hebrew poems stand alone in this respect among the literatures of nations. They are "universal poetry, the poetry of all languages, and of all peoples." We may clearly trace here the overruling providence and wisdom of Him who designed the Scriptures to be the fountain of spiritual light and life, of faith, hope, and charity, to all the peoples of every tongue.

§ 9. We propose to close this examination of the fundamental form by citing at length Psalm cxxx., as illustrative of nearly all the species and varieties of parallelism enumerated; but also for the sake of its own marvelous beauty and excellence. It is known since the times of the early Church as the psalm *De Profundis*.

Out of the depths have I cried unto thee, O LORD.

I

Lord hear my voice; [tions.
Let thine ears be attentive to the voice of my supplica-
If thou, LORD, shouldest mark iniquities, O Lord, who
[shall stand?
For with thee is forgiveness, that thou mayest be feared.

✦   II

I wait for the LORD,
My soul doth wait, and in his word do I hope; [ing,
My soul, for the Lord, more than watchmen, for the morn-
— — — — — — — — watchmen, for the morning.

III

O Israel, hope in the LORD;
For with the LORD there is mercy,
And with him is plenteous redemption;
And He shall redeem Israel from all his iniquities.

NOTES.—In this psalm Jehovah (LORD) occurs four times; Jah (LORD) once; and Adonai (Lord), Sovereign Lord, three times. This frequent naming indicates passionate earnestness.

The Invocation.—**depths**, of sorrow and misery, including physical pain, the fruit of sin.—**have I cried**; referring to special prayers, perhaps frequent and recent, already offered during this distress, but as yet unheard.

Strophe 1. The Petition.—**For**; between the third and fourth lines interpolate the thought: But away with such dark anticipations; for, etc. (*Dean of Wells.*) But I would rather regard

This is one of the fifteen Songs of Degrees, the sixth of the seven Penitential Psalms, and one of the four Pauline Psalms, as Luther called them. It was a favorite with him, and he has imitated it in one of the best of his hymns, "Aus tiefer Noth." It is said that once when suffering sharp pain of body, and in great peril from his enemies, he consoled his spirit by reciting this precious little psalm, again and again. Let us peer into its depths, let us get it by heart—I do not say commit it to memory, that is too cold a phrase—no, get it by heart, that in the hour of pain and trial it may be to us also an angel of consolation.

The date and author are unknown, but the psalm

line third as parenthetical or interjectional, and take the illative *for* as connecting the second and fourth lines. The Revision reads adversatively: *But with thee*, etc.—feared, with holy and reverent fear, inducing obedience, but conjoined with love.

Strophe 2. The Meditation.—wait; "There are some," says Luther, "who instead of waiting for God, his time, his way, his help, take upon themselves to decide for him, how, when, and in what degree he shall aid. This is not to wait for him; it is to make God wait upon them, and aid them as they define the way."—word, of promise.—watchmen; perhaps alluding to the temple watchmen. Observe the comma after watchmen. The meaning is, not "they that watch for the morning," as in the Authorized Version; but, "more than watchers (wait and hope) for the morning." The ellipsis in the fourth line is very expressive of the length and weariness of the watching, and the partial repetition is very characteristic of meditative soliloquy. The supply of words here by the translators detracts greatly from the poetic effect.

Strophe 3. The Exhortation.—Israel, God's people, spiritual Israel.—He, is emphatic in the Hebrew.

is certainly older than the books of Chronicles, wherein it is quoted. (2 Chronicles vi. 40-42.) This quotation occurs in the prayer of Solomon, but we are not permitted therefore to throw it back to his day, for the biblical critics say that the part of the prayer where it occurs was probably a subsequent addition by the chronicler. As to authorship, it is one of the Orphan Psalms, as the Talmudists call those that are without title, and we are therefore left to conjecture. It has so much the spirit and style of David that we feel almost justified in ascribing it to him.

As already observed, this psalm illustrates nearly all of the points which we have discussed. It begins with an independent monostich. There are distichs synonymous, antithetic, and synthetic. Those synonymous *iterant, variant, augent.* Observe the first in strophe 1, for a synonymously parallel expansion of thought. These distichs are varied by additions, ellipses, repetitions, and inversions. Besides, there are variations in the structure of the strophes. Observe particularly the third, wherein the first line is parallel with the last (Jebb's "introverted" form), which last line is inverted and increased by an added phrase. The whole is worthy of the closest study. It is a gem, a small one, but of purest ray serene.

VII.—STANZAS

§1. THE distinction of lines (*pesukim*) in the Hebrew text of Job, Psalms, and Proverbs, by means of the poetic disjunctive accents, is commonly attributed to the Masorites, but probably had its origin in the traditional cantillation of the synagogue. It is not reliable; for, as Ewald has shown, it is in many places violative of the sense, and also is carried into portions of the text that are undoubtedly prose. The division of the entire text into verses (also called *pesukim*), by means of the *soph-pasuk* (:), is not primitive, but is the work of the Jewish Rabbis, and was not complete until the ninth century. It often arbitrarily breaks in upon the sense. These verse divisions are commonly retained in our English versions. The division into chapters was as late as the thirteenth century, made first in the Latin Vulgate, and thence transferred by the Jews to the Hebrew text. It also is often in disregard of the natural and true divisions as indicated by changes in the subject-matter. These erroneous divisions are a great evil, often seriously obscuring the sense.

The evil, however, would not be to us so serious were it not for the mode in which our English Bibles are commonly printed. Not only are the capital divisions made too prominent, but each verse, which is very often but a part of a sentence, is presented as a distinct paragraph, and numbered at that.[1] Thus the connection of thought is constantly and violently broken, so as greatly to embarrass one accustomed to books printed in the usual and sensible way. Also between prose and poetry there is no distinction to the eye, a distinction always made in secular works, although rendered far less needful by the presence of meter and rhyme. Then observe the double columns on a narrow page; then the penuriously small type, saving cost but wasting eyes, if indeed eyesight be expended on it; then the bulkiness of the little volume, the most unhandy of all shapes for a reader. There is no standard work in our literature that is persistently so wretchedly booked for the general reader. Only some of the unhandy

---

[1] This gross mode of indicating verses was first introduced into the English Scriptures in the Genevan version of the New Testament (1557), and of the whole Bible in 1560. It has never been carried into the Hebrew Scriptures. In critical editions of the Greek New Testament, and in the English Paragraph Bibles, including the Revised Version, the figures are retained in the margin for convenience of reference.

common editions of Shakespeare, in forms absolutely prohibitory of pleasure or profit, are comparable to it.

Everybody in a Christian land feels that he ought to have a Bible. He goes to buy one. Cost is a consideration with average humanity. He buys a cheap one. Perhaps he tries to read it. From some cause, of which this average man is unconscious, he has a very lively consciousness that it is hard, uphill work, in fact positively disagreeable. It is of course neglected. He rests satisfied with *owning* a Bible. Perhaps it is a present, expensive, handsomely bound, for the parlor table; perhaps it is one of those huge, unreadable forms of that obsolescent institution, the Family Bible. Either is a bar to getting another; and thus, by an ingenious device of Satan, working through well-meaning publishers, the Bible itself hinders the Bible from being read. For it is morally impossible to read such a book; indeed, except by remarkably good eyes, it is physically impossible to read the diamond editions. Certainly no one indifferent to religion will read in spite of such difficulties. Our Bible societies are multiplying these hindrances to Bible reading, and distributing them with lavish hand. Oh, for a Bible burning! I would gladly light the pile, in the full persuasion that the destruction of nine-tenths of all the English Bibles now extant, if their reproduction in this form could be prohibited, would be a great blessing, soon resulting in a far more general and constant reading of the Holy Scriptures.

But what we especially insist upon is that the lines of poetry parallel to each other should be so arranged as to exhibit this relation. This much can be done with an accuracy admitting of only occasional question. In several editions of our Paragraph Bibles, including the Revised Version, it is measurably accomplished, and this form ought entirely to supersede that of the common Bible. We would insist that the strophic structure also should be exhibited, only that this is a matter yet under discussion, a feature of Hebrew poetry not satisfactorily worked out. It constitutes the subject now before us.

§ 2. In the previous chapter we have considered the versification as appearing in the parallelism of lines; we are now to study the form as exhibited in more extended portions. In very many of the psalms, if the reader will mark off the principal divisions and the subordinate paragraphs, the result is a striking and unmistakable symmetry of parts. There seems to be a natural division into groups equally balanced, each group consisting of similar subdivisions. Whether this comes from the natural pauses of thought, marking in such cases, unintentionally and as it were accidentally, symmetrical and corresponding divisions, or whether it results from the premeditated design of the artist, can be better decided after a full illustration of the fact.

A preliminary consideration is that frequently in Hebrew poetry independent lines occur, not parallel with any other. Such a line we will call a monostich. Examples are the first line of Psalms xxiii., xviii., cxxx., and the last line in Psalms viii., xv., xxv. The Hallelujah which closes a number of the psalms is of this character.[1] A monostich sometimes occurs in the body of a psalm—*e. g.*, Psalm xxiv., in strophes 5 and 6 (pages 150, 151); and Psalm xix., strophe 6 (page 30). The failure to observe the monostich has embarrassed and confused many attempts to exhibit the strophic

---

[1] The last five psalms are therefore called the Hallelujah Psalms, or sometimes the Greek Hallel, to distinguish them from Psalms cxiii.–cxviii., known as the Egyptian Hallel. There are some other psalms with this appendage. The word Hallelujah does not occur in our English version, it having been always translated. Many of these psalms have " Praise ye the Lord " also prefixed, but this prefix was not originally a part of the psalm, but the title only, as in the LXX.

structure. It should be set apart to itself, but is hardly to be considered a stanza. We must not, however, be hasty in pronouncing a line that is not parallel a monostich. A line is often so incorporated by the thought with its neighbors that while not strictly parallel it must be considered as associated with them in the stanza. For example, the prophecy of Hosea closes thus:

Who is wise that he may understand these things?
Prudent that he may know them?
    For the ways of the Lord are right,
And the just shall walk in them;
But the transgressors shall fall therein.
                             (Hosea xiv. 9.)

The third line is not to be accounted a monostich. We may call it the added line, or odd stich. Other examples will occur as we proceed.

To groups of lines constituting an organic whole in formal versification, the term strophe is now commonly applied, derived from classical prosody. It is not, however, used strictly in the classical sense, and it is not clear why our more thoroughly naturalized word stanza should be superseded. We shall use both, with only this difference, that the latter term be applied to the subdivisions of the strophe, when there are any, as in Psalms xlii., xliii. (page 191). We shall use also the term antistrophe, of which there is occasional need, in a similarly accommodated sense.

§3. Let us now consider certain obvious and unquestionable groups of parallel lines.

First, there is, of course, the distich clearly separated and standing to itself, most frequently and notably in Proverbs x., ff. Such distinct distichs occur quite often in the Psalms and Prophets, but it is observable that generally they are antithetic in character and gnomic in style. If the strophic division be recognized, such distichs must be accounted as stanzas.[1]

Secondly, there are frequently unmistakable tristichs. These abound in the Psalms, and exhibit a considerable variety of structure—*e. g.:*

> Blessed is the man that walketh not in the counsel of the [ungodly,
> Nor standeth in the way of sinners,
> Nor sitteth in the seat of the scornful.
> (Psalm i. 1.)

Here the first clause is omitted in the second and third lines. The gradational structure is finely marked throughout, expressing progression in wickedness.

---

[1] *E. g.,* Psalm xv., strophes 1 and 4 (pages 154, 155); and Psalm xxiv., strophe 2 (page 148).

Arise, O Lord, in thine anger,
Lift up thyself because of the rage of mine enemies,
And awake for me to the judgment that thou hast or-
[dained.
(Psalm vii. 6.)

Praise waiteth for thee, O God, in Sion,
And unto thee shall the vow be performed,
O thou that hearest prayer, unto thee shall all flesh come.
(Psalm lxv. 1, 2.)

Thou art my hiding place,
Thou shalt preserve me from trouble,
Thou shalt compass me about with songs of deliverance.
(Psalm xxxii. 7.)

The lofty looks of man shall be humbled,
And the haughtiness of men shall be bowed down,
And the Lord alone shall be exalted in that day.
(Isaiah ii. 11.)

The last line is an antithesis to the other two. There is a series of parallel tristichs in Job iii. 4-9. See also Psalm xv. (page 154). The first three chapters of Lamentations consist entirely of tristichs. It is not infrequent that in a tristich but two lines are parallel, yet the third odd line or stich is so incorporated in the sentiment that the three must be regarded as one stanza—*e. g.*:

Lift up your heads, O ye gates,
And be ye lifted up, ye everlasting doors,
   And the King of glory shall come in.
(Psalm xxiv. 7.)

All we like sheep have gone astray,
We have turned everyone to his own way,
   And the Lord hath laid on him the iniquity of us all.
(Isaiah liii. 6.)

Thirdly, there are tetrastichs in which two distichs are so closely associated as to constitute one stanza—*e. g.:*

He that killeth an ox is as if he slew a man;
He that sacrificeth a lamb, as if he cut off a dog's neck;
He that offereth an oblation, as if he offered swine's [blood;
He that burneth incense, as if he blessed an idol.
(Isaiah lxvi. 3.)

Thou shalt not be afraid for the terror by night,
Nor for the arrow that flieth by day,
Nor for the pestilence that walketh in darkness,
Nor for the destruction that wasteth at noonday.
(Psalm xci. 5, 6.)

Here the lines in each distich are partially antithetic, and the distichs themselves synonymously parallel. Again:

> The ox knoweth his owner,
> And the ass his master's crib;
> But Israel doth not know,
> My people doth not consider. (Isaiah i. 3.)

Here the lines of each distich are synonymously parallel, while the distichs themselves are antithetic.

A very common form of the tetrastich is the quatrain, wherein the lines are alternately parallel —*e. g.*:

> For as the heaven is high above the earth,
> So great is his mercy toward them that fear him;
> As far as the east is from the west,
> So far hath he removed our transgressions from us.
> (Psalm ciii. 11.)

> The Lord is my light and my salvation,
> Whom shall I fear?
> The Lord is the strength of my life,
> Of whom shall I be afraid?[1] (Psalm xxvii. 1.)

> For thy maker is thy husband,
> The Lord of hosts is his name;
> And thy redeemer, the Holy One of Israel,
> The God of the whole earth shall he be called.
> (Isaiah liv. 5.)

---

[1] See the remarks on bi-membral lines, page 235.

> I will make mine arrows drunk with blood,
>> And my sword shall devour flesh,
> With the blood of the slain, and of the captains,
>> From the chief of the princes of the enemy.
>>>> (Deuteronomy xxxii. 42.)

In this passage from the Song of Moses the third line is, in sense, a direct continuation of the first, and not of the second; and the fourth, of the second, and not of the third. This peculiar structure is rare. An approach to it is seen in the example next above. The tetrastich in its several varieties seems to be the most natural, and by far the most frequent form of the stanza.

In the fourth place, pentastichs occur by the intimate connection of a distich and tristich—*e. g.:*

> And if I say: Only let darkness cover me,
> And let the light about me be night;
> Even darkness hideth not from thee,
> But the night shineth as the day,
> Darkness is as light. (Psalm cxxxix. 11, 12.)

Another form is where with four lines an odd line is associated, though not parallel—*e. g.:*

> A thousand shall fall at thy side,
> And ten thousand at thy right hand,
>> But it shall not come nigh thee,
> Only with thine eyes shalt thou behold,
> And see the reward of the wicked. (Psalm xci. 7, 8.)

This is similar in construction to the closing stanza of Hosea, quoted in the last section (page 260). Another form adds to a quatrain an odd line, as follows, the final odd line, in this case, giving the reason:

> And when ye spread forth your hands,
>   I will hide mine eyes from you;
> Yea, when ye make many prayers,
>   I will not hear;
> Your hands are full of blood. (Isaiah i. 15.)

Further, two tristichs may be combined to form a six-lined stanza—*e. g.*, Psalm xxxix., strophes 2 and 3 (pages 182, 183). Again, we may have an odd line associated with a double tristich constituting a seven-lined stanza—*e. g.*, Psalm vii., strophe 2 (page 56); the odd line, in this case, being inserted between the two tristichs.

It is obvious that there may be many variations other than those illustrated; and that as the length of the stanzas increase, the varieties of possible construction increase in geometrical ratio, and beyond practical enumeration. Many illustrations occur in the preceding chapters.

§ 4. There is one peculiar mode in which tetrastichs, and sometimes stanzas of a greater number of lines, are occasionally formed that deserves special mention. " These stanzas," says Bishop Jebb, " are so constructed that whatever be the number of lines, the first line shall be parallel with the last, the second with the penultimate, and so throughout, in an order that looks inward, or, to borrow a military phrase, from flanks to center " —*e. g*.:

>   My son, if thine heart be wise,
>   My heart also shall rejoice;
>   Yea, my reins shall rejoice,
>   When thy lips speak right things.
>   (Proverbs xxiii. 15, 16.)

This structure is cited by Jebb as a species of parallelism, which he calls " Introverted Parallelism," superadding it to the three species of Lowth. It is, however, manifestly not this, since it has no reference to the nature of the parallelism, but only to the order in which lines parallel shall be arranged. It relates to the structure of the strophe, and the phrase Introverted Strophe or Stanza would be more appropriate. Another and a very good name is given to it by Jebb, the *Epanodos*, literally *a going back*, replying in advance to the second of two subjects proposed; or, if these be more than two, resuming in a precisely inverted order. We subjoin other examples:

Lord, thou hast been our dwelling place in all genera-
Before the mountains were brought forth, [tions;
Or ever thou hadst formed the earth and the world,
Even from everlasting to everlasting thou art God.
(Psalm xc. 1.)

Unto thee lift I up mine eyes, O thou that dwellest in
[the heavens;
Behold, as the eyes of servants, unto the hand of
[their masters,
As the eyes of a maiden, unto the hand of her mis-
[tress,
Even so look our eyes to Jehovah our God, until he have
[mercy upon us.
(Psalm cxxiii. 1, 2.)

The idols of the heathen are silver and gold;
The work of men's hands.
They have mouths, but they speak not,
Eyes have they, but they see not,
They have ears, but they hear not,
Neither is there any breath in their mouths
They that make them are like unto them;
So is everyone that trusteth in them.
(Psalm cxxxv. 15-17.)

This is remarkably elaborate; of course, such cases are rare. We add two examples of unconscious epanodic stanzas from the New Testament:

> Give not that which is holy to the dogs,
>   Neither cast ye your pearls before swine,
>   Lest they trample them under their feet,
> And turn again and rend you.
>
> (Matthew vii. 6.)

Here the more dangerous act of imprudence, with its fatal result, is placed first and last, thus making and leaving the deepest practical impression.

> For we are unto God, a sweet savor of Christ,
>   In them that are saved,
>   And in them that perish;
>   To the one, the savor of death unto death;
>   And to the other, the savor of life unto life.
>
> (2 Corinthians ii. 15, 16.)

In this case of epanodos, the painful part of the subject is kept subordinate, while the pleasing part is placed first and last.

§ 5. The question now recurs whether these strophic divisions are artificial, designed by the poet; or whether they are not accidental, perhaps developed only by the fancy of the editor. If the examples accumulated above, and in the preceding chapters, were fully representative of Hebrew poetry, perhaps no unprejudiced reader would deny the reality of this structure, even though many distributions in detail might be objected to. But in fact, a considerable number of the psalms, and perhaps the great bulk of prophetic poetry, does not exhibit symmetrical structure, and in some cases apparently cannot be distributed into strophes at all. Some editors, as Merx on Job, find divisions symmetrical throughout, but these in many cases are so manifestly forced that they cannot be accepted. Granting that strophic structure is not to be found in Job, nor in the Prophets, this would not decide against its existence elsewhere; for these may correspond to our current verse, as Pope's *Messiah* or the epics, which are without stanzas. But again, we are startled in looking through those editions which exhibit the psalms strophically arranged, to see the wide differences between editors in cases of the simplest and apparently the most obvious kind. For a single, though extreme example, we refer to Psalm cxxx. (page 252). This seems evidently and indisputably to consist of an Invocation, a monostich, followed by three tetrastich strophes, respectively a Petition, a Meditation, and an Exhortation. Now Moll makes four strophes, two tetrastichs, and two pentastichs, marking the parallelisms also in some cases quite differently. Canon Cook cites this psalm as one example of those in which "each line forms a complete sense, not justifiably called a strophe." This shows how little reliance is to be placed on mere subjective impressions; and, unless we can find other ground, such differences make it a question whether strophic structure may not be altogether a fancy.

That there are artificial subdivisions is, in a number of cases, proved by certain original, primitive marks, almost as purely mechanical as punctuation marks. The *Selah* is of this character. For, whatever may be the meaning of this hopelessly obscure term, if indeed it be a word at all; whether or not we accept the usual view that it is connected with the liturgical use of the psalm wherewith it occurs, being a musical sign indicating a pause when, perhaps, the people prostrated themselves, or marking emphasis when they shouted Hallelujah; still this fact is pretty well established, that it is not a part of the text of the psalm.[1] In many cases it unquestionably marks subdivisions. In Psalm iii. it occurs at the end of the first and of the second tetrastich, and at the close. Now if we count off a third tetrastich, we find at its end a pause in the sense, made evident by an ejaculation; hence some exegetes have thought it

---

[1] The *Selah* occurs in thirty-nine psalms, altogether seventy-one times, besides three times in Habakkuk.

probable that originally there was a *Selah* here also, which has fallen out in copying. However this may be, if we assume this third tetrastich, the subdivision becomes quite symmetrical, and these parts, which may very well be called strophes or stanzas, we can hardly doubt were intended by the poet. But unfortunately, in the very next psalm the *Selah* does not coincide with the pauses in sense, and if we divide the psalm into strophes upon this latter basis, the *Selah* will fall each time in the middle of a strophe. If we turn to Psalm xlvi., we find the *Selah* again marking the divisions of thought quite accurately. Further examination will show that in general it does so; and hence, while the irregularities are so numerous that we do not find it a reliable guide, still it furnishes strong evidence of artificial structure in the distribution of parts.

We turn once again to the Alphabetic Psalms. These are a species of acrostic, wherein the initial letter of certain lines taken in order make the Hebrew alphabet.[1] The object seems to have been

---

[1] Altogether nine psalms may be accounted alphabetic. In Psalms cxi. and cxii., the alphabetic letters are the initials of each line; in Psalms xxv., xxxiv., and cxlv., they are the initials of each distich; in Psalms ix., x., and xxxvii., they are the initials of each tetrastich; in Psalm cxix., they are the initials of the distichs, but each letter is repeated eight times, making an

to assist the memory. "In the scatterings and wanderings of families," says Isaac Taylor, "and in lonely journeyings, in deserts and cities, where no synagogue service could be enjoyed, the metrical Scriptures, infixed as they were in the memory by the very means of these artificial devices of versets and of alphabetic order and of alliteration, became food to the soul. Thus was the religious constancy of the people, and its brave endurance of injury and insult, sustained and animated."[1]

There are in some cases a number of irregularities in the alphabetic order which have given much trouble to the critics, but which may perhaps be explained by saying that the poet adopted the acrostic plan, but refused to be fettered by it, especially since the purpose in adopting it, as an aid to memory, would not be hindered, but rather promoted, by some deviations. Another explanation is that these irregularities were occasioned by corruptions of the text. In any case, it is evident that the alphabetic arrangement is not a poetic element, but rather a mechanical mnemonic device. Ewald regards it as evidence of late date of composition, and De Wette of degenerate taste, but

---

alliterative strophe of eight distichs, and twenty-two strophes, the number of the letters of the Hebrew alphabet.

[1] *Spirit of Hebrew Poetry*, chapter xiii., note.

it happens that five of these psalms are ascribed to David by their titles, and these critics have failed to disprove his authorship.

This acrostic device is not confined to the Psalms. It is found in Proverbs, very notably in chapter xxxi. 10 ff., which is a regular alphabetic poem, delineating the virtues of the Hebrew matron. The Lamentations of Jeremiah consist of five poems, each a chapter of twenty-two verses, except the third, which should have had this number, but, by a mistake in the length of the verses, has sixty-six. All these are alphabetic except the fifth. In the first three the initials of the first lines of the tristichs make the alphabet. In the third, moreover, each of the lines in the tristich begins with the same letter. In the fourth the initials of each distich make the alphabet. The lines in these poems are longer than usual; and it is also worthy of remark that the Hebrew alphabetic poetry is mostly elegiac or didactic.

Now it is manifest, without further showing, that this highly artificial structure warrants the conclusion that, in those cases at least where the number of lines included under one alphabetic initial is more than two, the poet wrote in stanzas. Some editors go farther than this, and regard the alphabetic distichs as distinct strophes. So Moll presents Psalm xxxiv. He regards it as a mere florilege, a collection of gnomes. So also Canon Cook. From these views we dissent. See our presentation of this psalm on pages 69–72, and remarks. Also Psalms xxv. and cxlv. have each four well-marked divisions of nearly equal length. In the three, David seems to have had in view a strophic structure entirely independent of the alphabetic arrangement. But in Psalm xxxvii. and in ix., x., which last two were probably one continuous composition,[1] he has united the two forms, though in the latter case quite irregularly. Was not David the inventor of this alphabetic device?

The refrain, which occurs in a number of psalms, also indicates a symmetrical and a strophic structure. One of the finest examples is the grand hymn Psalm xlvi., which Luther so nobly imitated in his choral hymn *Ein' feste Berg ist unser Gott*, called the Marseillaise of the Reformation. The refrain occurs at verses 7 and 11, which confirms the conclusion drawn above (page 272) from the indications of the *Selah* in this psalm. Did not this refrain also occur, originally, between verses 3 and 4, having been lost by the copyists? Its insertion would perfect the symmetry. The refrain in Psalms xlii., xliii. (page 191) at stanzas 3, 6, 9,

---

[1] They are presented as one in the LXX.

has always been noted not only for its beauty, but also for its dividing the poem into three equal and balanced parts. The refrain is found in Psalm cvii., at verses 8, 15, 21, and 31. This poem has other characteristics of artistic regularity. Indeed, it impresses, if not oppresses, the reader with a sense of its elaborate structure. But a refrain indicating smaller divisions will be more to the present point. We turn to the allegoric Psalm lxxx., which is divided into four parts by the refrain in verses 3, 7, and 14 (varied in form), and 19. But observe particularly the beautiful little missionary hymn Psalm lxvii.; though here the irregular placing of the *Selah* is embarrassing. Disregarding it, and taking the refrain to begin strophes 2 and 3, we have a regular structure. The refrain in some psalms indicates their use by antiphonal choirs.[1]

These confessedly artificial features justify us in concluding that strophic division is original in Hebrew poetry. It is not meant that it was originated by the Hebrew mind. David had the poetry of Moses to suggest it to him; for Psalm xc., the only one in the Psalter earlier than David, and Moses's Song in Deuteronomy xxxii., both exhibit strophic structure. Moses probably received the

---

[1]See especially Psalm cxxxvi.; and *cf.* Ezra iii. 11.

idea in his Egyptian education. Egyptian papyri earlier than the Pentateuch are said to exhibit this division of poems into strophes. Each strophe in the Hymn to the Nile has the first word written in red ink; and so also the Litanies to the Sun in the Egyptian Ritual.[1] We do not suppose the Hebrews followed such models, but rather that they elaborated from this starting point a system of their own.

§ 6. Biblical scholars and commentators generally accept thus much, but the details of the subject have not been satisfactorily settled. No principle or principles have been agreed upon by which to determine what constitutes a stanza or strophe. The quasi-mechanical aids of the alphabetic arrangement, the *Selah*, and the refrain, occur too seldom to be of much service here. There is perhaps but one principle always at hand by which we may determine the association of lines in one organic whole, and this we will call the logical coherence. The inner sense and meaning may be relied upon to fix the extent of the stanza, assuming that commonly each involves a whole thought as completed by its accessories. This is generally true of the modern and classical stanza; though it sometimes occurs that a thought

---
[1]Birch's *Records of the Past*, Vol. IV., p. 106.

runs out into two or more stanzas, and sometimes, but more rarely, that two distinct thoughts are found in one. Our first principle, then, is that where clauses and sentences manifest a unity of thought, a logical coherence, they may commonly be taken as constituting a stanza.

When the extent of the stanza or strophe has thus been at least hypothetically fixed, we need then to determine its inner form. This is done by an examination of the parallelisms, and an adjustment of the lines so as to exhibit their several relations. The simple classification of stanzas, which we have given, by the number of lines, with the two varieties of the quatrain and the epanodos, will answer all primary purposes, at least in simple cases. But it is to be observed that, owing to the plasticity of the fundamental principle, there is an almost endless variety of forms which the stanza may assume.

When the stanzas of a poem have been provisionally adjusted, the whole should be revised and readjusted with reference to the general correspondence of forms and symmetry of structure whenever evidences of symmetry are discernible.

By these means can be restored what in some cases we may regard as the original structure designed by the poet. But in others the result is perhaps very questionable; for the principle of logical coherence often fails to indicate sharp distinctions, the pauses in thought not being always definite; and hence the form may be so indeterminate and conjectural as to accommodate itself to the individual taste of the editor for symmetry of parts and for rhythmical cadence.

The examples presented in these chapters have been thus worked out; it must be confessed with a result differing in each case from any to be found in the critical editions of Hebrew poetry. No apology, however, is offered for this fact, since these editions exhibit so little adherence to any principle, and often so great carelessness, and since the results in some cases are manifestly fanciful and forced.[1]

---

[1] J. B. Köster has done more than any other biblical critic to develop strophic structure. But his principle is purely artificial, and in the majority of cases wholly inapplicable, and in these he proceeds apparently without rule.

Having given form to the psalms separately, Köster proceeds to classify them according to this structure. His classification, which is generally admissible, and has been approved by many commentators, is as follows:

1. Those psalms having strophes of equal length. Examples cited are: Psalms iii., iv., xii., xxiv., xxxii., lx.

2. Those in which strophes of unequal length are arranged symmetrically in corresponding groups. Thus, letting the fig-

§ 7. There is another formative principle which, while not universal nor sharply definite, will, if recognized, confirm our faith in strophic structure, and in many cases assist in the restoration of form. It is merely the extension of the fundamental form, the primary principle of Hebrew versification, thus: Not only are lines parallel to each other, but distichs and tristichs are often parallel to each other, so also are stanzas and strophes, so also are larger general divisions. And moreover, the three kinds of parallelism, the synonymous, the antithetic, and the synthetic or rhythmical, are also traceable in this correspondence, in this balancing

---

ures represent the number of verses in a strophe, we may have the following groups:

2, 2, 3, 3; 2, 3, 2, 3; 2, 3, 3, 2.

The last inverted order is compared to the Greek antistrophe, and the following examples are cited:

Psalm vi.—3, 4, 3; Psalm xlvii.—4, 1, 4.

Psalm xxxv.—3, 3, 4, 4, 4, 4, 3, 3.

Psalm xlv.—1, 1, 3, 3, 1, 3, 3, 1, 1.

3. Those in which the strophes increase or decrease throughout the psalm, determined by the abundant matter, or by the overflow of feeling. Examples cited are Psalms xviii. and xliv.

4. Those of which the form is wholly irregular, like the Greek dithyramb. These mostly belong to a late age, and are found, with few exceptions, in the latter part of the Psalter. David's Psalm xxi. is cited as a dithyrambic pæan consisting of a short strophe of two verses with a *Selah*, two longer of five verses each, and an ejaculatory close.

of the larger parts with each other. In short, the principle of parallelism is thoroughgoing.

As examples of parallel distichs, we cite the following:

> Will the Lord cast off forever?
> And will he be favorable no more?
> Is his mercy clean gone forever?
> Doth his promise fail for evermore?
> Hath God forgotten to be gracious?
> Hath he in anger shut up his tender mercies?
> (Psalm lxxvii. 7–9.)

> His anger endureth but a moment,
> In his favor is life;
> Weeping may endure for a night,
> But joy cometh in the morning. (Psalm xxx. 5.)

In the first example, both lines and distichs are synonymously parallel. In the second, the lines in each distich are antithetic, the distichs synonymous. In the following the lines are synonymous and the distichs antithetic:

The Lord bringeth the counsel of the heathen to naught,
He maketh the devices of the people of none effect;
The counsel of the Lord standeth forever,
The thoughts of his heart to all generations.
(Psalm xxxiii. 10, 11.)

In the following the lines are antithetic, but in

inverted order, thus making the distichs also antithetic:

> A little that a righteous man hath
> Is better than the riches of many wicked;
> For the arms of the wicked shall be broken,
> But the Lord upholdeth the righteous.
>
> (Psalm xxxvii. 16, 17.)

We observe that this parallelism of distichs is essential in the very nature of the quatrain, and of the epanodos; for in the distichs taken severally the lines are not parallel, and hence parallelism must occur between the distichs: see examples in §2 and §3. For examples of parallel tristichs, see Psalm xxxix., strophes 2 and 3 (pages 182, 183).

Our space will permit only a reference to parallel stanzas, and we select a few of the more obvious sort. See Psalm xxix., strophes 3 and 4 (pages 35, 36); and Psalm cxxxix., strophe 1, stanzas 1 and 2; also strophe 4, stanzas 1 and 2 (pages 203, 206). These are synonymously parallel. The following are antithetic: Psalm xxvii., strophes 1 and 3 (pages 97, 98); and Psalm lxviii., strophe 1, stanzas 1 and 3 (page 136). In most cases we may consider the parallelism between stanzas to be synthetic only, giving rise to similar structure, and a certain rhythmical likeness. The general result is symmetry.

The parallelism between strophes including two

or more stanzas, or between the general divisions of poems, is sometimes quite striking. For example, Psalm i. consists of two parts of three verses each, which parts are clearly antithetic, possibly used responsively. It may be remarked that the second part is the shorter, expressing, perhaps, the shorter continuance of the ungodly, or more prompt dealing with him, or, perhaps, the subject being painful to the psalmist, he leaves it sooner. Also observe the parallelism of the parts of Psalm cvii. separated by the refrain. Also in Psalm xxiv., strophes 5 and 6 (pages 150, 151) are almost identical. The three parts of Psalms xlii., xliii. (page 191) are in elegant correspondence with each other. In many cases where a formal parallelism of the parts is not manifested by a symmetrical structure, a logical correspondence is nevertheless quite obvious.

It seems to the writer that no one who considers attentively these complex correspondences, such as we have already pointed out and are about to illustrate further, and who experiences the pleasing sentiment which the consequent graceful symmetry inspires, can withhold his assent from the statement that parallelism between members, small and great, is a thoroughgoing principle in Hebrew poetry. While it does not govern, but only serves; while it does not mold, but only clothes the thought in artistic robes; still it is to be accepted as that which distinguishes the poetic from the prosaic form of speech in the Hebrew, and as the fundamental principle which justifies the search for and the exhibition of strophic and symmetrical structure. We do not forget the entire freedom of the Hebrew poet from prosodial constraints, nor that always " the thought lords it over the form," even in the smallest members. Our theory does not assert that parallelism always or even generally goes through all members, but only that it is the principle of that poetic form which the Hebrew poet, more or less consciously, has constantly in mind, and according to which his phrases, lines, stanzas, strophes, and wider divisions tend to shape themselves whenever thereby the sentiment finds easy and happy expression. It may also be affirmed that extended parallelisms occur very frequently, and that an attentive consideration of passages in the original tongue, or in accurately literal translation, often reveals them in a clearness and beauty that is both delightful and surprising.

§ 8. In order to a fuller illustration of the preceding statements, we propose now to cite in full Psalm xcv., with comments on these and other points as they present themselves. It is one of the Orphan Psalms, but is ascribed to David in the LXX. It is quoted in Hebrews iii. 7–11, and iv. 3–7. In the latter place the words are said to be "in David;" but this probably only locates them in the Psalter, so largely the work of David as, *a fortiori*, to go by his name. The psalm was probably composed in a later age, as an anthem to be used in the temple service. It is very familiar, being a favorite with all Bible readers; and from its prominent sentiment is very appropriately called the Invitatory Psalm:

I

O come, let us sing unto the LORD,
Let us make a joyful noise to the rock of our salvation;
Let us come before his presence with thanksgiving,
And make a joyful noise unto him with psalms.

II

For the LORD is a great God,
And a great King above all gods.
In his hand are the deep places of the earth,
The strength of the hills is his also.
The sea is his, and he made it,
And his hands formed the dry land.

NOTES.—*Strophe 1.* **Come before,** rather, anticipate—*i. e.*, go forth to meet him.

Strophe 2. **Gods,** of the heathen.—**deep places,** valleys, caves.

III

O come, let us worship and bow down,
Let us kneel before the LORD our maker.

IV

For he is our God,
And we are the people of his pasture,
And the sheep of his hand.

V

To-day, if ye will hear his voice,—

VI

Harden not your heart, as at Meribah,
As in the day of Massah in the wilderness;
When your fathers tempted me,
Proved me, and saw my work.
Forty years long was I grieved with that generation,
And said: It is a people that do err in their heart,
And they have not known my ways;
Wherefore I sware in my wrath,
That they should not enter into my rest.

—**strength**, rather, heights, summits; LXX., τὰ ὕψη; Vulgate, *altitudines montium.*

Strophe 3. **Worship**, prostrate ourselves to the earth.—**bow down**; the LXX. has *weep.*—**our maker**; not our Creator, but our Constitutor—*i. e.*, he that chose us out of all peoples and made us his own; so also in Psalm c. 3, and Psalm cxlix. 2.

Strophe 4. **Our God**, the covenant God, in opposition to the gods of the heathen.—**hand**, guiding and protecting.

Strophe 5. See remarks following the psalm.

Strophe 6. **Meribah**; Authorized Version translates *provoca-*

We observe that in strophe 1 the first distich is parallel to the second, and so close is the correspondence that at first glance the four lines seem indiscriminately parallel. In strophe 2, the second and third distichs are parallel, and exhibit an approach to the introverted form.

Again, strophe 1 is parallel to strophe 3, though double in length. Strophe 2 is parallel to strophe 4, and also double in length, the first distich of 2 corresponding with the first stich of 4, and the remaining double distich of 2 corresponding with the remaining single distich of 4.

Moreover, there is evidently both a structural and a logical parallelism between these parts of the psalm. Structurally, the first part (strophes 1 and 2) is double the length of the second (strophes 3 and 4). Logically, the first, the Tehillah, is an invitation to praise, with a reason and its ground added; the second, the Tephillah, is an invitation to prayer, with a reason and its ground added. Some poetic reason, perhaps, may be given why the second part is but half the first; or, per-

---

tion.—Massah; Authorized Version translates *temptation.* (See Exodus xvii. 7.)—proved, tried.—work, retributions.—that: the LXX. has *that;* adopted in Revised Version.—sware, the oath of God. (See Numbers xiv. 23.)—rest: There remaineth therefore a rest to the people of God. (Hebrews iv. 9.)

haps, one more grave, founded on the difference of subject.

So far all is clear and unquestionable; but when we look at the remainder of the psalm, our principle of parallelism disappears. In this instance let us try to find poetic reasons to justify the poet in abandoning it; if we fail, there is at least an illustration of that freedom and independence of all prosodial law which is native to the Hebrew bards.

What we have for convenience marked as strophe 5 is a line standing alone, an unfinished sentence, a protasis without an apodosis. It may be considered an example of aposiopesis, similar to that already commented on in Psalm xxvii., strophe 10 (page 101). If so, then, as in a logical enthymeme, the ellipsis is to be supplied mentally, perhaps in substance thus: Ye shall be blessed. Or this line may be understood as continuing the reason for prayer (strophe 4), and that the stream of exhortation is then interrupted by the Oracle or *Bath kol* (daughter of voice). The proposed prayer God answers before the invitation is finished, responding so immediately to the heart movement that the expression of the prayer is anticipated. Or, lastly, the elision of the apodosis may be taken as equivalent to an optative sentence, which is syntatically admissible, and adopted in the Revised Version, thus: "O that to-day ye would hear his voice."

The sixth strophe is the oracular *Bath kol*. The two initial letters of each distich are, in the Hebrew, the same. Still there is here only synthetic parallelism between the lines, and none whatever with the other strophes or parts of the psalm. Now, can this be so explained that we may still hold our theory that parallelism is a thorough-going principle of Hebrew poetry?

The plain, prosaic character of this Oracle is certainly striking. We are surprised at the sudden change from the highly poetic diction and artistic finish of the previous portion, at the precipitous movement from a passage so exquisitely cheerful, earnest, and graceful, into this solid, grave, prosaic mass at the close. It almost seems to be a poetic failure. But when we remember that this portion is the voice of God, it is hardly credible that a poet capable of writing the first portion would fail to rise with the subject. The change is certainly precipitous, but is it downward?

In an entirely different connection Coleridge makes the following remark: "It has struck my feelings that, the Pherecydean origin of prose being granted, prose must have struck men with greater admiration than poetry. In the latter it was the language of passion and emotion; it was what they themselves spoke and heard in moments of exultation and indignation. But to hear an evolving roll or succession of leaves talk continuously in the language of deliberate reason, in the form of a continued preconception, this must have appeared Godlike."

Whether or not prose naturally produces this impression, it certainly is within its compass to express certain phases of thought far more impressively than can be done by poetry. Observe that the sleep-walking scene in *Macbeth*, which is more intensely tragic than any other even in Shakespeare, is all, except the closing speech, written in prose. The diction is of the very plainest and simplest texture. Yet what a fearfully sublime impression of retribution it carries! The matter is too austere to admit of anything so artificial as the measured language of verse, even though that verse were Shakespeare's. An instinct of genius taught him that any attempt to heighten the effect by such arts and by the charm of delivery would unbrace and impair it. The change to a metrical movement in the closing speech must be felt by every competent reader as a letting down to a lower intellectual plane, a movement toward common everyday life.

If Milton's majesty forsakes him anywhere in the *Paradise Lost*, it is in those parts of the poem where the divine persons are introduced as speakers. It is agreeable to our taste for Eve to talk blank verse, and even for Raphael, but when the Almighty Father is represented as declaring his eternal purposes in metrical cadences, we are shocked. For this reason, perhaps, Book III. is generally regarded as inferior in poetic merit.

Again, there are many parts of the New Testament which would be impaired by appearing in poetic forms. Yet it is only concerning matter of the most exalted character that this can be said; for that which is but one grade below the highest extreme of dignity is well suited to poetic forms and diction. The dedicatory prayer of Solomon is essentially, though irregularly, poetical in form; could our Lord's intercessory prayer in the latter part of John's gospel admit, without fearful loss, of similar form? The almost historical prophecy, Isaiah, ch. liii., the Great Passional, is one of the noblest of poems, and perhaps of all the most profoundly pathetic. Would not the plain story of the Passion, as told by the evangelists, be greatly marred if reduced to the same mode of expression? There is some matter of thought too majestic, too severely grand for poetic forms.

So it is in our psalm. Instead of descending, it rises at once to the highest height of majesty. In such ethereal regions the wings of poesy best serve, like those of the cherubim, to cover the eyes. Hence the garb of plain, simple words, culminating in that dread mystery, the oath of God. The effect, on one who can receive it, is powerful, massive. We said the change of style is precipitous. So it ought to be, rising squarely to a dizzy, immeasurable height. The beauties of the first parts are as flowers growing at the foot of a mountain of rock.

If these views are allowed weight, they justify on rhetorical grounds the disregard of the law of parallelism in the closing part of this psalm, which fact, therefore, does not invalidate the theory.

§ 9. In further illustration of the subject, we will now examine Psalm ii. It is one of the most interesting in the Psalter, and consequently has been very carefully studied and commented on by biblical scholars. They generally pronounce it wholly irregular in form. But let us suspend our judgment until we have entered into its spirit, and discerned its successive scenes.

The psalmist here is not merely a poet, nor yet merely a prophet; he is a seer. He describes what passes before his eyes in vision, and his psalm is a mirror of what he sees, and an echo of what he hears. So sharp is the representation that it assumes almost a dramatic tone. From some celestial height the seer looks abroad over the earth and beholds the nations in wild tumult, preparing to resist the rule of God's Messiah (strophe 1). Their kings and princes have assembled, and he hears their consultation against the new and supreme kingdom (strophe 2). His eye now turns to the open heavens, and he sees Jehovah on his throne, laughing with scorn, and poising his thunderbolt; and he hears him declare his unalterable will (strophe 3). Behold! Messiah the Son intervenes, and announces the decree of Jehovah, committing to him universal empire, and fixing the doom of his enemies (strophe 4). The seer now turns again, and addresses the refractory kings, counseling wisdom and submission and homage, in view of the invincible might arrayed against them. Finally, he announces the blessedness of all who give in their allegiance to the kingdom of Messiah (strophe 5).

Let us endeavor to see with his eyes, to hear with his ears. Behold the turmoil of the nations:

I

Why do the nations rage,
And the peoples meditate a vain thing?

II

The kings of the earth set themselves,
And the rulers take counsel together,
Against Jehovah,
And against his Anointed:
Let us break their bands asunder,
And cast away their cords from us.

NOTES.—*Strophe 1.* **Rage**, indicating speedy rebellion.—**peoples**, meaning, perhaps, those of Israel, combining with the heathen nations.—**meditate**, intend.—**a vain thing**, that which is naught, and will prove naught. "We will not have this man to rule over us" (Luke xix. 14); "We have no king but Cæsar" (John xix. 15).

Strophe 2. **Set themselves**, in a posture of defiance, as did Herod the Great. (Matthew ii.)—**rulers**: this was literally fulfilled in the persons of Herod Antipas, the Tetrarch, and of Pilate; the one representing the effete monarchy of the people of Israel, and the other the imperial power of Rome, mistress of the heathen world. (See Acts iv. 25-28.)—**his Anointed**, his Messiah, his Christ. The word *Anointed* is retained here so as not to lose sight of its primary historic reference to an early king of Israel.—**bands** and **cords**, figures from yoked bulls, furious to cast off the yoke. A case of onomatopœia; the sound of the words in the Hebrew and the rhythm express finely the precipitancy and rage of the speakers.

III

He that sitteth in the heavens shall laugh,
The Lord shall have them in derision.
Then shall he speak unto them in his wrath,
And vex them in his sore displeasure:
    Yet have I set my King
    Upon my holy hill of Zion.

Strophe 3. The futures in this strophe are imperfects in the Hebrew. Many Hebraists agree that those of the first distich should be rendered by the present, thus:

> He that sitteth in the heavens laughs,
> The Lord holds them in derision.

The others are properly rendered by the future. The laughter here is either in scorn (*cf.* Psalm xxxvii. 13, and Proverbs i. 26), or expressive of conscious security and superiority. The quiet laughing passes over, through derision, to the agitation of wrath, breaking out in words and acts. This is one of the boldest passages in all poetic literature.—**Then shall he speak;** *i.e.*, presently in vengeance. This distich is another case of onomatopœia. Herder calls attention to the roll and whiz of the words in the Hebrew. The first line reminds us of thunder, and the syllabication of the second might be called zigzag.—**Yet have I,** the words of Jehovah in almost plain prose. *I* is emphatic in the Hebrew. The condensed power of the words of these strophes, and their vivid presentation of a majestic scene, are wonderfully sublime, and, by comparison, reduce the best passages of Homer, Pindar, and Milton to insignificance. They are only paralleled by these words:

> The nations raged,
> The kingdoms were moved;
> He uttered his voice,
> The earth melted. (Psalm xlvi. 6.)

IV

I will tell of the decree,
Jehovah said unto me:
Thou art my Son;
This day have I begotten thee.

Ask of me,
And I will give thee
The nations for thine inheritance,
And the uttermost parts of the earth for thy
[possession.
Thou shalt break them with a rod of iron;
Thou shalt dash them in pieces like a potter's vessel.

Strophe 4. Messiah now appears, almost dramatically, and speaks.—the **decree,** eternal and immutable of Jehovah, by which I shall reign.—**Thou art my Son.** These words are cited in Acts xiii. 33, and Hebrews i. 5, to prove the solemn recognition of Christ's sonship by God himself, and his consequent authority.—**Ask of me.** God requires to be asked, even of his Son. The swell of expression in this stanza is very fine. —**break,** rather, rule.—**rod of iron,** a scepter, stern and inflexible. (See Isaiah xi. 4; Revelation xix. 15.)—**potter's vessel,** a thing easily cast down from the hands and broken, and that cannot be made whole again. (See Jeremiah xix. 10, 11.)

Strophe 5. The Seer now speaks, in a sarcastic tone, with "divine irony," admonishing the refractory kings.—**Serve,** etc. "Work out your own salvation with fear and trembling." (Philippians ii. 12.)—**Kiss,** not in flattery, nor in conciliation, but in homage. (*Cf.* 1 Samuel x. 1.) Kiss his hand, or the hem of his garment, or his feet.—**in the way,** in your course of resistance.—**wrath,** of the Lamb. (Revelation vi. 15, 16.)

V

Be wise now therefore, O ye kings;
Be instructed, ye judges of the earth.
    Serve Jehovah with fear,
    And rejoice with trembling.

    Kiss the Son,
    Lest he be angry,
    And ye perish in the way,
    For his wrath will soon be kindled.

Blessed are all they that put their trust in him.

This psalm is anonymous, but Psalm cx., to which it closely corresponds, is ascribed to David, and hence some critics have inferred his authorship of this also. The reference in Acts iv. 25 is not decisive, according to the German critics, " because in the New Testament David's Psalm and Psalm are synonymous." (*Delitzsch.*) Ewald, followed by Stanley, assigns it, " by internal evidence," to David as author, and to the time of the conspiracy of Adonijah. Primarily, though subordinately, the psalm has plainly an historic reference, which may be to the establishment of Solomon's kingdom. But in a far deeper and wider sense, it relates to the Christ, the Messiah, the Anointed One, about to enter triumphantly upon his kingdom. It is repeatedly referred to in the New Testament as Messianic. All the early Jews regard it as prophetic and Messianic. Only in their opposition to Christianity have modern Rabbis abandoned and finally denied this interpretation, and limited its application to David. But the words of the psalm are too great, its tone is too lofty. The proclamation of the decree made by Messiah in strophe 4 would, in the mouth of any man, be grossly impious.

Let us examine the formal structure. It is plainly very symmetrical, almost perfectly regular. After the interrogative expression of astonishment (strophe 1), which is the introductory ground for the subsequent action, the psalm divides into two nearly equal parts. These parts, 2, 3 and 4, 5, differ in form, but in each the form is repeated. If we look into the sense, we see that strophes 2 and 3 are a thesis and antithesis, a strophe and antistrophe. This is true also, though less clearly, of strophes 4 and 5. The subordinate parts of strophe 2 are in close correspondence with those of 3, or, rather, are antithetically parallel, distich answering to distich throughout; for example, the words of Jehovah are in response to those of the kings and rulers. The parallelism between strophes 4 and 5 is not so perfect, but is sufficiently clear. Compare the stanzas beginning "Ask of me" and "Kiss the Son." Calvin has remarked that the closing monostich relieves the severity of the preceding distich. True, but structurally it stands as the antithesis to the last distich of strophe 4.

We now especially remark an introverted or epanodic logical structure of the whole. The psalm begins with the words of the Seer, bringing into view first the people, and then the kings. Then we have the words of the kings. Then, still rising, Jehovah speaks. Now, having reached the conclusion of the first part, the middle of the poem, the series is repeated, but in inverted order. First, corresponding to Jehovah, Messiah speaks. Then, descending to earth, the kings again come into view, in the admonition of the

Seer, whose last words, like his first, apply to all men. Is this complete vertical circle accidentally drawn? Looking more closely, we see in strophe 5 that the exhortation to do homage to the Son is in responsive contrast with the rebellious counsel of strophe 2; and the words of the stanza, "Be wise now therefore," etc., reply to the words of the kings in strophe 2. Also compare strophes 3 and 4, and observe that the first distich of 3 is logically correspondent with the last in 4; and the last distich in 3 with the first two in 4. If this duplex system of parallelism be admitted to exist in this psalm, surely its artistic structure is almost as wonderful as its rhetorical excellence.

VIII.—LYRICS

§1. THE Bible is not properly a book; it is a library. The Old Testament comprises all the extant works of the Hebrews from the earliest age down to about 400 B.C., a period of more than ten centuries. It is a collection of all the early literature of a wonderful people, who have surpassed even the Greeks in their influence on the history and development of mankind.

Now, is it a mere fancy that each literature has some peculiar distinctive mark? Is there not in every national mind one dominating thought whose influence pervades, often it may be *sub audite*, all its literature? Is not this fundamental characteristic in Greek literature, heroism? in the Roman, power? in the German, liberty of thought? in the English, liberty of person? In the late literatures there is, of course, much that is derived from the earlier. Each, besides its own dominant characteristic, is pervaded more or less by the thoughts of those preceding it; and in searching for that which is distinctively its own, this foreign element must be eliminated. But it may be questioned whether any literature can be entitled to an independent rank that has not within itself an original, informing element, one that constitutes a new point of departure for thinking and feeling.

Whatever may be true of other literatures, there can be no question that one thought dominates the Hebrew literature, becoming especially prominent in its poetry. It is more easily discriminated because there is no foreign admixture, no influence coming from prior antiquity. This thought is, Jehovah and his Messiah. There are other, subordinate characteristics which embellish Hebrew poetry; as, its passion, its love of nature, its austere dignity, its rich and bold imagery, its intense patriotism. Since these are shared more or less by other literatures, they become distinctive only by degree; whereas, the thought of Jehovah and his Messiah is peculiar, and separates this from and elevates it above all others. The psalms are all aglow with it. Jehovah is boldly apostrophized as their inmate:

> But thou art holy,
> O thou that inhabitest the praises of Israel.
> (Psalm xxii. 3.)

Thus this thought is woven into the innermost texture of every psalm, and imparts its hue to every sentiment. Although so obvious, it needs to be discriminated and named here; for in the discussion that follows, we propose to point out and illustrate certain other characteristics, which must be recognized as subordinate to the one constant and all-pervading element.

§2. Poetry is commonly divided into lyric, didactic, dramatic, and epic. These divisions are not rigidly exclusive of each other, and are otherwise logically objectionable, but they are familiar, and suited to our present purpose. In Hebrew poetry the chief forms are the lyric and didactic. Indeed, the existence of the other two has been denied by many eminent authorities. Says Perowne: "The Hebrews have no epic and no drama. Dramatic elements are to be found in many of their odes, and the Book of Job and the Song of Songs have sometimes been called divine dramas; but dramatic poetry, in the proper sense of the term, was altogether unknown to the Israelites." Renan attributes the absence of the drama to the absence of mythology, and Schaff attributes the absence of the epic to the same cause. The revealed religion excludes mythology and hero-worship, which control the epic, and substitutes for them monotheism, which is inconsistent with any kind of fiction or idolatry. It is admitted that there are epic elements in several lyric poems, as in the Songs of Moses, in the Song of Deborah, and in several of the historic psalms; but even here the lyric features predominate, for the subjectivity of the poet is not lost in the objective event, as is the case in the genuine epos. Leaving the further consideration of this question, we will confine our attention to the first form, the lyric.

The ode, or lyric, is the poetry of song and the lyre. From this original union with music we are to deduce its proper idea. Lyric poetry is eminently the language of feeling. "It wells up from the human heart, and gives utterance to its many stormy and tender emotions of love and friendship, of joy and gladness, of grief and sorrow, of hope and desire, of gratitude and praise." It is not distinguished from other kinds by the matter on which it is employed, it only subjects it to peculiar sentimental treatment. Music and song are naturally warm. They justify a bolder and more passionate strain than is admissible in a mere recitation. Hence the enthusiasm that belongs to the ode, and its liberty; the digressions, the abrupt transitions, and the disorder which it admits. These characteristics lie on the surface; beneath these is a substratum of thought which preserves unity, and which justifies its excursive passion. A mere imitator feels himself bound to appear all fervor. He flames away, gets up into the clouds, and becomes so eccentric that we cannot follow or partake of his raptures. A true poet, amid his bold flights and sudden alternations of feeling, keeps rein upon his fancy, and preserves a logical connection of ideas, so that with all his ardor he is clearly one who thinks, and not one who raves.

Pindar is called the "father of lyric poetry;" but five centuries before Pindar sang, lyric poetry attained among a despised people an excellence to which the boasted Greek did not rise. Milton, severe in his classical taste, says: "There are no songs comparable to the songs of Zion. Not in their divine arguments alone, but in the very critical art of composition they may be easily made to appear over all kinds of lyric poesy incomparable." We claim for Israel's king the title of preëminence. A prelude was sounded by Moses and Deborah, but with David's lyre the voice of song attuned its most dulcet notes, and after him we have, in Israel, only echoes growing fainter. When they had ceased, then Pindar sang the heroes and hero-gods of Greece in original and noble song, and his influence has flowed down the centuries, informing the best secular lyrics of subsequent ages. But the anthems of Israel are flooding the world. The Christian Church has caught up the strains, and, whatever deviations its doctrines have shown, its songs are one. Abyssinians, Nestorians, Greeks, Latins, Lutherans, Anglicans, and Independents all use the Psalter, and unite in harmonious devotion. How many millions of all nations are at this day singing these songs and offering these prayers, and how is their influence deepening and widening as the ages roll on!

§3. The earliest lyric extant is Lamech's Sword Song, coming to us through the Hebrew Scriptures from the antediluvian age. Other poetic remains of the pre-Mosaic age are the Prediction of Noah,[1] and the Death Chant of Jacob.[2] These are prophetic.

Moses, the leader and lawgiver, was also a poet of the highest genius. His Song of Deliverance from Pharaoh and his host overthrown in the Red Sea is the oldest patriotic ode in existence.[3] It might be called the Cradle Song of Israel, or, better, its National Anthem. It sounds through all

---
[1] Genesis ix. 25–27.   [2] *Idem.* xlix. 1–27.   [3] Exodus xv. 1–19.

the thanksgiving hymns of Israel, and is associated by the Apocalyptic Seer with the final triumph of the Church, when the saints shall sing the song of Moses and the song of the Lamb.[1] The style is simple, archaic and grand. The arrangement is antiphonal, chorus answering to chorus, the maidens playing the timbrels. We have also Moses's song celebrating Jehovah's wonderful dealings with Israel, called the Song of the Rock, from the frequent use of that figure.[2] "That this splendid ode must on every ground take the very first rank in Hebrew poetry, is universally allowed." (*Schaff.*) The parting Blessing of Moses on the twelve tribes is lyrical in form, but prophetic in character.[3]

A fourth ode of Moses, which concludes all that remains to us of his poetry, unless he be the author of Job, is Psalm xc. "This psalm sums up the spiritual experience of his long pilgrimage in the wilderness, and proves its undying force at every deathbed and funeral service." It is a solemn and sublime dirge over the transitoriness of human life, and was written probably in the midst of the desert of Paran. Here was the grave of a generation of wanderers; for God had said: As truly as I live, your carcasses shall fall in this wil-

---

[1] Revelation xv. 3.   [2] Deuteronomy xxxii.   [3] *Idem.* xxxiii.

derness. I, the Lord, have said, I will surely do it unto all this evil generation that are gathered together against me; in this wilderness they shall be consumed, and there they shall die.¹ And Moses beheld the term of life of his brethren, of the people that he led and loved, reduced to threescore years and ten, or to fourscore years. A melancholy experience was that of the thirty-eight long years of wandering and dying in silence, for there is no record of these years. At the close of this dark age, Moses, understanding the number of years whereof the Lord spake that he would accomplish the desolation of Israel, set his face to seek by the prayer and supplication found in this psalm that God would turn from his wrath and spare his people. The prayer, in spirit and ground, is exactly parallel to that of Daniel, asking the fulfillment of a known purpose. With him it cries: O Lord, hear; O Lord, forgive; O Lord, hearken and do; defer not, for thine own sake, O my God; for thy people are called by thy name.²

We will fail to appreciate the majestic dignity, the intense sadness, the sublime power of this grand composition if we lose sight of the circumstances. Let us conceive that shortly before the

---

¹ Numbers xiv. 28, 29, 35.   ² Daniel ix. 19.

final march from Kadesh down the Arabah, Moses retires alone from the camp to a distant, rocky height, and standing thereon, overlooks the scene. The multitudes of the living generation of sons cover the plain before him like grass springing in the morning dew. In the midst is the tabernacle and the pillar of cloud. All around spreads the great and terrible desert, glittering with the bones of the dead generation of fathers. Beyond, rises the everlasting granitic mountain mass of Seir. Above, the heavens maintain their dreadful composure. Toward them the aged intercessor looks with outstretched hands, and the primeval silence of the place is broken by A Prayer of Moses, the man of God:

I

Lord, thou hast been our dwelling place in all genera-
Before the mountains were brought forth,   [tions.
Before thou gavest birth to the earth and the world,
Even from everlasting to everlasting, thou art God.

NOTES.—*Strophe 1*. The eternity of God. It contrasts powerfully with the brevity of man's life.—**dwelling place**, home. The Israelites had no other for forty years.

> The eternal God is thy refuge,
> And underneath are the everlasting arms.
>   (Deuteronomy xxxiii. 27.)

—**the mountains**, emblems of eternity and strength. Mount Seir was in sight.—**brought forth**, born when they emerged from the deep. And the Spirit of God brooded upon the face

II

Thou makest man return to dust;
And sayest: Return to dust, ye children of dust.
For a thousand years in thy sight,
Are as yesterday when it passeth,
And a watch in the night.

Thou sweepest them away, they are asleep.
In the morning, as the grass that springeth up;
In the morning it flourisheth and springeth up,
In the evening it is cut down and withereth.

---

of the waters. (Genesis i. 2.) We remember that this psalmist wrote the history of the creation.—the world, the universe.—from everlasting to everlasting, eternity, past and future.

Strophe 2. The transitory nature of human life.—dust; the Hebrew means particles produced by crushing. Dust thou art, and unto dust thou shalt return. (Genesis iii. 19.)—a thousand years. One day is with the Lord as a thousand years, and a thousand years as one day. (2 Peter iii. 8.)—passeth; the words in the original glide rapidly.

Thou sweepest. But one word in the Hebrew is used here, and we have no one sufficient to give its full meaning, which is to sweep away and overwhelm with a flood, possibly an allusion to the Deluge.—asleep; *i. e.*, sleeping in death (*Köster, Delitzsch, Moll*). This is a consequence of "Thou sweepest." There is no comparison, as in the Authorized Version and Revised Version: "They are as a sleep." *They* refers to *men*, not to *years*, and the common interpretation, that "years pass as a dream," is altogether unwarranted. A generation of men passes away into the night slumber of death, but—in the **morning**, a new generation springs up, like grass in the dew; it

III

For we are consumed in thine anger,
And in thy wrath are we troubled.
Thou hast set our iniquities before thee,
Our secret sins in the light of thy countenance.

For all our days are passed away in thy wrath,
We end our years as a sigh.
The days of our years, all are threescore years and ten,
Or, if strength be great, fourscore years;
And their pride is labor and sorrow;
For soon it is gone, and we fly away.

Who knoweth the power of thine anger,
And, according to thy fear, thy wrath?
Teach us so to number our days,
And we shall ingather a heart of wisdom.

---

springs up, to be in its turn cut down, and to wither. This figure passes through David (Psalm ciii. 15, 16), over to Isaiah (ch. xl. 6–8), and down to Peter (First Epistle i. 23, 24).

Strophe 3. A transition from the general subject of fleeting human life to a particular view of it in his own people.—**consumed.** "For indeed the hand of the Lord was against them, to destroy them from among the host, until they were consumed." (Deuteronomy ii. 15.)—**troubled,** terrified.—**in the light of thy countenance,** so that the sins were completely known to them, and to all the universe. They could not endure the light shining from Moses's face, which was a mere reflection. (Exodus xxxiv. 29, ff.)

Passed away, literally *have turned,* as the day turns to evening. "Woe unto us! for the day turneth [same word in He-

IV

Turn, O Jehovah; how long?
Repent thee concerning thy servants.
O satisfy us in the dawning with thy mercy,
That we may rejoice and be glad all our days.
Make us glad according to the days thou hast afflicted us,
The years we have seen evil.

Let thy work appear unto thy servants,
And thy glory upon their sons.
And let the beauty of Jehovah our God be upon us;
And the work of our hands establish thou upon us,
Yea, the work of our hands, establish thou it.

---

brew], for the shadows of the evening are stretched out.". (Jeremiah vi. 4.)—as a sigh, or a fleeting sound, a murmur, a whisper, a word quickly spoken and forgotten.—our years, all; emphatic in the Hebrew. The fourth line of this stanza is parenthetical; the Authorized Version expresses the thought inaccurately—their pride; the *bona naturalia*, youth, health, and beauty.—labor and sorrow, toil and vanity—*i. e.*, without result.

And, according, etc., may be thus paraphrased: And who understands the terrors of thy wrath in the measure that a just fear of thee should impart?—teach us so; *so* connects with the preceding distich, not with what follows, as in the Authorized Version and Revised Version. Teach us in this measure (or thus)—to number our days, not arithmetically, but understandingly to estimate.—ingather, as harvest is gathered in, brought home.

Strophe 4. A special supplication for mercy and blessing on Israel.—Turn (not *Return*, as the Authorized Version and Revised Version) from thine anger.—how long shall it burn?—

The cloud which hangs over the beginning of the psalm is partially removed at the close. That intense confidence in God characteristic of Moses breaks forth at the last. (*Dean of Wells.*) It has been remarked that the psalm is like the pillar of cloud and fire which led the children of Israel. It is dark and bright. It is dark as it looks in sorrowful retrospect on man. It is bright as it is turned in hope and confidence to God. (*Perowne.*)

repent. "Wherefore should the Egyptians speak, and say, For mischief did he bring them out, to slay them in the mountain, and to consume them from the face of the earth? Turn from thy fierce wrath, and repent of this evil against thy people." The intercession of Moses, Exodus xxxii. 12.—**in the dawning;** or, in this morning of a new day of mercy and hope. Literally, *with thy mercy in the morning.* (Revised Version.) It does not mean "early"—*i. e., soon,* as in the Authorized Version. "The dawning denotes that there has been a night in Israel, but now there begins a new era of grace." (*Delitzsch.*)— **make us glad according to;** *i. e.*, make us to rejoice in some proportion to the days and years of our humiliation.

Let thy work appear. "God's work is first to appear, his majesty is to be revealed; then man's work, which is God's work carried out by human instruments, may look for his blessing." (*Perowne.*)—**beauty,** or favor; see Psalm xxvii. 4; a very expressive word in the Hebrew, signifying primarily what is sweet, pleasant, and delightful. It is not merely beauty in the widest sense, or glory or goodness, but a union of them all. (*McCurdy.*)—**the work of our hands;** an expression frequent in Deuteronomy to denote human achievements generally.—**establish,** prosper and confirm by an influence from above descending upon us; for without this, in our own strength, we can accomplish no good thing.

There is something in its tone wonderfully striking and solemn. It acquaints us with profound depths of the divine nature. These awful thoughts may well have occurred to Moses at the close of his wanderings, and the author is plainly grown gray with a vast experience. (*Ewald.*) All critics unite in their admiration of its majesty dignity, of its profound mystery. It strides with threatening tread above all the heights, and above all the depths of life. (*Moll.*) The psalm of eternity. (*Herder.*) The most sublime of human compositions, the deepest in feeling, the loftiest in theologic conception, the most magnificent in imagery. There is underlying this poem, from the first line to the last, the substance of philosophic thought, apart from which, expressed or understood, poetry is frivolous, and is not in harmony with the seriousness of human life. This psalm is of the sort which Plato would have written, or Sophocles, if only one or the other of these minds had possessed a heaven-descended theology. (*Taylor.*)

Between the time of Moses and David, we have the Song of Deborah from the heroic age of the Judges.[1] It is a stirring battle song, full of fire and dithyrambic swing, breathing the spirit of an age of disorder and tumult, when might was right. We have already seen how it influenced the tone and imagery of the great Processional Anthem, Psalm lxviii. Another and a very different specimen of female poetry is Hannah's hymn of joy and

---

[1] Judges v.

gratitude when she dedicated her son, Samuel, the last of the Judges, to the service of Jehovah.[1] It furnished the keynote to the Magnificat of the Virgin.[2]

We now reach the time of David and the Psalter; for Psalm xc. of Moses is the only one prior to his time in the collection. It connects the book of praises with the infancy of the nation, and makes it coextensive with the millennium of Hebrew literature. David's poetry, nearly one-half the whole book, has been partially examined. Before considering the lyrics of later authors, we will glance at the Psalter as a whole.

§ 4. The title, Psalter, originated in the Greek Alexandrian or Septuagint Version, and is a collective term for the Book of Psalms. It was originally the name of a stringed instrument, and the word psalm means the music and playing of the instrument. Tehillim, or Songs of Praise, is the Hebrew title. The Psalter is subdivided into five books, each of which is distinctly marked by a doxology at its close. The Hebrew Midrash on Psalm i. 1 says: "Moses gave the five books of the Law to the Israelites, and as a counterpart to them David gave the Psalms, consisting of five books." But beyond question this fivefold division

---
[1] 1 Samuel ii. 1-10.   [2] Luke i. 46-55.

was not complete until five centuries after David. Still, Delitzsch supposes that this remark may point to an internal harmony between the fivefold enunciation of the law and the fivefold response of the national heart; the subjective echo to the objective command.

There are good reasons for believing that the first book, containing forty-one psalms, almost all David's, was compiled by Solomon. The second, beginning with Psalm xlii., and containing thirty-one psalms, was probably compiled soon afterwards; but peculiar characteristics of the inscriptions, and a peculiar use of the divine names, indicate a different redaction. The third, beginning with Psalm lxxiii., contains seventeen psalms, which were probably collected in the reign of Jehoshaphat. The fourth, beginning with Psalm xc., containing seventeen, and the fifth, beginning with Psalm cvii., and containing forty-four psalms, were compiled after the Captivity, though containing, besides Moses's psalm, some psalms that are undoubtedly David's, preserved probably by tradition. "If any more general subdivision of the book is needed as a basis or a means of a more convenient exposition, it may be obtained by taking as the central column of this splendid fabric its most ancient portion, the sublime and affecting Prayer of Moses, and suffering this, as a landmark, to separate the whole into two great parts, the first composed entirely of psalms belonging to the Monarchy, the other of a few such, with a much greater number of late compositions." (*Alexander.*) The canon was closed not later than 400 B.C. What principle governed the compilers, in the order of arrangement, has been a subject of much discussion without satisfactory result. The arrangement was regarded by the Jews with that profound, not to say superstitious, reverence for antiquity so characteristic of them, and probably has never been disturbed. This is illustrated by the Midrash Tillin (ch. 27) on Psalm iii., which says: "When Joshua Ben Levi undertook to revise the arrangement of the Psalms, an echo from heaven (*Bath kol*) cried to him, Wake not David from his slumbers."

The old canonical tradition of the Hebrews, preserved in the titles to many psalms, assigns, out of the total one hundred and fifty, one to Moses, seventy-three to David, two to Solomon, eleven to the Sons of Korah, twelve to Asaph, one to Heman the Ezrahite, and one to Ethan the Ezrahite. Of the remaining forty-nine, twenty-four have titles not indicating authorship, and twenty-five are untitled. These last are the Orphan Psalms, as they are called by the Talmudical writers. In the Authorized Version the untitled psalms are thirty-seven, twelve being psalms which in the Septuagint have Hallelujah as a title, in our version translated and improperly made the first line of the psalm. The titular ascriptions of authorship have undergone searching criticism within the present century, and the result on the whole seems favorable to their correctness. The twelve assigned to Asaph cannot all have been composed by Asaph the Levite, the renowned chorister of David, for some of them are as late as Hezekiah and the Chaldean exile. It has therefore been generally concluded that Asaph is a family name, similar to that of the family of Levitical musicians and psalmists, the Sons of Korah.

In the titles to the psalms are found a number of terms so obscure that their meaning is still in doubt. Some seem to be musical terms, others terms classifying the kinds of odes. The system is far from being scientific or accurate in any sense, but is of archaic interest. We give a few of these terms:

1st. Tĕhillâh, a hymn of praise; occurs in the title of Psalm cxlv., David's hymn of praise. The plural, Tehillim, is the title, as already stated, of the whole Psalter.

2d. Tĕphillâh, a prayer. A large proportion of the psalms, as we have seen, fall into this class. Ewald says that all lyric poetry partakes of the nature of prayer.

3d. Kênâh, a dirge or lament, including all elegies.

4th. Mâshêl, an ode skillfully constructed, a similitude, a parable in the Old Testament sense— *e. g.:*

> I will incline mine ear to a parable,
> I will open my dark saying upon the harp.
>
> (Psalm xlix. 4.)

There are several other classes, which, however, fail to exhaust the kinds of odes, and which trespass upon each other most illogically. Altogether the system, if it can be so called, affords a curious illustration of the unscientific habit of Hebrew thought.

We have seen that lyric poetry originated in the pre-Mosaic age, that with Moses it attained unsurpassed excellence, and that it flourished with a rude vigor during the period of Judges. Its culmination was in the reign of David, the prince of songsters, who set his royal seal upon the lyric art, and made it his own. Thenceforth it declined. Through the reigns of the earlier kings, when the nation was quiet and at peace, or, at least, was no longer struggling for existence, gnomic poetry blossomed and bore fruit. Ewald calls this the artificial period of Hebrew poetry. From the end of the eighth century before Christ, the decline of the nation was rapid, and with its glory departed the chief glories of its literature. The lyrics of this period are distinguished by a smoothness of diction and an external polish which are tokens of labor and art. The style is less flowing and easy, and, except in rare instances, show none of David's dash, vigor, impulsive abruptness, and tempestuous passion. After the Captivity there are only a few hymns, compiled for the liturgical services of the temple. Israel's right hand had forgot her cunning.

The New Testament contains four lyrics: The Magnificat of the Virgin (Luke i. 46–55); The Benedictus of Zacharias (Luke i. 68–79); The Gloria in Excelsis, a single distich (Luke ii. 14); The Nunc Dimittis of Simeon (Luke ii. 29–32). These are the only passages of the New Testament, other than quotations, that can be reckoned as poetry. We have already indicated that there are a number assuming an unintentional poetic style, but these alone are avowedly odes. Their spirit is thoroughly that of the Old Testament, and, indeed, the longer ones are made up of quotations or adaptations. They are specimens of Hebrew poetry composed in Greek, and impress us with the fact that this people, in adopting the Greek language, did not become Greeks, but used that wonderfully flexible tongue to express Hebrew thought in Hebrew forms. This series of lyrics, of great beauty and interest, has been called the golden sunset of Hebrew poetry. But the sunset was long past. Rather it is the soft moonlight of its evening, the reflection of the departed king of day.

So, then, with a few scattered exceptions, we find all the sacred lyrics within the compass of the Psalter. This book stands apart from all the other books of the Bible. It is peculiar, not merely in the lyrical form of its teachings, but in the mode of teaching in a far deeper sense. Luther, in his preface to the Psalter, says: "The noble nature and art of the psalms consists in this, that while other books have much to tell us about the works of the saints, they give us few of their words. But the Psalter does still more, in that it does not set before us the poor, commonplace discourses of the saints, but the very best, even those which they held with God himself, in the greatest earnestness, and on the most important matters. By this means it lays before us, not simply their words and works, but their hearts, and the deep treasures of their souls, so that we may look upon the foundation and fountain of their words and works, that we can see in their hearts, what noble thoughts they had, and how their hearts were affected in all kinds of affairs, dangers, and necessities." Moreover, in the Psalter we are taught, as nowhere else are we taught, how acceptably to approach God in prayer and praise. For all the other books of the Bible are the words of God addressed to man, in law, in history, in prophecy, in doctrine. In this alone are the words of man addressed to God, in his griefs and fears, doubts and hopes, joys, cares, and anxieties—words, too, inspired by the Holy Spirit, so that we know that they are right words, moving words, acceptable words. So, then, if prayer and praise be our highest duties, our noblest exercises; if they be the keys opening the gates that bar our approach to the Eternal Presence; we have here the teaching that meets our greatest practical need, and lifts us to communion with our Maker.

§5. It remains to examine some other psalms not ascribed to David. Many of them are of wonderful power, and glow with delectable beauties. Of this class have already been presented Psalms ii., xlii., xliii., xc., xcv., and cxxx. A few others must suffice. The selections which follow are intended to illustrate in general the great variety of genius engaged in the sacred lyrics. They differ widely among themselves, and from any heretofore cited, yet are possessed of high poetic merit. Especially are they intended to illustrate, each one a particular characteristic of Hebrew poetry. The great thought of Jehovah dominates them all, and other special characteristics are more or less common; but in each of them some one mark comes out with an unusual prominence, which enables us the better to discriminate and emphasize it. The intensely concrete mode of Hebrew thought has already been particularly noted in Psalm cxxxix., and its austere dignity in Psalm xc. These two characters call for no further illustration.

Another character is the rich, glowing, oriental imagery, the high coloring of Hebrew poetry. Let us turn to Psalm xlv. It is a love song by one of the sons of Korah. In the title, the word Shoshannim means lilies, probably the equivalent to beautiful maidens, bridesmaids, or brides, and may indicate that it is adapted to a bridal ceremony. It celebrates the nuptials of a king. He is described as beautiful and gracious, as a hero and conqueror, as one anointed with the oil of gladness, as enjoying every earthly bliss, and about to make a foreign princess his bride. She is beautiful and glorious in her person and apparel, and is attended by a train of virgins. She is brought unto the king in his palace amid festal rejoicings.

The ode may have been suggested by some historic occasion; but this is no historic king of Israel, for there are insuperable objections to such interpretation. Solomon, the peaceful, was not a conqueror—but the point need not be considered in detail, for there are a number of expressions which cannot be construed as merely hyperbolical, and which it would be blasphemy to apply to any mere man. This king is blessed for evermore, he is addressed as divine, and his bride is exhorted to worship him. He occupies an everlasting throne, his dominion through his children shall extend over all the earth and endure to the end of time, and his praise shall be forever and ever. The only explanation of this exalted language is found in the old traditional interpretation of the Jews, confirmed by the author of the Epistle to the Hebrews,[1] and accepted by most critics, that this psalm is rhetorically an allegory, and intrinsically prophetic—Messianic. The king is Christ, the bride is his

---

[1] Hebrews i. 8, 9.

Church. It is a psalm full of mystery to the Jew, but luminous with brilliant glories in the light of the gospel and of progressing Christianity.

A strange Song of Loves this; but the title is confirmed by its erotic form and imagery; and nowhere will we find one more thoroughly oriental in tone, in the warm glow of its hues, and in the rich perfume of its spices. The poet begins by declaring his rapture:

I

My heart overflows with a goodly theme;
I speak, my words are for a king;
My tongue is the pen of a ready writer.

II

Fair, fair art thou above the sons of men;
Grace is poured into thy lips;
Therefore God hath blessed thee forever.

NOTES.—*Strophe 1.* Prelude.—a ready writer; the tongue moves fluently as the pen of a shorthand writer. Thus Ezra is called "a ready scribe" (ch. vii. 6).

Strophe 2. The king's personal excellence. The Hebrews regarded beauty as the outward manifestation of an inherent nobleness akin to divinity.—grace is poured into thy lips. The words that I speak unto you, I speak not of myself. (John xiv. 10.) The Spirit of the Lord is upon me, because he hath anointed me to preach the gospel to the poor. And all bare him witness, and wondered at the gracious words that proceeded out of his mouth. (Luke iv. 18, 22.)—forever. See also strophes 4 and 9.

III

Gird thy sword upon thy thigh, O Mighty One,
Thy honor and thy majesty;
And in thy majesty go forth,
Ride, for the sake of truth and lowly right,
And thy right hand shall teach thee terrible deeds.
>Thine arrows are sharp,
>>Peoples fall under thee;
>In the heart of the king's enemies!

IV

Thy throne, O God, is forever and ever;
A scepter of equity is the scepter of thy kingdom.
Thou hast loved righteousness, and hated wickedness;
Therefore, O God, thy God hath anointed thee
With the oil of gladness above thy fellows.

Strophe 3. His heroic prowess. And I saw, and behold a white horse, and he that sat on him had a bow, and a crown was given unto him, and he went forth conquering and to conquer. (Revelation vi. 2.)—**Mighty One**; this could very well be rendered Hero.—**honor** and **majesty**, array thyself in them. Kay takes these words to be in apposition with sword.—**ride, for,** etc.; a knightly motto.—**right hand,** is boldly personified. It leads the warrior onward, and teaches him the terrible things it executes.

Thine arrows, etc. The beauty of this vivid picture subjoined to the strophe is greatly obscured in the Authorized Version by a prosaic supply of ellipses, and an unwarranted transposition of clauses. The psalmist sees the battlefield, the sharp arrows fly, the foes fall; he approaches the slain, and behold, the arrows are in their hearts.

Strophe 4. His righteous rule.—**Thy throne, O God**; this is

V

Myrrh and aloes and cassia, are all thy garments;
From palaces of ivory strains of harps delight thee;
Daughters of kings are among thy precious ones;
The queen, in gold of Ophir, is stationed at thy right
[hand.

the literal, grammatical construction. He is over all, God blessed forever. Amen. (Romans ix. 5. See Hebrews i. 8, 9.) The rendering of the fourth line is not so unquestionable, but is defensible, and consists with the context.

Strophe 5. His pleasant delights.—Myrrh, etc.; his garments are as thoroughly perfumed with these spices as if made of them.—from palaces, etc.; out of his own many palaces, decorated with ivory, strains of joyous music greet him welcome. The common interpretation is that the king goes to a foreign kingdom to claim his princess bride, and that as he approaches her home he is welcomed with music. This accords with the ancient oriental custom, according to which the bridegroom went out after the bride, and conducted her to his own home. But it does not appear to have been practiced by royal bridegrooms, and for obvious reasons. There is not one word in the ode which indicates any such progress of the king. The notion has been thought into it by the interpreters, and accepted one from another; their fancy being caught by the allegorical correspondence to Christ's coming into the world. It is directly contrary to the plain statement in strophe 7, that the bride is brought unto the king, and this inconsistency is explained by violent suppositions. It is much better to understand that thus far in the ode no allusion has been made to the nuptials. The present strophe describes merely his royal pleasures and state within his own dominions. This is simple, clear, and consistent, and does not bring in a hard knot to be

VI

Hearken, O daughter, and consider, and incline thine ear,
Forget also thine own people, and thy father's house,
So shall the king greatly desire thy beauty;
For he is thy Lord, and worship thou him.

And the daughter of Tyre, with a gift,
The rich of the people, shall entreat thy favor.

afterwards cut. We must not let our fancy lead us beyond the record.—thy precious ones, thy treasures, thy jewels. "As polygamy had only the permission, not the sanction of God, it may seem strange that it should be mentioned as a feature in the splendor of this monarch. But polygamy was practiced by the best of kings; and the psalmist is describing the magnificence of an oriental court such as it actually existed before his eyes." (*Perowne.*)—the queen is stationed, the chief consort, not simply *stand*, as in the Authorized Version and Revised Version, but *is placed* at the post of honor. This queen has been variously explained, and the confusion has caused some to reject the Messianic interpretation altogether. Possibly she may be a different one from her of the next strophe, one already wedded, and now another is to be added to his wives; thus symbolizing the ancient Jewish and the Christian Church. It is better, however, to understand that the queen here and in strophe 6 is the same person. Here his happiness is spoken of as if already complete. The present tense, "is stationed," is used with prophetic confidence. In the next strophe, beginning the second part of the poem, the poet returns to the quasi-historic order, and exhorts her who is to be the queen, and stationed at the king's right hand. The Church of all the saints is the King's bride. But what do the "daughters of kings" in the previous line symbolize? Another hard knot for the inter-

VII

All glorious is the king's daughter within,
Her apparel is inwrought with gold.
In embroidered robes she shall be led unto the king,
Virgins her companions attending, brought in unto thee.

With gladness and rejoicing shall they be brought,
They shall enter into the palace of the king.

preters. It seems best to regard these, and the virgins of strophe 7, as unsymbolical. We must not push an allegory or a parable too far. Much must be accepted as merely filling in the picture.

Strophe 6. The bride exhorted. The scene is changed to a foreign kingdom, and the princess is addressed by the psalmist as an ambassador, and is promised gifts.—Hearken, etc.; the earnestness of this threefold address shows how difficult it is to gain the attention of the bride, to make her comprehend her complete change of sphere, the disruption of old ties, and the entire surrender of her heart now demanded. Yielding will win the king's love. The merchant princes of Tyre, the wealthiest commercial city in the world, and the rich of all nations, will entreat her favor with gifts.—daughter of Tyre, is a Hebraism for the city or for its inhabitants. (*Cf.* "daughter of Babylon," "daughter of Jerusalem.")

Strophe 7. The report of the ambassador to the king, and his account of the future festive progress of the bride to the palace of her Lord.—within, her own, or, rather, her father's royal house.—her apparel. Let us be glad and rejoice, and give honor to him, for the marriage of the Lamb is come, and his wife hath made herself ready. And to her was granted that she should be arrayed in fine linen and white; for the fine linen is the righteousness of saints. (Revelation xix. 7, 8.) And I John saw the holy city, the new Jerusalem, coming

VIII

In the place of thy fathers, shall be thy sons;
Thou shalt set them for princes in all the earth.

IX

I will make thy name to be remembered in all genera-
[tions;
Therefore shall the peoples praise thee forever and
[ever.

The psalm divides into two parts, the second beginning with strophe 6. Structurally, strophe 5 stands in the midst, and the parts before and after correspond in introverted order. In the first and last stanzas the poet speaks of his own work. Köster's arrangement is more symmetrical, but for the sake of symmetry he breaks the logical coherence, setting the distichs of strophe 5 apart in different strophes. This cannot be allowed. It belongs to his second class—see page 279, note.

Can it be without significance that this mystic

---

down from God, out of heaven, prepared as a bride adorned for her husband. (Revelation xxi. 2.)

Strophe 8. His posterity.—thy fathers, are those of whom as concerning the flesh Christ came. (Romans ix. 5.) He shall be yet more highly honored by his sons, who shall be the princes of the earth.

Strophe 9. Conclusion. The psalmist speaks as one in a long series of inspired heralds, and in behalf of all.

psalm is immediately followed by the great Song of the Church?

> God is our refuge and strength,
> A very present help in trouble.
>
> (Psalm xlvi. 1.)

Again, this is followed by one in which the nations are exhorted cheerfully to entertain the universal kingdom:

> Sing praises to God, sing praises;
> Sing praises unto our King, sing praises;
> For God is the King of all the earth.
>
> (Psalm xlvii. 6.)

To this succeeds another describing the glories and privileges of the Church, and saying:

> Let Mount Zion rejoice,
> Let the daughters of Judah be glad;
> For this God is our God forever and ever,
> He will be our guide even unto death.
>
> (Psalm xlviii. 11, 14.)

All of these successive psalms are by the sons of Korah.

§ 6. With the Song of Loves we will contrast one of very different tone; it might almost be called a Song of Hate. The imprecatory character of certain psalms is a familiar difficulty, and we have avoided it as belonging to doctrinal rather than to æsthetic exposition. But it is too marked a feature, in a purely rhetorical point of view, to be entirely unnoticed. A striking trait in the Jewish character is its intensity of feeling. The ardent love for Jehovah our God has its counterpart in a scorching hate of the wicked, his enemies. The friendship for Jonathan is not deeper than the abhorrence for Doeg. The profoundly intense patriotism, the exaltation of the Holy City, which is indeed the joy of the whole earth, is balanced by an equally intense and withering malediction of those who came up against her, or rejoiced in the day of her calamity. The Chaldean exile brought this patriotism into full blaze. There are not many songs belonging to this epoch, but they are remarkable. We merely refer to Psalm cii., but will cite in full the familiar Psalm cxxxvii. Its rhetorical beauty and strength, its profound pathos and bitterness, have won universal recognition. Modern literature abounds with allusions to it, imitations lie on every hand (as, for example, Byron's noted paraphrase), and a number of its expressions have become household words. The elegiac pathos of its rise passes over into patriotic feeling, which bursts into a flame of passionate fury, and hurls a curse upon the oppressor like a thunderbolt:

I

By the rivers of Babylon, there we sat down,
Yea, we wept when we remembered Zion,
We hanged our harps on the willows thereby.
For there our captors demanded of us songs,
And they that oppressed us, mirth, saying :
Sing us one of the songs of Zion.

II

How shall we sing the LORD's song in a strange land?
If I forget thee, O Jerusalem,
Let my right hand forget her cunning.
Let my tongue cleave to the roof of my mouth,
If I do not remember thee ;
If I prefer not Jerusalem above my chief joy.

NOTES.—*Strophe 1*. **Willows.** This has given the scientific specific name to our weeping willow, *Salix babylonica*. Hence also it is called *weeping*. The species are identical. Herodotus speaks (I., 194) of boats at Babylon whose framework was of willow. Before the Babylonish Captivity the willow was always the symbol of joyful prosperity. "It is remarkable for having been in different ages emblematical of two directly opposite feelings, at one time being associated with the palm, at another with the cypress. There can be no doubt that the dedication of the tree to sorrow is to be traced to the pathetic passage in the Psalms." (John's *Forest Trees.*)—**demanded**, in derision.

Strophe 2. **Forget,** what is due.—**her cunning.** These words, not in the Hebrew, are supplied by the translators. It is a case of aposiopesis. The meaning is, forget its skill in playing the harp; and my tongue nevermore sing. What intensity! The

III

Remember, O LORD, to the sons of Edom, the day of
[Jerusalem;
Who said: Raze it, raze it, to the very foundation
[thereof.

O daughter of Babylon, that art laid waste;
Happy he that shall reward thee as thou hast served us;
Happy he that shall take and dash thy little ones against
[the stones.

---

latter expression is derived from Job xxix. 10.—if I prefer not. Wordsworth translates literally: "if I advance not Jerusalem above the head of my joy"—*i. e.*, if I set not Jerusalem as a diadem upon the head of my rejoicing, and crown all my happiness with it.

Strophe 3. The maledictions.—to the sons of Edom, to their sorrow.—the day, is, according to common oriental usage of the word, the day of calamity. The Edomites were active in the destruction of Jerusalem; see Amos i. 11. Being the kinsmen of Israel, this was particularly odious.—O daughter of Babylon; a familiar periphrasis for Babylon itself.—art laid waste; prophetic anticipation.

The change of tense in the progress of this psalm has troubled the interpreters, and led to different suppositions as to the date of its composition. The traditional interpretation takes it to have been written in Babylonia during the Captivity. But the past and distant of strophe 1 may indicate a date after the taking of Babylon by Cyrus and the restoration of the Jews, and before its complete destruction by Darius Hystaspis. (*Hitzig, Hengstenberg, Hupfeld, Perowne, et al.*) This admits the future tense of the last distich. If the view be accepted, we must understand the poet in strophe 2 to be speaking in the person of the captives.

The last line of the ode is worthy of special remark. It is in accord with, and perhaps has reference to, the prophecy of Isaiah xiii. 16, in the Burden of Babylon: Their children also shall be dashed to pieces before their eyes. Powerful, shocking, terrible, this concluding sentiment at first glance seems repugnant, not only to the spirit of Scripture, but also to the spirit of poesy. But consider how vividly graphic it is. Seizing on a single culminating circumstance, it gives to our eyes all the horrors of the midnight sack at once, as by the flash of a search light. The spoiler has possession; defense has ceased. Where is the father? In the heap of the slain. Where is the mother? In the streets. Why there? Her home is in flames. And the avenging soldier snatches her babe from her breast, and dashes out its brains against the wall. This powerful condensation reminds us of the line in the Song of Moses: I will make mine arrows drunk with blood; and of the similar phrase of Homer: The sword of Achilles, hot with blood. We shudder as we read it, and must confess its poetic force to be as intense as the passion that flames through it.

§ 7. A marked feature of the Hebrew lyric is the love of nature which it manifests, These poets saw God in everything, and their adoration for Jehovah our God warmed their hearts with love for all his works. "No poetry in any age has shown a fuller appreciation of nature in all its moods, in its majesty and in its sweetness, in its terrors and in its repose. Thronged, as it were, with multitudinous forms of life, the atmosphere in which the Hebrew lyrist moves is bright with one all-pervading light, which gives a meaning and an object to them all." (*Cook.*) Hence, every mountain and river of Palestine, the cedars of Lebanon, the snows of Hermon, the fig, the olive, and the vine, the rock of the desert, the sands of the sea, the excellency of Carmel, the rose of Sharon, and the lily of the valley, all are consecrated and immortalized in the Scripture metaphors. Yet there is very little direct description of natural scenery, and that little is not for its own sake, as we find it in secular poetry, but for the sake of something beyond. All the means and resources of the loftiest poetry were at the command of the Hebrew bard, but he made them subservient to a nobler purpose than that which animates secular genius. He is charged with a message, his central theme is higher than nature, and all his powers are absorbed, and all his stores are exhausted in attaining its adequate expression,

In illustration we select Psalm civ., one in full sympathy with the beauties of creation, one more nearly descriptive than perhaps any of the sacred odes, and yet one which not less completely subordinates every sentiment to the praise of the Creator. The unknown psalmist, it will be seen, has in mind the seven days of the world's genesis, and without adhering closely to the order of the record, reproduces it in the form of a poetic panorama. Many interpreters discover a spiritual significance lying just below the surface of the psalm. To this we will not here attempt to penetrate, but only glance at that rhetorical beauty which has always been acknowledged, and very frequently praised. Humboldt, who seemed indifferent to its chief excellence, the religious sentiment, has in his *Cosmos* pronounced this Psalm of Nature unrivaled in poetical literature, as " presenting in itself a picture of the whole world." Certain linguistic peculiarities, also its smoothness, grace, and artistic polish, point to a late period of composition. Its calm sweetness contrasts finely with the unrestrained rapture and fiery passion of those odes we have just considered. It recalls that primeval anthem when—

> The morning stars sang together,
> And all the sons of God shouted for joy.

We may imagine that the psalmist opens the sacred Mosaic roll, and having read how in the beginning God created the heavens and the earth, calls up his powers to a service of praise:

Bless the LORD, O my soul.

I

O LORD my God, thou art very great;
Thou hast put on glory and majesty,
Who coverest thyself with light as with a mantle,
Who stretchest out the heavens like a curtain,
Who layeth the beams of his chambers in the waters,
Who maketh the clouds his chariot,
Who goeth on the wings of the wind,
Who maketh winds his messengers,
Flames of fire his ministers.

NOTES.—*Strophe 1.* And God said, Let there be light, and there was light. (Genesis i. 3.)—**Thou hast put on** a faint but real image of thine ineffable glory; the dazzling glory of God is dimmed and softened by his garment of light. And God said, Let there be a firmament in the midst of the waters. (Genesis i. 6.) He stretches out the canopy of heaven like a tent. He constructs his pavilion in the watery firmament above, as a man builds an upper chamber with joists and rafters. He rides thence in his chariot, or sends forth his messengers to do his commands. (*Dean of Wells.*) As God uses the agency of winds and flames to execute his will, so he employs the spiritual ministry of angels to minister to his world of spirits. See Hebrews i. 5.

II

Who laid the foundations of the earth,
That it should not be removed forever.
Thou didst cover it with the deep as with a garment;
The waters stand above the mountains,
At thy rebuke they flee,
At the voice of thy thunder they haste away,
The mountains rise, the valleys sink,
Unto the place which thou didst found for them.
A bound thou hast set, that they may not pass,
That they turn not again to cover the earth.

III

He sendeth forth springs in the valleys,
They run among the hills,
They give drink to every beast of the field,
The wild asses quench their thirst.
Above them dwell the birds of heaven,
Among the branches do they sing.
He watereth the hills from his chambers;
The earth is satisfied with the fruit of thy works.

Strophe 2. And God said, Let the waters under the heaven be gathered together unto one place; and let dry land appear; and it was so. (Genesis i. 9.)—found for them, for the waters. The previous line is a parenthesis.—a bound. Did the psalmist forget the deluge? No, but he is here speaking of the present and future.

Strophe 3. Yet provision is made for watering the earth.

IV

He causeth the grass to grow for the cattle,
And herbs for the service of man,
Bringing forth food out of the earth.
With wine, too, he maketh glad the heart of man,
With oil he maketh his face to shine,
And with bread he strengtheneth man's heart.
The trees of the LORD are satisfied,
The cedars of Lebanon which he planted,
Where the birds make their nests;
The stork, cypresses are her dwelling,
The high hills are a refuge for wild goats,
The rocks for the conies.

V

He appointeth the moon for seasons;
The sun knoweth his going down.
Thou makest darkness, and it is night,
Wherein all the beasts of the forest come forth.
The young lions roar after the prey,
And seek their meat from God.
The sun ariseth, they retire,
And couch them down in their dens.
Man goeth forth unto his work,
And to his labor, until the evening.

Strophe 4. And God said, Let the earth bring forth grass, the herb yielding seed, and the fruit-tree yielding fruit. (Genesis i. 11.) Oil makes man's face to shine, not by anointing, for it was the head, not the face, that was anointed, but by the

VI

How manifold are thy works, O LORD!
In wisdom thou hast wrought them all.
The earth is full of thy riches.

VII

That sea, great and broad,
Wherein are moving things innumerable,
Living creatures, small with great!
There go the ships;
That leviathan thou hast made to play therein.

VIII

These wait all upon thee
To give them their food in its season.
That thou givest unto them they gather;
Thou openest thine hand, they are satisfied with good.
Thou hidest thy face, they are troubled;
Thou takest away their breath, they die,
And return to their dust.
Thou sendest forth thy breath, they are created,
And thou renewest the face of the ground

---

cheerfulness it imparts as a condiment of food. It is still so used in the East. Corn, wine, and oil were the glory of the promised land. (See Deuteronomy xi. 14.) The trees are satisfied with moisture by the rain.

Strophe 5. And God said, Let there be lights in the firmament of heaven, to divide the day from the night. (Genesis i. 14.) ·And God said, Let the earth bring forth the living creature after his kind, cattle, and creeping thing, and beast of the

IX

Let the glory of the LORD endure forever;
Let the LORD rejoice in his works.
He looketh on the earth, and it trembleth,
He toucheth the mountains, and they smoke.

X

I will sing unto the LORD while I live;
I will sing praise to my God while I have being.
My meditation of him shall be sweet;
I, I will be glad in the LORD.
Sinners shall be consumed from the earth,
And the wicked, they shall be no more.

Bless thou the LORD, O my soul.
 Praise ye the LORD.

---

earth after his kind. (Genesis i. 24.) And God said, Let us make man in our image. (Genesis i. 26.)

Strophe 7. And God said, Let the waters bring forth abundantly the moving creature that hath life. (Genesis i. 20.)

Strophe 8. The dependence of all living things on God. The perpetual expiration and renewal of life in the mutations of time and races. Dust thou art, and unto dust thou shalt return. (Genesis iii. 19.) He breathed into his nostrils the breath of life. (Genesis ii. 7.)

Strophe 9. God rejoices in his creation. If he frowns, the earth quakes; if he touches the hills with lightning, they smoke. Volcanoes are not alluded to; they seem to have been unknown to the ancient Hebrews.

Strophe 10. The delight excited by the contemplation of God's works. Sinners, the only blot on this glorious scene,

§ 8. Humboldt says: "Nature is to the Hebrew poet, not a self-dependent object, but a work of creation and order, the living expression of the omnipresence of the Divinity in the visible world." Indeed, the Hebrew took no account of second causes; he bounded over the immediate enigmas of nature to the ultimate solution in a First Cause. He saw no chain of cause and effect; there was but one link, God the cause, and every phenomenon, however insignificant, the direct effect of his agency. The Scriptures do not deny the reality and efficiency of second causes, but there is little or no natural science in the Bible, as there is little or no philosophy. Not only are the phenomena of nature attributed to the direct agency of God, but the movements of history are also referred directly to Jehovah the King of kings, and Lord of hosts, who ruleth the hearts and trieth the reins of the children of men.

This brings us face to face with the true scriptural doctrine of the Providence of God. It admits the reality and efficiency of second causes, both material and mental, but denies that they are

---

shall finally disappear. Hallelujah! It is observed in the Talmud that this first hallelujah in the Psalter, where only it occurs, is coupled with the prospect of the destruction of the wicked.

independent of the Creator and Preserver of the universe. It teaches that an infinitely wise, good, and powerful God is everywhere present, controlling all events, great and small, necessary and free, in a way perfectly consistent with the nature of his creatures, and with his own infinite excellence, so that everything is ordered by his will, and is made to subserve his wise and benevolent designs. (*Hodge.*)

The thought that God is the Creator and Preserver of all things, and the Ruler of all events, pervades the entire Scriptures. With the recognition of this relation comes the sense of protection and safety. Since all the issues of life are in his hands, who is perfect in power and goodness, there springs up an abiding confidence that all things work together for good to them that love God. Especially does the voice of trust sound through the Psalter; it is the common keynote of all its anthems. That this characteristic may be fairly presented, we purpose to close our citations with Psalm xci., which in a peculiar manner emphasizes the security of those whose trust is in Jehovah.

The Talmudists call this psalm the Poem of Accidents, and seem to think that it possessed a talismanic virtue to protect one repeating it in time of danger. It were better to call it the Psalm of Special Providences, and the words of St. Paul, "If God be for us, who can be against us?" might be taken for its text. Delitzsch pronounces it not only one of the most beautiful, but one of the most original of the sacred odes. Indeed, there are several peculiarities that should be carefully noted. It is lyrical in form and spirit, but the general tone is didactic, and it therefore occupies the border ground between these two classes of poetry. It is one of the most clearly marked Dialogue Psalms, a class pointed out by Bishop Horsely. There are two responsive voices, and an oracle at the close, the words of the God of Providence, who, as it were, interrupts the last speaker. It has reasonably been surmised to be a Pilgrim Song, that is, one to be used by pilgrims during their journeys to the festivals at Jerusalem. It certainly seems to enumerate many of the dangers that in an unsettled time, in an unwholesome season, and in wild districts beset peaceful pilgrims. Accepting this view, we shall more readily appreciate its meaning if we set before our eyes a picture somewhat as follows:

An aged Jew, one of long experience in the ways of God to man, wise to give instruction, and devout, a sage in Israel, is on his way up to Jerusalem, accompanied by a young man whose ears are open to the words of the teacher. They have journeyed together afoot for some days, have encamped by night together, and are now passing through a lonely wilderness. They are conscious of the dangers of the way, but without fear they beguile the weary hours in holy conversation. The hoary sage speaks first, and sounds the theme. The youth promptly responds by a declaration of faith. Then follows instruction, broken in the midst by an exclamation of trust from the youth. The continued instruction is interrupted by the voice of God, approving it, and making precious promises to the youth who has avowed his trust in the name of Jehovah. With this scene in mind, attend now to the words of the inspired sage:

I

He that dwelleth in the covert of the Most High,
Abideth under the shadow of the Almighty.

> I say: The Lord is my refuge and fortress;
> My God, in him will I trust.

NOTES.—*Strophe 1*. First voice, and response of second voice.—**dwelleth**, makes his home.—**covert**, or, *secret place*, possibly referring to the Holy of Holies, where a devout man might tropically be said to dwell under the shadow of the wings of the cherubim.—**abideth**, literally, passes the night.

II

Surely he, he shall deliver thee from the snare of the
From the noisome pestilence.   [fowler,
He shall cover thee with his pinions,
And under his wings shalt thou be sheltered.
His truth, a shield and a buckler!

III

Thou shalt not be afraid for the terror by night,
For the arrow that flieth by day,
For the pestilence that walketh in darkness,
For the destruction that wasteth at noonday.

Strophe 2. Again the first voice, continuing through strophe 4. It names perils arising from enmity and craft of men, and from the noxious agencies of nature.—a shield and a buckler, the large *scutum*, as distinguished from the smaller *clypeus*.

Strophe 3. Dangers seen and unseen.—arrow, may refer to the hostile assaults of man; but the parallel word, rendered *destruction*, more literally means *contagion*, so that probably it is God's arrow—as in the following:

> I will spend mine arrows upon them;
> They shall be burnt with hunger,
> And devoured with burning heat,
> And with bitter destruction.
> (Deuteronomy xxxii. 23, 24.)

In the *Iliad*, book first, Apollo shoots arrows of pestilence into the Grecian camp. But here—

> The sun shall not smite thee by day,
> Nor the moon by night. (Psalm cxxi. 6.)

IV

A thousand shall fall at thy side,
And ten thousand at thy right hand;
   It shall not come nigh to thee.
Only with thine eyes shalt thou behold,
And see the reward of the wicked.

V

   Thou, O LORD, art my refuge!

Because thou hast made the Most High thy habitation,
There shall no evil befall thee,
And no plague shall come nigh thy tent.

VI

For he shall give his angels charge over thee,
   To keep thee in all thy ways;
They shall bear thee up on their hands,
   Lest thou dash thy foot against a stone.

Strophe 5. Line first is an exclamation of the second voice; the first voice then resumes, and continues through strophe 7. There is much dispute about the rendering here; that given seems clear, and is grammatically justifiable.

Strophe 6. The ministry of angels. (See Hebrews i. 14.) God promised Israel to send his angel, "to keep thee in the way." (Exodus xxiii. 20.) The same word for *way* is used in each case. The promise is the same in both, referring to protection, rather than to guidance, and meaning: to protect thee *while in the right way.* Satan, in Matthew iv. 6, and Luke iv. 10, 11, misquotes the words very adroitly, omitting the limitation and denying any with "lest ever" (μήποτε). There is no promise of protection if one goes out of the right way. To do

VII

Thou shalt tread on the lion and adder;
The young lion and dragon shalt thou trample under
[feet.

VIII

Because he hath set his love upon me,
   Therefore will I deliver him;
   I will set him on high,
Because he hath known my name.

IX

He shall call upon me, and I will answer him,
   I will be with him in trouble,
   I will deliver him and honor him,
With long life will I satisfy him,
And will shew him my salvation.

so, claiming protection, is to tempt God, and "It is written, Thou shalt not tempt the Lord thy God."

Possibly when writing these stanzas, the psalmist had in view the following:

> Then shalt thou walk in thy way safely,
> And thy foot shall not stumble.
> When thou liest down, thou shalt not be afraid;
> Yea, thou shalt lie down, and thy sleep shall be sweet.
>
> Be not afraid of sudden danger,
> Neither of the desolation of the wicked when it cometh;
> For the Lord shall be thy confidence,
> And shall keep thy foot from being taken.
>   (Proverbs iii. 23-26.)

Compare also Isaiah v. 27: None shall be weary, nor stumble among them.

Strophe 7. Observe how the second line amplifies the

The author is unknown. The LXX. ascribes it to David; a surmise, probably, on the ground of certain Davidic expressions, which may have been unconscious imitations. The ancient Rabbins ascribe it to Moses, and make the youth here instructed Joshua. This is a very captivating conjecture, but seems to have no ground except that the psalm follows anonymously Psalm xc. of Moses,[1] and that the first line of one is similar to that of the other. But this correspondence may have determined the position in the Psalter, and a similarity of introductory lines is a ground too weak for fixing authorship. There are, however, verbal coincidences with Moses's Song, and with his Blessing; but these also may have been unconscious imitations. The psalm very closely resembles Job v. 17–23. Professor Plumptre calls it

---

thought at every point, partially inverting the order. Open violence and secret malignity are here figured. Behold, I give you power to tread on serpents and scorpions. (Luke x. 19.) The lion, the stone, the ways, the tent, the exposure by day and by night, all comport with the idea of a pilgrimage. I have ventured to express by a blank line the view that this stanza is incomplete, being interrupted by what follows.

Strophes 8 and 9. The *Bath kol.* The voice of God is heard, endorsing the words of the sage in an address to him concerning his companion. Its literalness and dignified simplicity contrast finely with the highly tropical and ornate character of the preceding portions.

---

[1] It was a canon with the Rabbins that a title ascribing authorship applied not only to the psalm to which it was prefixed, but also to all the untitled psalms which immediately followed it in the Psalter.

"an echo, verse by verse almost, of the words in which Eliphaz the Temanite describes the good man's life."

Ewald fixes the date of composition in the time of Antiochus Epiphanes, four hundred years after the Captivity; Hitzig gives it a similar date, 162 B.C. These are mere guesses. Certain linguistic peculiarities point to a post-Solomonic age. One well-supported view is that the ten anonymous psalms, xci.–c., have a mutual connection, a common authorship,[1] and a common dependence on the later prophecies of Isaiah; for there are striking coincidences in the subject-matter, style, and phraseology with each other, and with these prophecies. (*Elliott.*) It does not follow that this series was composed by Isaiah, as some have supposed; but we may infer with some confidence that the date of composition is in the time of Hezekiah, whose accession to the throne may have formed the historical groundwork of the remarkable revival of the regal prophecies, both in the writings of Isaiah and in this series of psalms. In any case there seem to be good grounds for assigning a date earlier than that of the Captivity.

The Emperor Alexander I. of Russia is said to have been awakened by means of this psalm. The Countess Tolstoj gave it to him in writing on the evening before his march against Napoleon in the year 1812. This was presenting apples of gold in a basket of silver; for, besides the striking and graceful appropriateness of her gift, it is most precious truth, conveyed in a beautifully wrought artistic form.

---

[1] Early Jews of the Christian era ascribe the authorship of Psalm xcii. to Adam.

§ 9. The Monarchy opened with the Psalms of David; it closed with the Lamentations of Jeremiah. We have here a series of elegies, the most pronounced in the Hebrew literature.[1] They constitute the funeral dirge of the theocracy, and of the holy city. Patriotism finds nowhere a more intense expression, and the sorrows of bereavement have no more passionate language. "Every letter is written with a tear, every word is the sob of a broken heart." The life of the mourner had been stormy, and when it finally dissolved in tears his genius gathered into one harmonious composition the spirit and truth of his eloquent prophecies, to remain forever the crown and glory of his ministry.

The overthrow of the Monarchy by eastern Babylon, and the exile that followed, were typical of that greater overthrow by western Babylon, and of the longer exile not yet at end. The scattered nation, whose chief bond is its ancient literature, keeps alive a patriotic fervor by fondly dwelling on its past glories, and by lamenting its desolation in the wailing of these elegies. They are read throughout the world, year after year and century after century, in the month Ab (July),

---

[1] Their strophic structure has already been noted. See page 274.

with fasting and weeping, by the people who are again wandering in prolonged exile, finding a home nowhere, a grave everywhere; a people whose scepter has departed, but who have given songs to the world.

How hath the Lord covered with a cloud in his anger
    the daughter of Zion!
He from heaven hath cast down to the ground
    the beauty of Israel,
And hath not remembered his footstool in all
    the day of his wrath.

"O land of the godly, how lone and deserted!
    Thy tribes wander friendless, thy glory is gone.
Thy prophets are silent, their glory departed,
    And hushed is the voice of the monarch of song.

"No longer the sounds of rejoicing and gladness,
    No longer the voice of thy harp thrills the ear;
Thy mirth is departed, thy joy changed to sadness,
    Thy relic is ruin, thy fate is despair."

www.ingramcontent.com/pod-product-compliance
Lightning Source LLC
Chambersburg PA
CBHW030304240426
43673CB00040B/1054